Mastering Game Development with Unreal Engine 4
Second Edition

Build high-performance AAA games with UE 4

Matt Edmonds

BIRMINGHAM - MUMBAI

Mastering Game Development with Unreal Engine 4
Second Edition

Acquisition Editor: Shweta Pant
Content Development Editor: Flavian Vaz
Technical Editor: Ralph Rosario
Copy Editor: Safis Editing
Project Coordinator: Alinka Dias
Proofreader: Safis Editing
Indexer: Rekha Nair
Graphics: Jason Monteiro
Production Coordinator: Shraddha Falebhai

First published: June 2016
Second edition: September 2018

Production reference: 1270918

Published by Packt Publishing Ltd.
Livery Place
35 Livery Street
Birmingham
B3 2PB, UK.

ISBN 978-1-78899-144-5

www.packtpub.com

To my wife, Nicole, and my amazing daughter Svetlana. The patience and support of the former helped see this through, and the blossoming love of games by the latter makes it all worthwhile!

– Matt Edmonds

mapt.io

Mapt is an online digital library that gives you full access to over 5,000 books and videos, as well as industry leading tools to help you plan your personal development and advance your career. For more information, please visit our website.

Why subscribe?

- Spend less time learning and more time coding with practical eBooks and Videos from over 4,000 industry professionals

- Improve your learning with Skill Plans built especially for you

- Get a free eBook or video every month

- Mapt is fully searchable

- Copy and paste, print, and bookmark content

Packt.com

Did you know that Packt offers eBook versions of every book published, with PDF and ePub files available? You can upgrade to the eBook version at www.Packt.com and as a print book customer, you are entitled to a discount on the eBook copy. Get in touch with us at customercare@packtpub.com for more details.

At www.Packt.com, you can also read a collection of free technical articles, sign up for a range of free newsletters, and receive exclusive discounts and offers on Packt books and eBooks.

Contributors

About the author

Matt Edmonds has been a lover of games for as long as he can remember, and a professional maker of PC, console, and mobile games since summer 2000. Having graduated with a degree in physics and mathematics, and while doing graduate studies in computer engineering, it became clear all of Matt's free time was going toward learning the technical and creative skills to build amazing 3D games. After making games on his own for around a year, he finally got a break after showing his work making a real-time strategy game in an open source 3D engine with Surreal Software and has never looked back: he now leads teams in creating amazing titles across generations of hardware. With a love of Unreal and 7 years of professional experience with it now, this book is a testament to that passion.

I'd like to thank Stuart Denman for being the leader who gave the young physics graduate just mentioned a chance to prove that he could become a leader of his own in the industry one day. Thanks to my wife and daughter, who have patiently watched weeks go by where for hours on end I was holed-up in a closed room working away at this book. Thanks to my good friend Brandon Mann for help reviewing. And thanks, Mom; you made it all possible... literally!

About the reviewer

Brandon Mann is a professional game engineer working at Z2 / King with over 10 years of professional game development experience. He has worked on games from indie, to AAA, to mobile. Brandon has worked with a wide variety of game engines, from Unreal Engine 4 and 3, to Unity, to a wide variety of other proprietary engines.

> *I would like to thank my fiancée for her constant support and her encouragement for me to continue to grow and progress both personally and professionally.*

Packt is searching for authors like you

If you're interested in becoming an author for Packt, please visit `authors.packtpub.com` and apply today. We have worked with thousands of developers and tech professionals, just like you, to help them share their insight with the global tech community. You can make a general application, apply for a specific hot topic that we are recruiting an author for, or submit your own idea.

Table of Contents

Preface   1

Chapter 1: Making a C++ Project for a First-person Shooter   7
  Introduction   7
  Technical requirements   8
  Building the FPS C++ project   9
    Installing and building UE4   9
    Running the editor and picking a template   12
    Building and running the game project   13
  Modifying our game with C++   14
    Overriding the character class   14
    Editing our class in VS and hot-reloading the editor   19
  Summary   22
  Questions   23
  Further reading   23

Chapter 2: Inventory and Weapons for the Player   25
  Introduction   25
  Technical requirements   25
  Adding the Weapon and Inventory classes   26
    Creating our Weapon class   26
    Converting the existing gun   28
    Creating an inventory and adding a default gun   30
  Adding a WeaponPickup class   39
    Creating a new actor class   39
    Setting up our blueprints   43
    Back to code to finish up   46
  Putting our inventory to use   50
    Adding controls to cycle weapons   51
    Adding swapping of weapons to our character   51
    Bringing it all together   53
  Summary   54
  Questions   54
  Further reading   54

Chapter 3: Blueprint Review and When to Use BP Scripting   55
  Introduction   55
  Technical requirements   56
  Blueprint review and Blueprint-only games   56
    Blueprint overview   57

Blueprint-only games – is this right for you? 62
Blueprint scripting and performance 63
Blueprint scripting example – moving platform and elevator 64
Blueprint tips, tricks, and performance hits 74
Summary 75
Questions 75
Further reading 76

Chapter 4: U.I. Necessities, Menus, HUD, and Load/Save 77
Introduction 77
Technical requirements 78
Integrating UMG into our player's HUD class 78
Building icons for the inventory with screen captures 78
Using UMG to display inventory icons on screen 93
Synchronizing your inventory and HUD 94
Using UMG and game save slots 100
Creating a widget for save slots 101
Creating a save game file 103
Save and load from our menu 108
Summary 115
Questions 116
Further reading 116

Chapter 5: Adding Enemies! 117
Introduction 117
Technical requirements 117
Creating an AI controller and a basic brain 118
Proving out the basics 118
Adding C++ decision making to the behavior tree 123
Attacking the player 127
More polished combat – spawn points, hit reactions, and dying 139
Spawn points for enemy placement 139
Hit reactions and dying 141
Notes on load/save 146
Summary 149
Questions 149
Further reading 150

Chapter 6: Changing Levels, Streaming, and Retaining Data 151
Introduction 151
Technical requirements 151
Traditional level loading 152
The basics 152
Using load/save to transition 155
Perchance to stream? 170

Streaming advantages and disadvantages   170
Example streaming and best practices   172
Summary   175
Questions   175
Further reading   175

Chapter 7: Getting Audio in Your Game   177
Introduction   177
Technical requirements   178
Basic sounds and triggering by animation   178
Sounds, cues, channels, dialog, FX volumes, and more!   180
Triggering sounds from animation   183
Environments and sound   190
Hitting different surfaces   190
Player footfalls and environment FX   196
Summary   202
Questions   202
Further reading   202

Chapter 8: Shader Editing and Optimization Tips   205
Introduction   205
Technical requirements   206
Knowing and building materials   206
Overview of materials, material instance creation, and use   207
Working on material networks and performance tips at editor time   210
Materials at runtime and various platforms   217
Runtime tools and techniques to quickly iterate shaders   218
Know Your Platform and How to Adapt Shaders!   220
Summary   230
Questions   231
Further reading   231

Chapter 9: Adding an In-game Cutscene with Sequencer   233
Introduction   233
Technical requirements   234
Sequencer – UE4's newest cutscene tool   234
Why use sequencer?   234
Adding a scene and triggering it   240
Alternatives to sequencer   249
Fast and easy in-game scenes   250
Matinee   250
Summary   253
Questions   253
Further reading   253

Chapter 10: Packaging the Game (PC, Mobile)   255
  Introduction   255
  Technical requirements   256
  Know your platform(s)   256
    Setting up an installable PC version and general settings 257
    Android setup   260
    iOS setup   266
  How to build, test, and deploy   267
    UE4's play options vs package project   268
    When and how to build and test on device   268
    Making standalone builds and installing them   269
    Avoiding rebuild-hell on platforms near releases   270
  Summary   270
  Questions   271
  Further reading   271

Chapter 11: Volumetric Lightmaps, Fog, and Precomputing   273
  Introduction   273
  Technical requirements   274
  Volumetric lightmaps, lightmass, and fog   274
    Adding volumetric lightmaps with lightmass volumes   275
    Using Atmospheric Fog   277
    Using Volumetric Fog   282
  Lightmass tools   286
    Learning Lightmass settings and previewing tools   287
    Profiling lightmaps   293
  Summary   295
  Questions   296
  Further reading   296

Chapter 12: In-scene Video and Visual Effects   297
  Introduction   297
  Technical requirements   297
  Playing in-scene video with Media Framework   298
    Creating our assets   298
    Building and playing the video in-scene   302
  Adding physics particles   305
    Creating our initial emitter on projectile hit   306
    Orienting and adjusting physics of the particles   310
  Summary   312
  Questions   312
  Further reading   313

Chapter 13: Virtual Reality and Augmented Reality in UE4   315
  Introduction   315

Technical requirements   316
Making a VR project and adding new controls   317
   Making the initial VR project   317
   Building and deploying for GearVR   318
   Adding HMD controls   323
Making an AR project and porting our projectiles   328
   Making the initial AR project   328
   Android deployment specifics   330
   Porting our projectiles and firing them in AR   331
Summary   336
Questions   336
Further reading   336

Other Books You May Enjoy   337

Index   341

Preface

Unreal Engine 4 is an incredibly powerful set of technologies that are now made available to anyone and everyone for free. For students learning and the largest of teams working on all manner of games and platforms, it provides a means to bring all manner of apps and games to the public. This book is all about building the confidence of those who use it and raising the level of developers to a master level where any problem, any challenge in any project is a solvable problem.

Who this book is for

Developers experienced with UE4 development should regard this book as a reference for best practices, practical examples, and a broad dive into the major systems of the technology to build leadership skills and confidence.

What this book covers

Chapter 1, *Making a C++ project for a first-person shooter*, is our starting point for the whole book and its corresponding UE4 project on GitHub. We'll start by installing the engine and building it in C++. Then we'll add a first-person shooter template Unreal supplies for us, go over building it in C++ as well, then adding a new player class and controls.

Chapter 2, *Inventory and weapons for the player*, here we are adding some basics for gameplay and further getting comfortable adding C++ classes and connecting them to blueprints in the editor. In the end, the player has a fully functional inventory system including item pick-ups and cycling them with new controls.

Chapter 3, *Blueprint review and when to use BP scripting*, is a section where we examine UE4's Blueprint scripting system and its advantages and disadvantages in some detail, including a practical implementation in our game's map.

Chapter 4, *U.I. necessities, menus, HUD, and load/save;* in this chapter, we quickly accelerate into some deeper topics: after first getting our U.I. and HUD setup and hooked to our inventory, we'll deep-dive into UE4's file system and other classes to implement a save-anywhere load/save system and hook that up via U.I. as well.

Chapter 5, *Adding enemies!;* here we will import a new character and build and hook up its entire A.I. system to notice, animate to, and attack our player.

Chapter 6, *Changing levels, streaming, and retaining data;* switching maps (levels) in UE4 or utilizing one of its streaming options are a must for all games. We'll take some time to get familiar with Unreal's options here and then move on to retaining data when changing maps. Using our load/save system from above, we'll adapt it to allow our player to persist inventory across levels while also retaining the state of each map as it was left.

Chapter 7, *Getting audio in your game;* audio is an often overlooked piece of games that can make or break their immersion! After an overview of UE4's major audio systems, we'll dive into topics such as material-based impact sounds and environmental effects.

Chapter 8, *Shader editing and optimization tips;* materials and the shaders they create are arguably Unreal's most obviously important system. The visuals possible in UE4 are nearly limitless, but one needs to have an understanding of the limits and costs when using it. We'll go through some practical examples creating new materials and profiling them to get familiar with how to optimize your shaders and adapt to different platforms.

Chapter 9, *Adding an in-game cutscene with Sequencer;* this chapter introduces the reader to Sequencer, the in-game cutscene tool mainly used and supported in UE4 now. After making an in-game scene with our player and enemy A.I., we'll discuss some alternatives to Sequencer.

Chapter 10, *Packaging the game (PC, mobile);* no game is complete if it can't be put and run on its target platform! Here we'll go through some examples of packaging the game and installing, as well as discuss some of the differences in UE4 between launching on a device and doing a standalone build.

Chapter 11, *Volumetric lightmaps, fog, and precomputing;* UE4 offers a ton of amazing graphics systems, but its lighting is one well known and respected in the industry as top-notch. This chapter explores some of the advanced lighting available and adding it to our game, as well as adding and modifying both atmospheric and volume fog.

Chapter 12, *In-scene video and visual effects;* here we explore UE4's Media Framework and some of the cool things it provides. Specifically, here we'll take some video captured of the game's earlier in-game scene and play it in-game as a video file (MP4). We'll also explore Unreal's particle systems and physics particles, adding these to our projectile impacts.

Chapter 13, *Virtual Reality and Augmented Reality in UE4;* two of the newest major additions to Unreal's growing list of platforms are VR and AR. In this final chapter, we'll create two standalone projects (one for each), and modify and implement unique features of each, including porting our projectiles from the main project into our AR project!

To get the most out of this book

Fundamental comfort with using Unreal Engine 4 is an important starting point, but not mandatory. The objective of this book is to take those who work in the technology to a level where they are comfortable enough with all aspects to be a leader and driver of that technology on a project. While UE4 is a multi-platform set of technology, a Windows PC with Visual Studio is the primary development platform, also used frequently is a MacBook Pro and XCode, and Android phones (including GearVR) and iOS devices are also represented.

Download the example code files

You can download the example code files for this book from your account at `www.packt.com`. If you purchased this book elsewhere, you can visit `www.packt.com/support` and register to have the files emailed directly to you.

You can download the code files by following these steps:

1. Log in or register at `www.packt.com`.
2. Select the **SUPPORT** tab.
3. Click on **Code Downloads & Errata**.
4. Enter the name of the book in the **Search** box and follow the onscreen instructions.

Once the file is downloaded, please make sure that you unzip or extract the folder using the latest version of:

- WinRAR/7-Zip for Windows
- Zipeg/iZip/UnRarX for Mac
- 7-Zip/PeaZip for Linux

The code bundle for the book is also hosted on GitHub at `https://github.com/PacktPublishing/Mastering-Game-Development-with-Unreal-Engine-4-Second-Edition`. In case there's an update to the code, it will be updated on the existing GitHub repository.

We also have other code bundles from our rich catalog of books and videos available at `https://github.com/PacktPublishing/`. Check them out!

Download the color images

We also provide a PDF file that has color images of the screenshots/diagrams used in this book. You can download it here: https://www.packtpub.com/sites/default/files/downloads/9781788991445_ColorImages.pdf.

Conventions used

There are a number of text conventions used throughout this book.

CodeInText: Indicates code words in text, database table names, folder names, filenames, file extensions, pathnames, dummy URLs, user input, and Twitter handles. Here is an example: "Mount the downloaded WebStorm-10*.dmg disk image file as another disk in your system."

A block of code is set as follows:

```
/** Muzzle offset */
UPROPERTY(EditAnywhere, BlueprintReadWrite, Category = Projectile)
class USceneComponent* MuzzleLocation;
```

Any command-line input or output is written as follows:

```
$ mkdir css
$ cd css
```

Bold: Indicates a new term, an important word, or words that you see onscreen. For example, words in menus or dialog boxes appear in the text like this. Here is an example: "Select **System info** from the **Administration** panel."

Warnings or important notes appear like this.

Tips and tricks appear like this.

Get in touch

Feedback from our readers is always welcome.

General feedback: Email `feedback@packt.com` and mention the book title in the subject of your message. If you have questions about any aspect of this book, please email us at `questions@packt.com`.

Errata: Although we have taken every care to ensure the accuracy of our content, mistakes do happen. If you have found a mistake in this book, we would be grateful if you would report this to us. Please visit `www.packt.com/submit-errata`, selecting your book, clicking on the Errata Submission Form link, and entering the details.

Piracy: If you come across any illegal copies of our works in any form on the Internet, we would be grateful if you would provide us with the location address or website name. Please contact us at `copyright@packt.com` with a link to the material.

If you are interested in becoming an author: If there is a topic that you have expertise in and you are interested in either writing or contributing to a book, please visit `authors.packtpub.com`.

Reviews

Please leave a review. Once you have read and used this book, why not leave a review on the site that you purchased it from? Potential readers can then see and use your unbiased opinion to make purchase decisions, we at Packt can understand what you think about our products, and our authors can see your feedback on their book. Thank you!

For more information about Packt, please visit `packt.com`.

1

Making a C++ Project for a First-person Shooter

Introduction

Welcome to Mastering Unreal Engine 4! The goal of this book is to take individuals who are familiar with UE4 and C++ development to the next level in a holistic way. While some chapters will focus on specific system implementations and best practices in depth, others may give a more broad view of the large UE4 systems that are often used by content creation team members. By the end, you should have a solid foundation on which to make the best decisions concerning the use of UE4's technology with any scope or platform of project, and you will be able to guide a whole team towards seeing the project through to the end. There will be many areas in which you can directly implement these systems into game projects, but the overall goal of this book is to be able to address any needs from a technical direction side, giving you a base of knowledge that's a step above that of those who simply write code.

In this chapter, we will start a project for a basic combat game so that we have a basis for adding and working on more advanced features when we go forward. While some of this is automatically managed from UE4's game templates, we will go through all the necessary steps to make sure that the core setup referenced through the rest of the book is added, built, and tested, and that some new gameplay systems are implemented and demonstrated.

The major topics to be covered through the rest of this chapter are as follows:

- Setting up and creating a new first-person shooter project
- Overriding existing UE4 classes
- Adding and implementing simple C++ functions for them
- Quick review of build and running options

Technical requirements

For this chapter, you will need the following components:

- Visual Studio 2015 or 2017 (any edition)
- Unreal Engine 4.18.3 or higher built from source code

Some quick notes on platforms and installations: the aforementioned components assume that you will be using a Windows 10 PC, but there is no reason that a Mac running a current version of Xcode cannot benefit from and perform all the same work explored in this book. As the work presented will be from VS and reference some of its features, this is the recommended working environment as we progress through the chapters, but it is not specifically required. Samples will be tested from time to time and built on Mac mainly for iOS purposes in later chapters, but this book will not focus on IDE specifics other than giving steps (typically in Visual Studio terms) and tips. Code samples may reflect formatting that comes from `wholeTomato.com`'s Visual Assist tool, which I highly recommend for Visual Studio users, but their tool does not affect building or results.

You can find all the sources referenced in all of this book's chapters at `https://github.com/mattedmonds404/Mastering`, with revision history for the work presented in each chapter

For this chapter and its work, be sure to select the branch named `Chapter1`, the branch's dropdown on the top left of GitHub's web interface, or use the direct link for this chapter's branch at `https://github.com/mattedmonds404/Mastering/tree/Chapter1`.

Two notes on using the project directly from GitHub: You still need to have the engine installed from source locally so you can right-click the project (`Mastering/Mastering.uproject`) and click **Select Unreal Engine Version**, and you will need to choose your installation file, which will also build the proper project files. Upon launching the `Mastering.sln` file in VS, please go through the following steps:

1. Right-click the `Mastering` game project in the solution explorer and select **Set as Startup Project** so when running from VS, you launch directly into the editor for this project.
2. Set the configuration to **Development Editor**, with the platform set as **Win64**.
3. It may be necessary to right-click directly on the **UE4 Project** in the solution explorer and click **Build**. Sometimes, when building a game project, it will not pick up the full dependencies needed for building the engine, if this was not already done separately.

The engine version that we will be using is 4.19.0.

Building the FPS C++ project

In this section, we will go through the steps of creating a new project from scratch using the Unreal Project Browser. For those familiar with these steps already, the process should be relatively quick and straightforward. For anyone new to this setup, which can be typical of team members joining projects that are already in full development, there are some necessary steps to getting started. Since we will be working in C++ and using Visual Studio, I will make a quick aside here for users of the engine without the source code: Since this book will endeavor not to modify the engine source directly, it is still necessary for you to build C++ projects, as this is what this book will focus on. A blueprint-only project can be made without building source, and some pros and cons of this are explored in Chapter 3, *Blueprint Review and When to Use BP Scripting*, but again, this is not the way this book's information is presented in most implementation cases. It is also worth noting that Epic Games are quite receptive to users of their technology finding issues or improvements that they can help resolve, and if given proper debugging information, they typically respond to these raised issues much more readily on their answer hub forums, such as http://answers.unrealengine.com. Additionally, if your project needs a fix or change to engine code immediately before Epic Games can help, you will need to be comfortable debugging and building the engine. Lastly, if you would like to make pull requests of the types of changes or fixes that are to be integrated by Epic Games, you will also want to bind it to their GitHub project in Git. So, going forward, we will proceed as if we are installing the engine and project on a fresh computer with the full ability to rebuild from source code.

In the following section, we will do some modifications to the game mode and player, recompile these, and see the results in-game. For those wishing to skip ahead, all of the work that will be presented is available on the GitHub repository in the Chapter1 branch, as noted previously.

There are three major steps to getting a brand new project up and running:

1. Download and install the UE4 source and compile it.
2. Run the editor to the project browser for the first time and pick a template.
3. Build and run that project.

Installing and building UE4

Our first step is to download the UE4 source code and build it. This can be done in a number of ways. If this is your first time doing this, the simplest way is to go to their GitHub site to acquire the engine, at https://github.com/EpicGames/UnrealEngine.

For the link above to work, you must be signed in to GitHub, and have applied as an Unreal Developer. See: `https://wiki.unrealengine.com/ GitHub_Setup` for details.

Click the **Clone or download** button to see your options. From here, the simplest solution is simply to select the option to download the project as a ZIP file and unzip it wherever you like on your hard drive, as shown in the following screenshot:

Using the website is always a viable option with Git. While I am not personally a fan of the GitHub Desktop app, it is also a possibility that you can explore at this point in the process. And while I would say there are some user-experience issues with SourceTree, it is a free app that I do recommend for managing GitHub projects. For those comfortable with command-line work, there are a number of options, as well as a terminal that you can open in order to use these commands in SourceTree. The important part, for now, is to get the UE4 tree installed so that we can get to building!

The first thing to do when downloading a new version of the engine, be it an update or fresh install, is to always run Setup.bat (or the setup command on Mac) in the main installation folder before doing any other steps. Make sure that the pop-up window is getting all the platforms you use, ensuring that it pulls the required files for the platform that are described in the README.md file in the same folder.

Once the Setup.bat/setup command has completed, run the GenerateProjectFiles.bat file, and a UE4.sln file will appear in the same folder. A quick note on the state of UE4-generated solutions and VS 2015 and VS 2017: UE4 generates VS 2015 project files by default. It is possible to specify -2017 as a batch file argument. It is currently not necessary to build for 2017, and the 2015 project files open, build, and run perfectly well in both VS 2015 and VS 2017. However, if you have both versions of VS installed, then by default it will try to open them in VS 2015, which can be very annoying. As of writing this book, using either version of Visual Studio should grant the same results, and this was tested here, but going forward, what is in GitHub will force you to use VS 2017 for building in the editor. There is a discussion about why and how this is set later in this chapter in the *Overriding the Character Class* portion of the *Modifying Our Game with C++* section.

The steps that we need to go through to have the engine built are now very straightforward:

1. Double click the .sln and open it in VS.
2. For now, right-click the UE4 project in the solution explorer and select **Set as Startup Project**.
3. Select **Development Editor** as the **Configuration** (or **DebugGame**; more on this later), and **Win64** as the **Platform**.
4. Build the project. This can take an hour, depending on your hardware setup. Some build recommendations are listed at the end of this section.

Running the editor and picking a template

Our next step is running the editor. Launch the engine in VS by pressing *F5*. Without a game or app project in the solution, this will take you directly to the Unreal project browser. You can also easily do this any time later by right-clicking the UE4 project in the solution explorer and debugging or running it directly. I also recommend simply creating a shortcut to your UE4 install folder's `/Engine/Binaries/Win64/UE4Editor.exe` file, as sometimes it can be beneficial to quickly launch this outside of your programming IDE. From the Project Browser, go through the following steps:

1. Click the **New Project** tab, and under it, the **C++** tab.
2. Pick the **First Person** icon as our type to make our **first-person shooter (FPS)** base.
3. Pick a destination folder and a project name, and click **Create Project**.
4. If you choose a project name other than **Mastering**, please read the following information box.

The choices for **Desktop/Console**, **Quality**, and **Starter Content** can be left as their defaults, but feel free to hover over them and click their drop-down arrows to see the options for each, as well as the brief descriptions of what they do. **Starter Content** is actually an Unreal content pack, and we will be adding it manually in a later chapter.

 As the project presented here is set on GitHub as **Mastering**, that will be the name used throughout this book to refer to the project name. Unreal's templates use this for making several of the basic files added to the project, too. So, for example, when referring to `MasteringCharacter.h`, if you chose another name, please reference `(Your Project's Name)Character.h` from what the template built. For simplicity, it is recommended that you simply name it the same.

At this point, UE4 will close the project browser, generate the game's project files, and attempt to open it in VS. Naturally, at this point, it is a good idea to simply close the engine-only IDE session, as the engine project is also opened in the project solution. As you can see, the project you named should now be the startup project, and should contain several source files for the C++ template.

Building and running the game project

Now, we can finally build and run our game. Building the FPS sample project should go very quickly, and unless you change to another configuration or platform, it will not require the building of any of the engine code again. As a general rule, it is a good idea to build DebugGame versions for testing. Using this, you will get some extra runtime information and safety checks for your project's code, but typically without a significant change to performance when testing. So in our case, I recommend using DebugGame Editor, even though we built the engine in development. DebugGame Editor, as a standalone configuration (DebugGame) running on you PC, will build only the game project's code in debug, but will continue using the engine in its faster-running development configuration. Changing the configuration to Debug Editor, for example, would force the engine to fully build in debug as well. The engine also runs rather slowly in areas in debug builds, and maintaining both debug and development builds of the engine is time-consuming and usually unnecessary, unless it is actually debugging engine code directly. Once the project finishes building, simply run it using *F5*, like we did with the engine-only solution session. This will launch the editor with your game as the game project. The editor in UE4 is where all developers, including programmers, will do a huge amount of work and testing while building a game or app. **Play In Editor** (**PIE**) is one of Unreal's greatest strengths, as is the hot-reload of the game library while working in the editor. As projects grow in complexity, and the game flow may change from the simple starting of a level, hot-reloads and PIE itself may not always be a viable option for testing, but for our work in this section, it is perfect for showing off some of its advantages. Generally, when working on gameplay systems or debugging new code, PIE will be your best friend.

So, "sounds great!", you say. Feel free to give it a shot with the **Play** button near the right side of the top bar of the editor's default layout. Immediately, you'll notice that you can move around with the traditional WASD FPS keyboard controls, fire a weapon (with some physics impact on its projectile when it hits the cubes in the level), and even jump with the spacebar.

At this early stage, it is always a good idea to consider your controls. It is always recommended that you maintain viable PC controls for any game type for any team to use while working in the editor and PIE. Even if a game or app will not use a PC as its native platform, such as those using a mobile or VR, the speed and ease of testing in PIE makes maintaining parallel PC controls very valuable. In fact, if you go to the game project and open the `MasteringCharacter.cpp` file and browse through some of the input code, you will notice that it specifically supports two methods of turning in order to correspond to a control stick or virtual control stick on mobile, as well as direct axis input, such as a mouse. There is also commented-out code to support one-touch movement and turning on a touch-screen device, such as a phone or tablet. In the next section, we will add a new input. You are welcome to browse the existing inputs to see what was already set up and bound across the various platforms. Just keep in mind that at a time like this, it is typically much easier to begin maintaining controls across multiple platforms earlier than it is to add controls for a whole platform later.

Modifying our game with C++

In this section, we will look at some quick ways to add new features and gameplay to a project by adding a new mechanic to this FPS game: stealth. We will do this by overriding some of the existing supplied classes in the template, and adding a new input and some new code. At the end of this section, we will run the game, test that our code is definitely doing what we want, and see those results in game as the character crouches when the input is down. We will go through the following steps:

1. Add a new C++ class from the editor.
2. Modify this class and let it hot-reload back into the running editor.
3. Add a new input and gameplay mechanic and see it in action.

Overriding the character class

To facilitate our future work and start some good practices, we will add a bit of specialized game code here by subclassing the existing `MasteringCharacter` native (implemented in C++) class that supplied. This can be done directly in Visual Studio by hand, but Epic Games have once again supplied us with some shortcuts in Unreal that we will use from the editor. So, let's begin with the editor opened to our project, as we left it in the previous section.

We will begin in the content browser window, which is typically docked to the bottom section of the editor by default. If it is not already open for you, or was closed for some reason, just reopen it by clicking on the **Window** at the top and scroll to **Content Browser**, then **Content Browser 1**, and it will reopen as a free-standing window. I would dock this wherever you are comfortable in the editor, or, of course, it can be a free-standing window. What is important, however, is on the left-hand side. Just under the **Add New** dropdown is a small icon with three lines and a little arrow. Click this to open the **Sources** panel, which I find extremely helpful for navigating content in the editor. In there, under **Content,** is a folder called `FirstPersonCPP`, and in that is a `Blueprints` folder. Click on that folder and you should see a `FirstPersonCharacter` item on the right panel. This is the blueprint representation of the character we currently play when the game is started, and it is required to have an instance in the map for the game to function properly, given the way this C++ FPS template is made. This is one of the only blueprints used in the C++ FPS template, but let's open it and take a look at what is available from our native class in C++ code in the `MasteringCharacter.h/.cpp` file, which shows up here in a blueprint representation in the editor. Right now, it just looks like a collection of variables, with a line at the top starting with **NOTE:** and ending with a blue link to **Open Full Blueprint Editor**. A much more in-depth discussion of blueprints and their classes and interaction with C++ will be made in `Chapter 3`, *Blueprint Review and When to Use BP Scripting*. For now, just click the blue link so that we can see a bit of how these variables define our character in the game. The strict C++ style of the template makes very little use of this blueprint; it really is just a collection of some variables for the use of the template. But if you now click the **Viewport** tab at the top, you can see just what some of these variables do. For example, on the right in the **Details** tab, there should be an open flyout labeled **Camera**. Under this, the first variable is **Base Turn Rate** with a greyed-out value of 45.0. In code, this is used to determine how fast our character can turn, but it can't be edited. Let's go see why.

Switch back a moment and look in Visual Studio at `MasteringCharacter.h`. Down in one of the class' public sections, you should see the following lines:

```
/** Base turn rate, in deg/sec. Other scaling may affect final turn rate.
*/
UPROPERTY(VisibleAnywhere, BlueprintReadOnly, Category=Camera)
float BaseTurnRate;
```

The UPROPERTY macro is the method in which a C++ variable is bound into a blueprint class, where it can be seen and/or edited. In this case, the flags specified in the VisibleAnywhere BlueprintReadOnly macro are why we can view it in the blueprint, but not edit it, and the Category=Camera is why it is under the **Camera** flyout. Variables are automatically displayed in blueprints based on their camel case from C++, so each capital letter makes a word in the blueprint representation, such as BaseTurnRate, in our case. In the MasteringCharacter.cpp file, you can see in the constructor that BaseTurnRate = 45.f is specified, hence its value is shown in the editor. Again, this will all be used more and more, but a quick overview is needed for the changes that we will make shortly.

Our next steps are going to create a build of our game in the editor, so we will mention again the issues that will arise from having both VS 2015 and VS 2017. If you do not have VS 2015 installed and only use VS 2017, feel free to skip to the steps past this paragraph.

To force everything to open in Visual Studio 2017, follow two steps. First, in the project's readme.md file from GitHub, you will see instructions on how to make a batch file, or use the same line by copy-pasting in a command prompt, to generate your project files in VS 2017 from Explorer. In addition, when the editor generates these files, as noted, it will also default to VS 2015, which can be very annoying if you have both IDEs installed, as you may be working in VS 2017 and then the editor will make a build and try to open your project in VS 2015! You will want to go to the **Settings** tab at the top of the editor, open **Project Settings**, then scroll down under **Platforms** to the **Windows** flyout, as shown in the following screenshot:

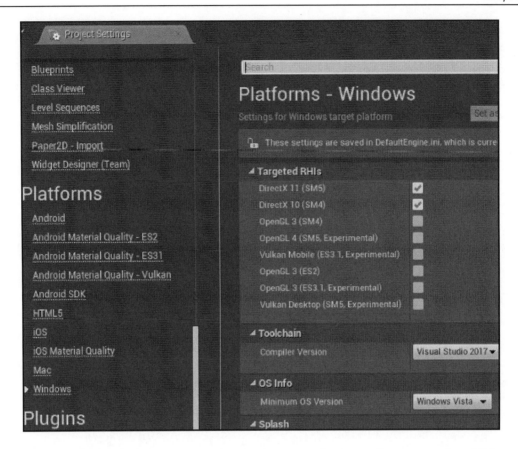

Select **Visual Studio 2017** as the compiler, as shown in the preceding screenshot. This should fix the problem of unwanted VS 2015 project files once and for all. This is what is checked in to GitHub, and if you are using only VS 2015 or don't want this behavior, just go to that same **Compiler Version** line and set it to **Default** or explicitly back to **2015**.

So, back in the main editor window, we will add our new class, derived from `MasteringCharacter`, by going through the following steps:

1. From the top menu bar, click **File** and select **New C++ Class**.
2. In the **Choose Parent Class** window, click the **Show All Classes** box on the top right.
3. In the **Search** field, start typing **MasteringCh** until it shows only **MasteringCharacter**, and then click on this option.
4. Make sure that the **Selected Class** field reads **Mastering Character** and click **Next**.
5. Change its name from **MyMasteringCharacter** to **StealthCharacter** and click **Create Class**.

In step 1, note that you can also access the **New C++ Class** option from the popup by simply right-clicking in a normal content browser window. Also, in step 2, over time it will just become a habit for you to always immediately click the **Show All Classes** box. It is nice that Epic Games filters it to some useful classes by default for new users, but as projects grow, you are typically using your own custom classes far more than these.

The editor should then tell you that it is compiling the new C++ code, and notify you when it has finished successfully on the bottom right. One very important note to bear in mind with this hot-reload concept is that if you now return to Visual Studio, it will want to reload the game project solution. This will prompt you to stop debugging, and if you say yes, it will close the editor! A technique I frequently use is just to attach and detach the debugger to the editor as needed. In VS, under the **Debug** menu is the **Detach All** command (I like this bound to *Ctrl + D*). This allows the editor to continue, and you can reload the solution safely as many times as needed. Once you want to debug some code, just reattach it to the running editor. To do this, go back to **Debug** and **Attach** it to **Process** (I like this bound to *Alt + D*). Click in the big field of **Processes,** and just tap the *U* key, and look for `UE4Editor.exe`. Double click this, and you are right back to debugging.

Editing our class in VS and hot-reloading the editor

So, now that our class is added with the **MasteringCharacter** as its parent, let's edit it in C++ and see our changes over in the editor. I suggest detaching the debugger as described in the last paragraph, but stopping debugging and restarting the editor is not a problem if you decide to do that. If you do detach, note that you need to right-click on the **Mastering** project in the solution explorer, select **Unload Project**, and then right-click it again and click on **Reload Project** to make sure that everything matches the current state (this is much faster than closing and reopening VS). In the solution explorer, you can now find the StealthCharacter.h and .cpp files under **Source/Mastering**. Open these. There's not much to them yet, but let's quickly add a new variable so that we can go look at it in the editor later. Add the following lines in the StealthCharacter.h file after the GENERATED_BODY() line:

```
public:
        /** Modifier to our turn and pitch rate when in stealth mode */
        UPROPERTY(EditAnywhere, BlueprintReadWrite, Category = Gameplay)
        float StealthPitchYawScale = 0.5f;
```

Back in Visual Studio, we will add the following to StealthCharacter.h after the StealthPitchYawScale variable that we added earlier:

```
public:
        virtual void SetupPlayerInputComponent(UInputComponent*
PlayerInputComponent) override;

        virtual void AddControllerPitchInput(float Val) override;
        virtual void AddControllerYawInput(float Val) override;

        void Stealth();
        void UnStealth();

protected:
        bool bIsStealthed = false;
```

Here, we are following the patterns from `MasteringCharacter`, which you can study further, but the short version is that we will bind a new input to two functions (`Stealth` and `UnStealth`), then override a base class's functions for using yaw and pitch input to slow these down by our scale. We will do this by adding the following code to `StealthCharacter.cpp`:

```cpp
void AStealthCharacter::SetupPlayerInputComponent(UInputComponent*
PlayerInputComponent)
{
        // Bind jump events
        PlayerInputComponent->BindAction("Stealth", IE_Pressed, this,
&AStealthCharacter::Stealth);
        PlayerInputComponent->BindAction("Stealth", IE_Released, this,
&AStealthCharacter::UnStealth);

        Super::SetupPlayerInputComponent(PlayerInputComponent);
}

void AStealthCharacter::AddControllerPitchInput(float Val)
{
        const float fScale = bIsStealthed ? StealthPitchYawScale : 1.0f;

        Super::AddControllerPitchInput(Val * fScale);
}

void AStealthCharacter::AddControllerYawInput(float Val)
{
        const float fScale = bIsStealthed ? StealthPitchYawScale : 1.0f;

        Super::AddControllerYawInput(Val * fScale);
}

void AStealthCharacter::Stealth()
{
        bIsStealthed = true;
        Super::Crouch();
}

void AStealthCharacter::UnStealth()
{
        bIsStealthed = false;
        Super::UnCrouch();
}
```

Most of this should be clear to experienced UE4 C++ programmers, but do note that our overridden functions for `Stealth` and `UnStealth` call existing functions in the `ACharacter` class that we distantly derive from. This uses existing mechanics to crouch and uncrouch our character, saving us the trouble of making these ourselves. You can build the project now, or after adding the following input, which causes an editor restart anyway, so make sure you did indeed save the editor changes that we made!

There are two ways to add our new input binding. The best way is to once again open **Project Settings** in the **Settings** tab in the main editor window. From here, scroll to **Engine** and **Input** in the flyouts, and you will see a section for **Bindings** on the right, and under it, **Action Mappings**. Click the small plus symbol to the right of **Action Mappings** and it will display a new line under it. We will rename the **NewActionMapping** that it added to **Stealth**, and then we will click the small plus symbol to the right of our new **Stealth** line. Click the **None** drop-down menu and scroll down to **Left Shift**, as shown in the following screenshot:

We have now bound the action named **Stealth** to the left *Shift* key of the keyboard. This will add a line to the game's `/Config/DefaultInput.ini` file and update the running editor version at the same time. If you were to instead manually add this line right at the top after `[/Script/Engine.InputSettings]` (that is, +ActionMappings=(ActionName="Stealth", Key= Left Shift)) and then save that file, the engine will not automatically reload the `.ini` files, which requires the relaunching of the editor to pick up the changes, if you were to modify it this way! So, always remember to try to edit settings from the **Settings** window, and if you do modify things in a `.ini` file, always remember to restart any running editor or standalone versions of the game on your PC to pick those up.

We need one last change in our `FirstPersonCharacter` blueprint to bring things all together, so open it in the full blueprint editor window again. At the bottom left, under its **Components** tab, is `CharacterMovement (Inherited)`. Click on this. There are now many properties on the right, but scroll down until you see the **Nav Movement** flyout and open it. At the top, there is the **Movement Capabilities** flyout, and in that we need to check the **Can Crouch** checkbox so that it is true. Note that the **Compile** button near the top left went from having a green checkmark to having an orange question mark. Click the **Compile** button to update the blueprint with this change and press *Ctrl + S* again to save.

Now, when running the game, note that when you press and hold *Shift*, the player's perspective moves down a small distance, which is set by a couple of other existing blueprint parent class variables, and our turn and pitch speed is slow down by our `StealthPitchYawScale`. Success! Now, feel free to modify the pitch and yaw scale value, even as the game is running, and see how much we speed up and slowed down while stealthed. This is also a great time to set some breakpoints in our functions and just step through how things are working on the C++ side, but at this stage, our mechanic is in and proven.

Summary

In this chapter, we have gone from having potentially no engine, zero source code, and no projects to having a local build of the UE4 engine and an FPS project of our own, and added code and overriding functions to add new gameplay to it. This is a great start, and gets us past many of the hurdles in making games and gives us a great foundation to build upon in subsequent chapters.

Next, we'll be looking much more in-depth at controls and improvements we can make on the basics that we mentioned in this chapter. We will also learn how to add some more game features, including inventory and weapon pickups. After that, there will be a much more in-depth discussion of blueprints and what they do for us, why they are so valuable, and when they can be a problem. Rounding out our initial efforts in this section, we will look at the UI, loading and saving, and adding an AI creature, before we quickly accelerate into several more advanced and varied topics in the following chapters!

Questions

Work through the following questions to test what you have learned:

1. What are some advantages to building the engine from source code?
2. Where is the source code for UE4 found?
3. What step always needs to be done after getting any updated version of UE4 before building anything?
4. How are variables exposed in the blueprint declared in C++?
5. How do we quickly add and test our functionality without needing to create a new blueprint in the editor?
6. Why is DebugGame a good choice to use as your configuration during development?
7. Why is requiring changes to `.ini` files in order to add new features a poor choice?
8. When changing a blueprint property, what step do you have to perform before saving it?

Further reading

https://docs.unrealengine.com/en-us/Programming/Introduction

Inventory and Weapons for the Player

2

Introduction

Welcome to our next chapter. In this chapter, we will build upon the Mastering project as it stands so far with a brand new system for handling the inventory and changing weapons. Wherever possible, any hardcoded types of systems will also be removed at this point, such as referencing assets by name from C++. When making such changes, there will typically be an accompanying discussion of why this is important to a given project. By the end of this chapter, though, we should be referencing all of our classes and assets in an easy-to-modify way, and have a very fast iteration time, changing things like adding new weapons and weapon pick-ups. In order, we will cover the following topics:

- Adding a `Weapon` class
- Inventory for weapons in C++
- Creating and using a `WeaponPickup` class
- Cycling weapons with new control bindings

Technical requirements

All requirements found in `Chapter 1`, *Making a C++ Project for a First-Person Shooter*, including its output Mastering project or one at a similar point of development, are required for this chapter.

Following our chapter progress branching theme, the GitHub work done in this chapter can be found here:

```
https://github.com/PacktPublishing/Mastering-Game-Development-with-Unreal-
Engine-4-Second-Edition/tree/Chapter-2
```

Engine Version used: 4.19.0.

Adding the Weapon and Inventory classes

Our goal for this section is to add these two new classes to our game and convert the hardcoded weapon template made for us into the new weapon class and add it to our new inventory class for our player. We will start with the editor running and take a moment to examine the existing weapon and see how it was made in the template, as a means to gather the information needed for designing and implementing this new weapon class.

Creating our Weapon class

While the FPS template gives a great jump-start to a project like this, it's very limited in a number of ways. It is intended to be the most minimal and agnostic implementation allowing us, the developers, to build in whatever direction is needed. As a theme throughout our improvements and expansion of this game project, as our needs for new systems and features arise, this is the motivation for our work. While the very simple weapon the template implements demonstrates all the core pieces of an FPS weapon, it is not at all easily modified, so thus, we need a new class. In a typical FPS game you are often switching between multiple unique weapons on a character, so we will make that possible step-by-step here.

To first see how the existing weapon was made, we need to open up **Content | FirstPersonCPP | Blueprints | FirstPersonCharacter** again in the Content Browser, and if you are re-opening it, click on the **Open Full Blueprint Editor** option again. In the main window, click the **Viewport** tab and as you click on some of these other items, you can see how they are shown or represented currently in the blueprint as it stands. The first thing to click, however, is in the **Components** tab, the very first item you can select, **FirstPersonCharacter(self)**. This is the overall class used for our player currently, and if you picked up where we left off in the previous chapter, is currently set to the StealthCaracter class, which is derived from our MasteringCharacter of course. Upon selecting that in the **Components** tab, you can see on the right in the **Details** tab you can see several variables under the **Gameplay** and **Projectile** fly-outs that we are going to want to move to the new weapon class:

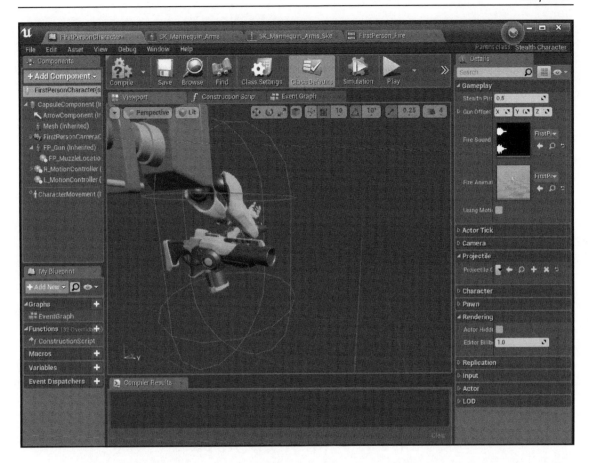

The **Gun Offset**, **Fire Sound**, **Fire Animation**, and the **Projectile Class** should all be moved into our new class as, of course, these will naturally vary from weapon to weapon. Looking back to the **Components** tab, you can also see there is an **FP_Gun (Inherited)** component, and under it, an **FPMuzzleLocation (Inherited)** component. These are a Skeletal Mesh Component and simple Scene Component, respectively, but also belong with the weapon and not with our character here directly.

So, back to the main editor window and the Content Browser, let's use the shortcut mentioned in Chapter 1, *Making a C++ Project for a First-Person Shooter*, and right-click in the main window to get the popup with **New C++ Class** near the top and add one. In this case, we want the parent class to simply be Actor, so for once we don't need to click the Show all classes option. Select it and then click **Next** as before. Here, we'll name the class MasteringWeapon, and click **Create Class**. And once more we'll get a hot-reload. Once that finishes, it's back to Visual Studio to add all the variables mentioned earlier that our new weapons will need.

Converting the existing gun

Opening up `MasteringWeapon.h` and `.cpp`, let's add some variables as `UPROPERTY` items again, and our goal now is to replicate what is currently done in `MasteringCharacter` in our weapon and then remove those items from the character class. As a reminder, the things our weapon needs to contain are as follows:

- Gun Offset (`FVector`)
- Fire Sound (`USoundBase`)
- Fire Animation (`UAnimMontage`)
- Projectile Class (`TSubclassOf<class AMasteringProjectile>`)
- Weapon Mesh (`USkeletalMeshComponent`)
- Muzzle Location (`USceneComponent`)

At this point, as we have a bit of code work to do and don't want to be hot-reloading a lot, I recommend shutting down the editor until we're ready to add a new instance of `MasteringWeapon` to the game. So, let's get to adding those variables to our new `.h` file. These first four you can literally cut (not copy, as we're removing them) and paste from the `MasteringCharacter.h` file after making a public section under GENERATED_BODY(), and add the declaration of the constructor while we are here:

```cpp
public:
        AMasteringWeapon();

        /** Gun muzzle's offset from the characters location */
        UPROPERTY(EditAnywhere, BlueprintReadWrite, Category = Gameplay)
        FVector GunOffset = FVector(100.0f, 0.0f, 10.0f);

        /** Projectile class to spawn */
        UPROPERTY(EditAnywhere, BlueprintReadWrite, Category = Projectile)
        TSubclassOf<class AMasteringProjectile> ProjectileClass;

        /** Sound to play each time we fire */
        UPROPERTY(EditAnywhere, BlueprintReadWrite, Category = Gameplay)
        class USoundBase* FireSound;

        /** AnimMontage to play each time we fire */
        UPROPERTY(EditAnywhere, BlueprintReadWrite, Category = Gameplay)
        class UAnimMontage* FireAnimation;
```

Do note, however, that the `ProjectileClass'` UPROPERTY line has been set to match the others, and it did not previously in `MasteringCharacter.h`. Now all we need is our Skeletal Mesh and Muzzle Location; we'll add the following:

```
/** Muzzle offset */
UPROPERTY(EditAnywhere, BlueprintReadWrite, Category = Projectile)
class USceneComponent* MuzzleLocation;
```

Now, keep in mind that we are departing from the template's hardcore C++ implementation of all of these game objects so that we can move to a more logical and helpful hybrid using blueprints. So, since all of our weapons will be instances of this class, for now let's just give the `GunOffset` the same default value it currently has (this variable is not very important right now) by changing its line in the `.h` file to the following:

```
FVector GunOffset = FVector(100.0f, 0.0f, 10.0f);
```

There will be a more in-depth discussion of the topic of blueprint/C++ balance in Chapter 3, *Blueprint Review and When to Use BP Scripting,* but for now you can always at least think of blueprint instances of classes as great containers for data, especially things that will be tuned during game design, such as weapon properties here. We now have all the variables we will be using in our weapon and could add a blueprint for our new gun, but it won't do anything yet, and also, by removing these variables from our `MasteringCharacter` class, of course, it won't compile now. Thus, our best course is to carry on a bit more and have our code in a better position. Back in `MasteringCharacter.h`, find and remove the `FP_Gun` and `FP_MuzzleLocation` variables. Then, search and remove all references to them *and* the four variables that we migrated to `MasteringWeapon.h` from the `MasteringCharacter.cpp` file. We can also remove the `VR_Gun` and `VR_MuzzleLocation` variables now as we'll make a whole new project when finally tackling a VR game later, so these are currently unimportant (but you can imagine otherwise converting them similarly in such a VR game).

 As a tip for how I work here, as I know I need to replicate the same functionality later in my weapon class that's currently in our character class, I just commented out those sections currently used in the character and then will remove them entirely as each is now handled by the weapon as we continue.

We can now also remove this line from `MasteringCharacter.cpp`, and we can be sure that we will need this in `MasteringWeapon.cpp`. Also cut and paste the line to there after `MasteringWeapon.h` include:

```
#include "MasteringProjectile.h"
```

Next, to get our components to show up in our blueprint instance, we need to add them in the constructor like so in our .cpp file (similar to how they were made in the character's constructor), and we also need to add some required headers, starting right after the preceding line:

```
#include "Runtime/Engine/Classes/Components/SkeletalMeshComponent.h"
#include "Runtime/Engine/Classes/Animation/AnimInstance.h"
#include "Kismet/GameplayStatics.h"


AMasteringWeapon::AMasteringWeapon()
{
        // Create a gun mesh component
        WeaponMesh =
CreateDefaultSubobject<USkeletalMeshComponent>(TEXT("WeaponMesh"));
        WeaponMesh->SetOnlyOwnerSee(true); // only the owning player will
see this mesh
        WeaponMesh->bCastDynamicShadow = false;
        WeaponMesh->CastShadow = false;
        WeaponMesh->SetupAttachment(RootComponent);

        // Our muzzle offset object
        MuzzleLocation =
CreateDefaultSubobject<USceneComponent>(TEXT("MuzzleLocation"));
        MuzzleLocation->SetupAttachment(WeaponMesh);
}
```

At this point, our character will be pretty broken if we play the game as they'll have no weapon, but as we need to do some editor work (adding a blueprint instance and another new class), this is a good time to build the game and start the editor back up. At this point, there is an intermediate commit submitted to GitHub's Chapter 2 branch available if you need to check that things match.

Creating an inventory and adding a default gun

Back in the editor once more, we can work on the two remaining pieces needed to get back to the level of weapon functionality we began with, while having abstracted out the functionality to the new class: a rudimentary inventory system, and an actual blueprint instance of a weapon like the one we just removed from our MasteringCharacter class.

First, let's add the new `MasteringWeapon` to the Content Browser. Right-click in the browser's main window again and select **Blueprint Class**:

Much like when we are creating a new C++ class, here, we need to click the **All Classes** flyout at the bottom and search for and click MasteringWeapon, and then the **Select** button at the bottom. Rename the item in the content browser to BallGun and open it in the BP editor. Once again, I find it best here to click the full blueprint editor to view the changes in the viewport tab as we edit. In the **Components** tab, select **WeaponMesh (Inherited)** and in its details, open the **Weapon Mesh** fly-out, go down to the **Mesh** fly-out, and there the **Skeletal Mesh** variable has a drop-down we can click. There are so few to choose from, so simply pick the SK_FPGun asset here. Back to the **Components** tab, select next the **MuzzleLocation (Inherited)** under the WeaponMesh and in the **Muzzle Location** and **Transform** flyouts, edit the **Relative Location** vector to be the same values we hardcoded previously: 0.2, 48.4, -10.6.

Now, back to the **Components** tab, and above the two components we were just editing, let's select the base class again, **BallGun(self)**, at the top. On the right, we have our **Gameplay** fly-out with our sound and animation variables. Select them from the drop-downs as the only assets we can, **FirstPersonTemplateWeaponFire02** and **FirstPersonFire_Montage**. Under the **Projectile** fly-out, select **FirstPersonProjectile** from its drop-down, and building our blueprint for this gun is now done! Click on the compile button and then save it:

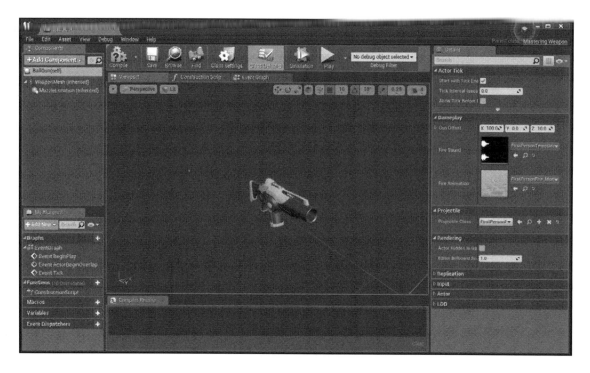

Lastly, we just need to get this very minimal inventory set up and we can return to code up the use of our weapon. Right-click in the Content Browser again and click New C++ Class. We'll make this one a very simple `UActorComponent` by choosing ActorComponent for the parent class, either in the filtered group or typing into the search in all classes. For the name, use MasteringInventory, click **Create Class**, and we will rebuild once more. In `MasteringInventory.h`, first we can this function as it will be unused (and remove the implementation in the `.cpp` file):

```
public:
        // Called every frame
        virtual void TickComponent(float DeltaTime, ELevelTick TickType,
FActorComponentTickFunction* ThisTickFunction) override;
```

We will need two variables and a couple of functions like so added after `BeginPlay()`:

```
protected:
        // Called when the game starts
        virtual void BeginPlay() override;

public:
        UPROPERTY(EditAnywhere, BlueprintReadWrite)
        TSubclassOf<class AMasteringWeapon> DefaultWeapon;
        /** Choose the best weapon we can of those available */
        void SelectBestWeapon(class AMasteringCharacter *Player);

        /** Select a weapon from inventory */
        void SelectWeapon(class AMasteringCharacter *Player,
TSubclassOf<class AMasteringWeapon> Weapon);

        /** Add a weapon to the inventory list */
        void AddWeapon(TSubclassOf<class AMasteringWeapon> Weapon);

        /** Add any default weapon we may have been set with */
        void AddDefaultWeapon();

        /** Get the currently selected weapon */
        FORCEINLINE TSubclassOf<class AMasteringWeapon> GetCurrentWeapon()
const { return CurrentWeapon; }

protected:
        TArray<TSubclassOf<class AMasteringWeapon> > WeaponsArray;
        TSubclassOf<class AMasteringWeapon> CurrentWeapon;
```

Notice here that our inventory component is only going to be dealing with class types, not with actual in-game actors. They will still be spawned by the `MasteringCharacter` class as they are equipped. We'll do that right after the implementations for the preceding functions are added to `MasteringInventory.cpp`, beginning directly after the `#include MasteringInventory.h` line:

```cpp
#include "MasteringCharacter.h"


// Sets default values for this component's properties
UMasteringInventory::UMasteringInventory()
{
        PrimaryComponentTick.bCanEverTick = true;
}

// Called when the game starts
void UMasteringInventory::BeginPlay()
{
        Super::BeginPlay();

        if (DefaultWeapon != nullptr)
        {
                AddWeapon(DefaultWeapon);
        }
}

void UMasteringInventory::SelectBestWeapon(class AMasteringCharacter
*Player)
{
        for (auto WeaponIt = WeaponsArray.CreateIterator(); WeaponIt;
++WeaponIt)
        {
                //TODO: add criteria for selecting a weapon
                {
                        SelectWeapon(Player, *WeaponIt);
                        break;
                }
        }
}

void UMasteringInventory::SelectWeapon(class AMasteringCharacter *Player,
TSubclassOf<class AMasteringWeapon> Weapon)
{
        Player->EquipWeapon(Weapon);
}

void UMasteringInventory::AddWeapon(TSubclassOf<class AMasteringWeapon>
```

```
Weapon)
{
        WeaponsArray.AddUnique(Weapon);
}
```

In `MasteringCharacter.h`, we need to add three things. In each of the following additions, I have also included the line of code that currently exists above where I placed the new line, so you can find where to place them. For the first, add UPROPERTY after `uint32 bUsingMotionControllers : 1`, which already exists in the `.h` file. Then, add the `AMasteringWeapon` pointer after `TouchItem`. And lastly, add the two function prototypes at the end of the third block after `GetFirstPersonCameraComponent()`:

```
uint32 bUsingMotionControllers : 1;

UPROPERTY(EditAnywhere, BlueprintReadWrite, Category = Gameplay)
class UMasteringInventory *Inventory;

class AMasteringWeapon* EquippedWeaponActor;

FORCEINLINE class UCameraComponent* GetFirstPersonCameraComponent() const {
return FirstPersonCameraComponent; }

FORCEINLINE class UCameraComponent* GetFirstPersonCameraComponent() const {
return FirstPersonCameraComponent; }

/** Equip a weapon */
void EquipWeapon(TSubclassOf<class AMasteringWeapon> Weapon);

/** Get the currently equipped weapon */
FORCEINLINE class AMasteringWeapon* GetEquippedWeapon() const { return
EquippedWeaponActor; };
```

Now, in the `.cpp` file, we'll need the new headers:

```
#include "XRMotionControllerBase.h" // for
FXRMotionControllerBase::RightHandSourceId
#include "MasteringInventory.h"
#include "MasteringWeapon.h"
```

We need one line added to the bottom of the constructor, and we can now delete all the previously commented-out code for equipping and firing the old gun:

```
Inventory = CreateDefaultSubobject<UMasteringInventory>(TEXT("Inventory"));
```

Our `BeginPlay()` is now very simple as well:

```
void AMasteringCharacter::BeginPlay()
{
```

```
        // Call the base class
        Super::BeginPlay();

        // Equip our best weapon on startup
        if (Inventory != nullptr)
        {
                Inventory->SelectBestWeapon(this);
        }
}
```

OnFire() is also much nicer looking; as you can see here, it is very compact and readable:

```
void AMasteringCharacter::OnFire()
{
        // try and fire a projectile
        if (GetEquippedWeapon() != nullptr)
        {
                UAnimInstance* AnimInstance = Mesh1P->GetAnimInstance();
                GetEquippedWeapon()->Fire(GetControlRotation(),
AnimInstance);
        }
}
```

And lastly, at the bottom of the file is the implementation for equipping a weapon:

```
void AMasteringCharacter::EquipWeapon(TSubclassOf<class AMasteringWeapon>
Weapon)
{
        UWorld *World = GetWorld();
        if (World == nullptr)
                return;

        if (EquippedWeaponActor != nullptr)
        {
                World->DestroyActor(EquippedWeaponActor);
        }

        const FRotator SpawnRotation = GetActorRotation();
        const FVector SpawnLocation = GetActorLocation();
        FActorSpawnParameters ActorSpawnParams;
        ActorSpawnParams.SpawnCollisionHandlingOverride =
ESpawnActorCollisionHandlingMethod::AlwaysSpawn;
        ActorSpawnParams.Owner = this;

        EquippedWeaponActor =
Cast<AMasteringWeapon>(World->SpawnActor(Weapon, &SpawnLocation,
&SpawnRotation, ActorSpawnParams));
        if (EquippedWeaponActor != nullptr)
```

```
        {
                //Attach gun mesh component to skeleton
                EquippedWeaponActor->AttachToComponent(Mesh1P,
FAttachmentTransformRules(EAttachmentRule::SnapToTarget, true),
TEXT("GripPoint"));
        }
}
```

Note that the actual spawn location and rotation are not really significant as we immediately attach a successfully spawned weapon to our mesh, but it's usually a good idea to have some reasonable defaults there to be safe.

At this point, we return to our MasteringWeapon files, first the .h file where we add this line near the bottom of the class:

```
public:
        /** Fire the weapon */
        void Fire(FRotator ControlRotation, class UAnimInstance* AnimInst);
```

And then implement it like so in the .cpp file to do all the work we were previously doing in the character:

```
void AMasteringWeapon::Fire(FRotator ControlRotation, class UAnimInstance*
AnimInst)
{
        // try and fire a projectile
        if (ProjectileClass != nullptr)
        {
                UWorld* const World = GetWorld();
                if (World != nullptr)
                {
                        // MuzzleOffset is in camera space, so transform it
to world space before offsetting from the character location to find the
final muzzle position
                        const FVector SpawnLocation = ((MuzzleLocation !=
nullptr) ? MuzzleLocation->GetComponentLocation() : GetActorLocation()) +
ControlRotation.RotateVector(GunOffset);

                        //Set Spawn Collision Handling Override
                        FActorSpawnParameters ActorSpawnParams;
                        ActorSpawnParams.SpawnCollisionHandlingOverride =
ESpawnActorCollisionHandlingMethod::AdjustIfPossibleButDontSpawnIfColliding
;

                        // spawn the projectile at the muzzle
World->SpawnActor<AMasteringProjectile>(ProjectileClass, SpawnLocation,
ControlRotation, ActorSpawnParams);
                }
```

```
        }

        // try and play the sound if specified
        if (FireSound != nullptr)
        {
                UGameplayStatics::PlaySoundAtLocation(this, FireSound,
    GetActorLocation());
        }


        // try and play a firing animation if specified
        if (FireAnimation != nullptr)
        {
                // Get the animation object for the arms mesh
                if (AnimInst != nullptr)
                {
                        AnimInst->Montage_Play(FireAnimation, 1.f);
                }
        }
    }
```

Now, all that's left to do is add a default weapon to our particular player's inventory component and we're back in business. Open the **FirstPersonCharacter** BP again in the editor. At the bottom of its **Components** tab now is our **Inventory (Inherited)**. Select it, and in the **Details tab**, under the **Gameplay**, **Inventory**, and **Mastering Inventory** fly-outs, click the **Default Weapon** drop-down and select **BallGun**. Now, playing the game should have everything looking just like it was before, but with a system in place that can accept all manner of new weapons for our character, simply by adding more **MasteringWeapon** blueprint assets and adding them to our inventory for selection, which is what our next section focuses on.

This is a great time to take a moment and set some breakpoints in these new functions and step through, making sure everything looks right in the debugger. Note that if you try to step through some functions and it steps right over them, check whether you're building the game in the Development Editor and set it to DebugGame Editor instead. Oftentimes, these smaller functions are simply optimized away in development.

Adding a WeaponPickup class

Now that we have a working inventory, if minimal, and a weapon class for creating new weapons, we need one more key piece: a way to add these new items to that inventory. There are functions now ready to receive this, but how do we get that into the game in a meaningful way? Well, there are a number of approaches here based on the type of game and its design needs. In the following case, we'll stick to a fairly traditional FPS-style game and add a weapon pickup that can be dropped into our game world either during level design or dynamically.

Creating a new actor class

As noted already, different games have different design needs in this area. If your game only ever had, for example, slots for weapon items (as many popular 3D action games do), then we wouldn't really need an inventory class, nor a weapon pickup class. You could save yourself some trouble by just adding a couple of `AMasteringWeapon` pointers to your player class and in that weapon, override the `AAcotr's Tick(float DeltaSeconds)` function to give it a behavior when on the ground, and stop that behavior while it is stored and hidden or shown when equipped by the player. In this case, we have a very flexible and open-ended system that can be used for a large variety of weapons all being stored at the same time. The reason for adding a pick-up here is to demonstrate a different behavior when the item is on the ground, and add some additional data that helps us expand the usefulness of our inventory. As in many action FPS games, we will give the item pickup a visibly noticeable rotation while it sits at the proper height on the ground, set up its collision settings so the player can pick it up, and add an ammo count and power level to our weapons so that we can automatically equip the best item we have when one is available or our equipped one becomes unusable. Of course, the pickup item will also reference the MasteringWeapon it represents, so we will quickly build a new one here with a new MasteringProjectile to differentiate it since we're currently working with limited assets.

For the curious, yes, this book will delve into some of the wonderful, but free, UE4 assets from the marketplace in future sections to address advanced visuals and give us some variety in the characters and more in our sample game. At the moment, however, we will simply work with what we have in the FPS template to quickly establish these core game concepts.

At this point, creating a new class is quite familiar, so hopefully we can speed through the steps a bit. If anything seems incorrect or not what is expected, naturally it is a good idea to skim through the steps previously presented regarding making a new class and begin work on its functionality. So, back in the editor, let's add yet another new C++ class, with the parent as a simple **Actor**. We'll name it `MasteringWeaponPickup`, and its implementation should actually go rather quickly compared to the more complicated classes we have been working on.

We have a decision to make on where the actual pick-up functionality is implemented. At this point, let's take a moment to revisit encapsulation. For any readers who may have been around to experience Unreal Engine 3, most have a similar story about looking at Actor.h and Actor.cpp and thinking their eyes were going to fall out. These were, no pun intended, epic files, with tens of thousands of lines of code that implemented a myriad of possible in-game behaviors for every single actor (no matter how simple) in the game. Those files are still a bit large, but thanks to massive efforts by Epic between UE3 and UE4, they managed to move huge amounts of specialized code into components and specific plugins, greatly reducing the volume of code and number of variables on such a widely used class. The easiest way to get this pickup working would be to simply drop it into our `MasteringCharacter` class and let our character colliding with a pickup do all the work. However, if you begin doing this for all the systems you add to a medium or large project, your character class will find itself in a state like UE3's actor files, and new team members will have a hard time figuring out where functionality is and will have to familiarize themselves often with the entire voluminous class to competently make changes. If we encapsulate the functionality needed into the items that generally "own" that game behavior, it makes learning the project much easier and modifications become less risky and more manageable in scope for newer developers on the team.

So in this case, let's start early with this practice, and put the pickup functionality as much as possible into our `MasteringWeaponPickup` class itself. Here are the set of functions and variables we will need in the body of the header:

```
public:
        // Sets default values for this actor's properties
        AMasteringWeaponPickup();

protected:
        // Called when the game starts or when spawned
        virtual void BeginPlay() override;

        virtual void NotifyActorBeginOverlap(AActor* OtherActor) override;

public:
        // Called every frame
        virtual void Tick(float DeltaTime) override;
```

```
UPROPERTY(EditAnywhere, BlueprintReadWrite)
TSubclassOf<class AMasteringWeapon> WeaponClass;

/** How fast the pickup spins while on the ground, degress/second
*/

UPROPERTY(EditAnywhere, BlueprintReadWrite, Category = Gameplay)
float RotationSpeed = 30.0f;

/** How much ammunition is provided for this weapon on pick-up */
UPROPERTY(EditAnywhere, BlueprintReadWrite, Category = Gameplay)
uint8 Ammunition = 10;

/** This weapon's relative weapon power to compare it to others */
UPROPERTY(EditAnywhere, BlueprintReadWrite, Category = Gameplay)
uint8 WeaponPower = 1;
```

A quick note on the `uint8` items at the end: it has been a known issue for some time that only this one is supported by classes exposed in blueprint. Adding `uint16` and `uint32` types would require a massive amount of work for several systems on Epic's part, so it is not ever a high priority on their list of features (the amount of work versus the benefit to developers isn't very high). In this case, it's no problem, so we can take the benefit of the 8-bit version to force all values in our blueprint instances to always be between 0-255. If you need a larger range, you're forced to use a normal full-sized (but signed) `int` and then the burden is on the code side for you to check that designers modifying these blueprints don't enter a value that's not valid. So, an ongoing theme through all the work done in this book will be to tailor your needs to your design. Weapon power here is just an arbitrary value, so we can differentiate which weapons are better than others. Something this basic and abstract may be perfect for your game, depending on the number of weapons, or maybe should be computed from various damage and speed types of factors.

An important part of being a top-level developer is good communication, and sitting with a designer to discuss a system, and (depending on the project size) putting this into a wiki page or another source of document storage, is key. An exaggerated example would be: if we knew with certainty that our game was never going to use more than one weapon, all of this inventory and weapon abstraction is largely unnecessary. Since I want to demonstrate how we can make it scale to a large number of weapons, that is the motivation for getting these systems in place early and as encapsulated as possible as we go.

So next, here are the implementations in the pickup's `.cpp` file:

```
#include "MasteringCharacter.h"
#include "MasteringInventory.h"


// Sets default values
```

```cpp
AMasteringWeaponPickup::AMasteringWeaponPickup()
{
    // Set this actor to call Tick() every frame.  You can turn this off to
improve performance if you don't need it.
        PrimaryActorTick.bCanEverTick = true;

}

// Called when the game starts or when spawned
void AMasteringWeaponPickup::BeginPlay()
{
        Super::BeginPlay();
}

void AMasteringWeaponPickup::NotifyActorBeginOverlap(AActor* OtherActor)
{
        AMasteringCharacter *player =
Cast<AMasteringCharacter>(OtherActor);

        if (player == nullptr)
        {
                return;
        }

        UMasteringInventory *Inventory = player->GetInventory();
        Inventory->AddWeapon(WeaponClass, Ammunition, WeaponPower);

        // here we automatically select the best weapon which may have
changed after adding the above,
        // NOTE: this should probably be an option the player can turn on
and off via UI
        Inventory->SelectBestWeapon();

        // and now that we've done our job, destroy ourselves
        Destroy();
}

// Called every frame
void AMasteringWeaponPickup::Tick(float DeltaTime)
{
        Super::Tick(DeltaTime);

        FRotator rotationAmount(0.0f, DeltaTime * RotationSpeed, 0.0f);

        AddActorLocalRotation(rotationAmount);
}
```

So, you can see, it's fairly simple. Most of what it does is spin around on the ground at the speed specified by RotationSpeed, allows itself to be picked up by a player, and then destroys itself. We'll talk about its collision filtering when we set up an instance, but notice that we cast the OtherActor pointer to a mastering character type: this of course works for subtypes (such as our StealthCharacter class), but any other Pawn classes will fail to cast there, returning null, so (as seen in that next line) we can ignore them now.

Setting up our blueprints

Next, we need an actual new weapon. This will be very quick as again, right now we have very little to work with in the way of art assets, so we will demonstrate things creatively using those same art assets. Right-click on our BallGun weapon blueprint and click **Duplicate**. Rename the duplicated one BigBallGun and do the same trick, duplicating the FirstPersonProjectile blueprint and renaming it BigFirstPersonProjectile. We'll edit each of these quickly to get them ready to be pickups that can be added to our inventory and used by the player.

Open their full blueprints. In the projectile's components, pick **ProjectileMovement (Inherited)** and on the right you'll see the **Projectile** fly-out. Set the speeds to about double their current values, so to 6,000 to really give this one some punch compared to the other. In its **CollisionComp (Inherited)** under the **Transform** fly-out, set its scale to 2. I prefer when possible to click the lock icon on the right since we're doing universal scaling here, so you only have to type in the number once rather than in all three components. Then, click on its **StaticMesh1** component under its **CollisionComp (Inherited)**, and here we make one small visual change: under its **Static Mesh's Materials** fly-out, pick the drop-down and set it to **M_FPGun**. This material's texture is obviously set up for the gun and not a ball, but it makes our new bullet silver to really help differentiate it and let us know which gun we're firing (since the guns themselves otherwise look identical at this point). With both of these made, now go back to the BigBallGun blueprint's window and click its class (**BigBallGun(self)**), under components. Now, under the **Projectile** fly-out, we naturally set it to our new **BigFirstPersonProjectile**.

With the weapon and projectile done, now we can finally set up our weapon pickup. In the Content Browser, make a new blueprint class, show all classes, and select our **MasteringWeaponPickup**. Name this BigBallGunPickup and double-click it to check it out. Click **BigBallGunPickup(self)**, and under **Gameplay** you're welcome to change the rotation speed or amount of ammo in this pickup; however, be sure to at least change the weapon power to 1 or greater so it can "sort" above our default gun we'll still add from code.

The only components at the moment should be the (self) one and a scene component. We'll leave the scene component, and now use a bit of blueprint work directly as preparation for further blueprint discussions in the next chapter. We could of course add these components that we're about to use in the constructor in C++ like the template has done to date, but it's much quicker and easier to customize here in the blueprint. But again, depending on your project's needs, the C++ way might be the better choice. Doing it the way it is done here requires no code, but would require adding the components manually every time a new pick-up is made.

This is another area of managing a project an expert developer will know how to balance: what is the bandwidth of the team compared to the project's goals? If, for example, the game had many systems designers who were comfortable working in blueprint, it might make sense to simply allow them to do the duplicated work a number of times, adding these components in blueprint and require no coding help. On the other hand, if programmers themselves may have to set these up and their time is limited (hint: it always is!), it's probably best to add the components into the constructor to reduce the setup time needed to make these pick-ups. Always keep in mind your team's capabilities before committing to a workflow such as this.

Back to the pick-up, I renamed the scene component here so that I know it's really only for making an offset from the ground. Click on that scene component now (top component) and click the **Add Component** button at the top. Pick skeletal mesh as the type (you can rename it BallGunMesh).

Note: In all likelihood in a major game, you would have separate art assets here, so you would use a static mesh on the pickup that is a simplified version and not an animated character such as the gun that is held and equipped; but again, we work with what we have.

On the mesh's details pane, find its mesh fly-out and set it to SK_FPGun. Similarly, set its material to M_FPGun. So that when placed on the ground it doesn't actually sit flat on the ground, under its **Transformation** flyout, set the **Location** to be about 50.0 in Z so that it's half a meter in the air. Now, we need to click the mesh and add a child component to it so that the whole pickup can be, well, picked up! Click the green add button again, and this time add a **Sphere Collision** component. We need to change only one thing out of good practice: under its **Collision** fly-out, change its Collision **Preset** in the drop-down to **OverlapOnlyPawn**:

What this does is allow the collision system to ignore all objects when deciding whether one has collided (or, specifically in our case, overlapped, which means items can pass through it), but will get this event that overlapping is happening, "hit" events are the ones that stop movement. This way, things like our projectiles won't have to be considered by the collision system, only pawns walking around, which is always important to limit these interactions as much as possible to keep performance high. Lastly, click and drag our **BigBallGunPickup** (the icon in the content browser) into the main level editor window where the environment is shown (the boxes and walls) and place it on the ground. Place a few if you like, so we can walk around and pick them up.

Back to code to finish up

Having everything set in the editor and level, we have a few more code changes to make. First, we make some changes in `MasteringInventory.h`:

```
USTRUCT()
struct FWeaponProperties
{
        GENERATED_USTRUCT_BODY()

public:

        UPROPERTY()
        TSubclassOf<class AMasteringWeapon> WeaponClass;

        UPROPERTY()
        int WeaponPower;

        UPROPERTY()
        int Ammo;
};
```

We add this `struct` to the very top of the file, just after the `#include` header section. We will use this in the inventory list to reference weapons from now on, instead of referencing the `MasteringWeapon` class itself directly (but, of course, this is now a member in the `struct` for our use). We use the `struct` to track two new properties we associate with weapons: ammo and weapon power.

Next, after the `DefaultWeapon` variable, modify the first three functions (we remove passing the player for selecting weapons, and add ammo and power to the adding of weapons):

```
    /** Choose the best weapon we can of those available */
    void SelectBestWeapon();

    /** Select a weapon from inventory */
    void SelectWeapon(TSubclassOf<class AMasteringWeapon> Weapon);

    /** Add a weapon to the inventory list */
    void AddWeapon(TSubclassOf<class AMasteringWeapon> Weapon, int
AmmoCount, uint8 WeaponPower);

    /** Get the currently selected weapon */
    FORCEINLINE TSubclassOf<class AMasteringWeapon> GetCurrentWeapon()
const { return CurrentWeapon; }
```

```
        /** Change a weapon's ammo count, can't go below 0 or over 999 */
        void ChangeAmmo(TSubclassOf<class AMasteringWeapon> Weapon, const
int ChangeAmount);

protected:
        TArray<FWeaponProperties> WeaponsArray;
        TSubclassOf<class AMasteringWeapon> CurrentWeapon;
        int CurrentWeaponPower = -1;
        class AMasteringCharacter* MyOwner;
```

In the MasteringInventory.cpp file, add this:

```
#define UNLIMITED_AMMO -1

// Sets default values for this component's properties
UMasteringInventory::UMasteringInventory()
{
        PrimaryComponentTick.bCanEverTick = true;

        MyOwner = Cast<AMasteringCharacter>(GetOwner());
        check(GetOwner() == nullptr || MyOwner != nullptr);
}

// Called when the game starts
void UMasteringInventory::BeginPlay()
{
        Super::BeginPlay();

        if (DefaultWeapon != nullptr)
        {
                // NOTE: since we don't use a pick-up for the default
weapon, we always give it a power of 0
                AddWeapon(DefaultWeapon, UNLIMITED_AMMO, 0);
        }
}
```

At the top, right under our `#include` section, notice the `#define` used to show clearly that when we see this, a weapon has unlimited ammo. This is much safer than using -1 directly, as new team-members might not understand seeing the magical properties of -1 in other areas of the code. In the constructor, notice also that we do a trick because we know this object is a component, and thus has to have (when used) an owning actor, and we save this as `MyOwner`. If you set a breakpoint there, you'll notice as the level editor starts, you get one instance with a null owner. This is the default object being constructed and thus is nothing to worry about. However, notice the `check`. It, well, checks for that case, but then will assert whether someone tried to add an inventory component to anything that isn't `MasteringCharacter`, just to be safe. This check is done very rarely (once each time an inventory is created), so is fine being a normal `check`. Below, there's a `checkSlow` I'll explain just for contrast. This line of saving a pointer already cast to the right type of our owner saves us some time later when adding weapons, and then we also don't have to keep passing a `MasteringCharacter` pointer through all these functions since, once again, we know that every player has one and only one inventory, and every inventory exists as part of a player. We also add the default weapon with unlimited ammo and a weapon power of 0. After this, we basically replace the old `SelectBestWeapon`, `SelectWeapon`, and `AddWeapon` so that they now look like this:

```
void UMasteringInventory::SelectWeapon(TSubclassOf<class AMasteringWeapon>
Weapon)
{
        MyOwner->EquipWeapon(Weapon);
}

void UMasteringInventory::AddWeapon(TSubclassOf<class AMasteringWeapon>
Weapon, int AmmoCount, uint8 WeaponPower)
{
        for (auto WeaponIt = WeaponsArray.CreateIterator(); WeaponIt;
++WeaponIt)
        {
                FWeaponProperties &currentProps = *WeaponIt;
                if (currentProps.WeaponClass == Weapon)
                {
                        checkSlow(AmmoCount >= 0);
                        currentProps.Ammo += AmmoCount;
                        return; // our work is done if we found the gun
already in inventory, just update ammo
                }
        }

        FWeaponProperties weaponProps;
        weaponProps.WeaponClass = Weapon;
        weaponProps.WeaponPower = WeaponPower;
        weaponProps.Ammo = AmmoCount;
```

```
            WeaponsArray.Add(weaponProps);
}

void UMasteringInventory::ChangeAmmo(TSubclassOf<class AMasteringWeapon>
Weapon, const int ChangeAmount)
{
        for (auto WeaponIt = WeaponsArray.CreateIterator(); WeaponIt;
++WeaponIt)
            {
                FWeaponProperties &currentProps = *WeaponIt;
                if (currentProps.WeaponClass == Weapon)
                {
                    if (currentProps.Ammo == UNLIMITED_AMMO) //
unlimited ammo gun, we're done
                            return;

                    currentProps.Ammo = FMath::Clamp(currentProps.Ammo
+ ChangeAmount, 0, 999);
                    if (currentProps.Ammo == 0) // gun is now empty!
                    {
                        CurrentWeaponPower = -1; // force us to
select any better weapon that does have ammo
                        SelectBestWeapon();
                    }
                    return; // our work is done if we found the gun
already in inventory, just update ammo
                }
            }
}
```

Notice that changing ammo uses a non-const iterator and a reference to the structs it is iterating. This way, we can simply directly modify the ammo count in the struct that exists in the array. Always be careful as it's very easy to simply use a local variable in the iterator, make a change, and not have that saved as you'd like in the array! Also notice checkSlow. Adding weapons doesn't happen very often either, so it is perfectly fine being a normal check for performance. I just put it there to remind myself to discuss them. checkSlow is only used in debug builds, so if content developers use a development build, they would never have it assert on them (which can be annoying for artists and designers if it were to happen, because it basically causes a crash that they can do nothing about). So use these wisely.

In any case where a check is used that could happen in a live build and could be very severe, always use the `checkf` variants instead because this will also output whatever you format into its string output into the game's .log file. This way, if a player with a live version of the game has a problem, or a release build crashes, you can look at that log and it may immediately give you a clue as to what happened.

Lastly, keeping with our theme of encapsulation, we'll have the weapon inform the inventory as it spends ammo (as the gun does the firing and the inventory does the ammo-tracking in our game). When a gun runs out of ammo, the inventory will automatically try to pick the next best option, and since our default weapon has unlimited ammo, we always know at least something will be available. This, of course, can vary wildly in different styles of games, with a "dry fire" sound when out of ammo and trying to fire, or switching from a gun to a melee attack when out of ammo. Here, we'll add this parameter to our firing function:

```
void Fire(FRotator ControlRotation, class UAnimInstance* AnimInst, class
UMasteringInventory* Inventory);
```

And we'll implement it in the .cpp like so at the bottom of the `Fire` function:

```
// reduce ammo by one
Inventory->ChangeAmmo(GetClass(), -1);
```

That's it! We can now run around our level, pick up the big gun, and watch its projectiles really make those boxes fly... until it's out of ammo and we're back to the default gun.

Putting our inventory to use

Don't worry, all the hard parts are done! But we do still have one last important, if less challenging, thing to do to make this more like a viable normal inventory in a game: swapping weapons. We'll need an input for cycling them, and keep in mind that we currently auto-equip the best weapon you pick up at the time of pick-up, and at the moment have no way to choose anything else.

Adding controls to cycle weapons

Much like before, when we added an input for stealth and bound it to left-shift, let's head back to the editor's project properties and engine/input/bindings fly-outs. Here, we'll add two **Action Mappings** with the + button, and name them **InventoryUp** and **InventoryDown**. I like to bind these to **Mouse Wheel Up** and **Mouse Wheel Down**, respectively, but you're free to choose any inputs you prefer. We now have our means of cycling, and just need to set it up like our stealth mechanic once more in our character.

Adding swapping of weapons to our character

First, we need to add cycling to our inventory. There are a number of ways to do this, and with a plan, you could, for example, simply sort the array based on the power of the items going in and store the current weapon's array entry. There are dangers to this, but it would make for very fast and clear switching of weapons. The implementation here will be a bit rough, but is not critically important. Knowing ahead of time how extensively a system will get used is very important to long-term healthy development as well. If a system has a very rough but fully functional implementation, and will never likely change or be reused by other areas of code in the life of the project, just leave it be. We all want to always write perfect code, but code oftentimes comes from outside contributors or less experienced developers. While keeping to best practices ourselves is always encouraged, it's also important to know when you don't need to over-engineer something of limited scope or use; just get it working and move on. Game development relies on speed, and there is nothing wrong with revisiting code that was written under one set of requirements (such as "the game will only ever have at most two weapons" changes to "we now need 10 or more weapons for the player!"). Clean up and build things the best you can for the job they do. It's just a classic downfall of many developers to not realize when something is good enough, even if it's not perfect or the way we'd ideally like it. So, with that huge disclaimer, here's the rough inventory cycling code to finish up this section:

```
int UMasteringInventory::FindCurrentWeaponIndex() const
{
        int currentIndex = 0;
        for (auto WeaponIt = WeaponsArray.CreateConstIterator(); WeaponIt;
++WeaponIt, ++currentIndex)
        {
                const FWeaponProperties &currentProps = *WeaponIt;
                if (currentProps.WeaponClass == CurrentWeapon)
                        break;
        }

        checkSlow(currentIndex < WeaponsArray.Num());
```

```
            return currentIndex;
    }

    void UMasteringInventory::SelectNextWeapon()
    {
            int currentIndex = FindCurrentWeaponIndex();

            if (currentIndex == WeaponsArray.Num() - 1) // we're at the end
            {
                    SelectWeapon(WeaponsArray[0].WeaponClass);
            }
            else
            {
                    SelectWeapon(WeaponsArray[currentIndex + 1].WeaponClass);
            }
    }

    void UMasteringInventory::SelectPreviousWeapon()
    {
            int currentIndex = FindCurrentWeaponIndex();

            if (currentIndex > 0) // we're not at the start
            {
                    SelectWeapon(WeaponsArray[currentIndex - 1].WeaponClass);
            }
            else
            {
                    SelectWeapon(WeaponsArray[WeaponsArray.Num() -
    1].WeaponClass); // select the last
            }
    }
```

Add the prototypes for the functions to your .h file. Then, add these lines below all of our previous input binding in AMasteringCharacter::SetupPlayerInputComponent:

```
// Cycling inventory
PlayerInputComponent->BindAction("InventoryUp", IE_Pressed, this,
&AMasteringCharacter::SelectNextWeapon);
PlayerInputComponent->BindAction("InventoryDown", IE_Pressed, this,
&AMasteringCharacter::SelectPreviousWeapon);
```

And in the character, add these functions (with their prototypes near the other control handling functions in the header):

```
void AMasteringCharacter::SelectNextWeapon()
{
        Inventory->SelectNextWeapon();
}

void AMasteringCharacter::SelectPreviousWeapon()
{
        Inventory->SelectPreviousWeapon();
}
```

And if you were to test things like this, it would look like it's partly working and then breaks. Stepping through the code, a line that wasn't important before was missing, but seeing that CurrentWeapon was always null, it was very easy to add this last line to `SelectWeapon`. It's always great to keep those debugging skills up!

```
void UMasteringInventory::SelectWeapon(TSubclassOf<class AMasteringWeapon>
Weapon)
{
        MyOwner->EquipWeapon(Weapon);
        CurrentWeapon = Weapon;
}
```

Bringing it all together

Now, our inventory and pickups are all complete. If you launch the editor, you can step through the cycling up and down code to make sure everything is working correctly. We redundantly re-equip the default weapon if that's our only one, but the real work in the character's `EquipWeapon` already handles trying to switch from a weapon to that same weapon class and returns to the top. We now have a fully functional inventory that we can use to cycle through our, albeit only two, weapons, both up and down. Mission accomplished!

Summary

We started this section with a hardcoded weapon made by bolting some components and input onto a character. We now have a system to make infinite unique weapon types, make a cool pick-up item for them, add them to the inventory, switch to the best weapon, track ammo, switch to another weapon automatically when one runs out of ammo, and cycle those weapons as we want with input. This is just one example of many game systems that will be implemented over the course of even small game projects, but it has shown several fundamentals of design (in the coding sense) as well as game design and how they mesh together. Never over-engineer what you won't need, but always plan for the future and make sure that your requirements are all there. We've also done a bit more work directly with blueprints and its editor. In the next chapter, we will go in depth into what blueprints can do and understand a bit deeper about how it works. A major point of discussion will be how games can (and are!) built only using blueprint scripting and no project C++ code. This approach has many risks, but for smaller projects or working with limited resources to get something demonstrated, it can be a huge benefit, and those benefits are there even for a C++ project such as ours if you know when to use them.

Questions

1. Is there any reasonable way we could have swapped weapons on the character the way the template originally set it up?
2. Why move firing functionality out of the character and into our weapon class?
3. Why do we only store actor classes, and not actors, in the inventory?
4. What is the purpose of a weapon pickup class? Why not just use the weapon directly as the pickup?
5. What advantages are there to adding components to a class in code versus adding them to an instance in blueprint?
6. What are the differences between `check`, `checkSlow`, and the `checkf` variants?
7. Which one should always be used for live game builds checking critical code?
8. Why is finding the current weapon index in its own function?

Further reading

https://docs.unrealengine.com/en-us/Programming/Assertions

Blueprint Review and When to Use BP Scripting

3

Introduction

Welcome to our next chapter. This will be our first departure from focusing on C++ code, but not the last. Unreal has many systems with great capabilities that exist in a form you can access from the editor without writing any code. The most flexible and most closely related to actually writing code will be explored here, delving into UE4's blueprint system and its capabilities and limitations. Up until now, most of our work has been implementing things in C++ and minimally showing how these are interacted with as blueprint objects in the editor. Blueprint is capable of much more, including making whole games. In this chapter we'll cover:

- Blueprint review/overview
- Blueprint-only games, pros and cons
- Scritping an object with blueprint (elevator)
- Blueprint tips & tricks

Technical requirements

Like last time, the work in this chapter will be done by utilizing what was finished in Chapter 2, *Inventory and Weapons for the Player*. This, however, is not strictly required and the contents here should be implementable with the Chapter 1, *Making a C++ Project for a First-Person Shooter*, project or even a new UE4 template.

As usual, the GitHub branch for this chapter is here:

```
https://github.com/PacktPublishing/Mastering-Game-Development-with-Unreal-
Engine-4-Second-Edition/tree/Chapter-3
```

Engine version used: 4.19.0.

Blueprint review and Blueprint-only games

It's fair to ask: just what exactly is "blueprint?" There are really two main areas to be concerned with. The first we have already touched on previously and used: integrating C++ classes with the UE4 editor. Classes used in the editor are typically derived from UObject at some level, and this allows for them to utilize things such as the UPROPERTY and UFUNCTION macros that then allow these to be accessed by blueprint instances of those classes, such as StealthCharacter. With a few exceptions of some basic geometry and other essential game objects, almost everything placed directly in a level by yourself or designers or artists will be an instance of a blueprint class, such as our character in the level now. The other area to be aware of that every project should evaluate for its needs is the **blueprint visual scripting (BVS)** system. Almost all gameplay concepts you can think of doing in C++ are possible in blueprint scripting. It also has an integrated debugger you can use with breakpoints during runtime. Here, we will delve into these concepts a bit more deeply and look at some of the advantages and limitations for scripting.

Blueprint overview

As we have shown multiple times in our previous chapters, the advantages of exposing variables that will be iterated upon or made unique in many instances of the same class type is fairly obvious: these variables can be modified while running the editor by content creators with no programming knowledge whatsoever. System designers in particular depend on having the right variables exposed so they can tune and build variants of systems quickly and test them equally quickly. Doing this almost entirely from C++ as the FPS template begins means that changing those values at best requires compiling and doing a hot-reload of the game while in the editor, and at worst, shutting down the editor, building, and restarting it. Much like scripting in blueprint, discussed in the next paragraph, much of blueprint's exposure and utilization in your game comes down, once again, to your team's and project's needs. If the design of a class for your game is almost certain to never change or change very minimally over the course of the project, and you have plenty of C++ programmers as resources, maybe it makes sense to get things done in a very direct way like the FPS template's character started for us. However, if you have designers (system-level or otherwise) who are anxious to get started building a variety of game objects and are constantly changing them, adding new variations, and testing these quickly in levels, the more blueprint flexibility you can give them, the better! As noted previously, at the most basic level, blueprint classes are excellent data containers: even if designers or artists are never going to use them, programmers directly benefit from having access to view and often modify as much data as possible in classes while staying in the editor. The iteration time is instantaneous, and you can always check your values without switching context from the editor to Visual Studio or other windows. Of course, there are sensitive, critical values that you may not want anyone arbitrarily modifying from blueprint, but with UPROPERTY flags such as `BlueprintReadOnly`, you can easily give people the availability to view what is currently set for a property without letting someone accidentally modify it and save a bad value. Hopefully the point is made well enough here that other than making sure you keep inexperienced people from changing critical data, there is almost no downside to exposing any interesting variables of a class that can be viewed in the editor as UPROPERTY types.

Now, on to visual scripting. This is so far wholly untouched in our prject, but that is about to change with a fully utilized example in the next section (*Blueprint scripting and performance*). For those new to using blueprint scripting, as it's possible also to make entire games while never using it at all, don't worry, there will be lots of screenshots and direct work in it in that section. For now, though, we will simply discuss from a high level the capabilities and drawbacks of using scripting. First, what are some major things that you can do in blueprint scripting?

- Game logic: Including `for`/`while` loops, using local and class variables of most types, and access to huge numbers of functions in existing UE4 classes.
- Game mechanics: Interaction between objects in the world, collision responses, movement, and even pathfinding.
- Access shareable Blueprint Function Libraries: These are groups of stateless/static utility functions you can write in both C++ or blueprint scripting, and share with different teams or projects.
- Easily integrate with UI in the UMG editor, often crucial for UI/UX designers' workflow.
- No rebuilding any executable or code, and easy referencing of one object to another: as will be discussed in the section immediately following this one, you can (and people do) make whole games just using scripting for logic.

Sounds great, right!? Well, before you think there's a very big *but* coming, let's be clear: blueprint scripting *is* quite great, and powerful. Here is a quick list of some drawbacks to be aware of, but comparing those to the capabilities blueprint scripting gives out of the box to teams who invest in getting familiar and comfortable with it, well, the drawbacks are overall very minor:

- Performance costs can be significant: It's generally possible to minimize these, but profiling them and determining problem areas is harder and requires a different skillset than profiling C++ code for issues.
- Loss of access to certain data types: C++ is only dependent on your platform compiler settings, but blueprints must be usable and accessible across all platforms UE4 supports (32 and 64 bit, mobile, web, and so on).
- Debugging can be... buggy: Often, the context of how you got to a breakpoint is missing, or certain variables won't be available when you hover over them. It's great to have the debugger, but when it doesn't work, you're on your own.
- Anyone can modify or add things to blueprints: *anyone!* This means your team needs to have very well-defined roles for who can modify what types of things, to prevent someone without expertise introducing bugs that are hard to find.

- Switching back and forth between C++ code and blueprint scripting can be distracting: Often, to get the whole picture of what's going on, you need data from both, and switching contexts can slow down development.

First, a brief discussion of a few of these points and how to mitigate them. For performance profiling, the editor has a very good tool built into it that if you're not already familiar with, take some time and see what it can do. This is the **Profiler** in the **Session Frontend** window, which can be accessed from the **Window** toolbar under **Development Tools**:

If a team is disciplined about tracking performance from the start, it is usually a bit easier to track down what has changed and caused a problem. But again, keep in mind, something as simple as changing a value of one variable might be detrimental to performance, and if you use compiled blueprints, there may be no way to easily search for that change in version tracking history. Two strategies to mitigate this are to integrate source control to the editor, and "nativize" blueprints. If you have a supported source control package (this book's project is using Git), you can enable source control integration by right-clicking any blueprint asset in the editor, and at the bottom of the popup is the option to connect to source control.

Once it's set up, you can right-click on any blueprint asset again, such as the FirstPersonCharacter, and different. versions of it:

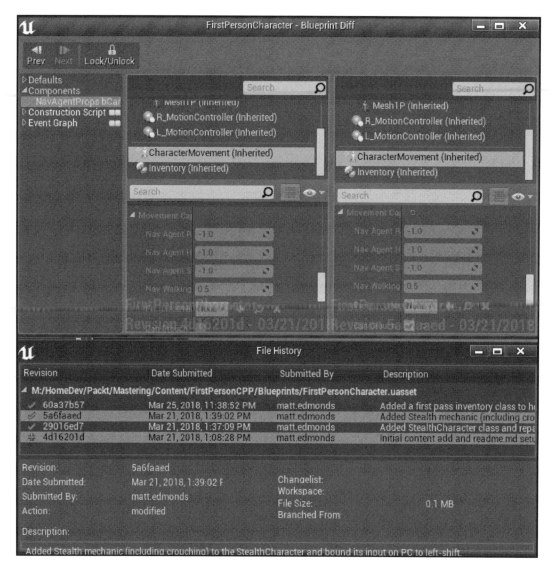

Finding data changes can be difficult at times (look closely and you'll see where **Can Crouch** was changed in the preceding screenshot), but when it works right, showing script changes as visual graphs side by side can be incredibly helpful in tracking down where a new change may have caused a problem.

A tutorial on setting this up for Git can be found in the *Further reading* section of this chapter. Nativizing blueprints can be enabled under **Project Settings | Packaging | Blueprints**. This turns all blueprint classes in the editor into intermediate C++ classes, and packages them to your project. You may have a few reasons to do this. It's something to experiment with if your project is having trouble understanding why some blueprints are not working as expected, but we won't spend further time on this option here.

Lastly, regarding the loss of data types, it's entirely possible with Blueprint Function Libraries. You can use native (compiler) types for your platform and return results in types that blueprint can then use. For example, if you had some UI using the existing UE4 FDateTime values and want the difference between them in seconds, this is not doable in blueprint directly because the values of those date-time structs is natively in int64 format. So you could easily make a function such as this, which takes the two dates from blueprint, does the math natively (ToUnixTimestamp returns an int64) and then returns the result as an int32, which blueprint can then access (and thus the UI can display):

```
UCLASS()
class UDateTime : public UBlueprintFunctionLibrary
{
        GENERATED_BODY()

public:

        UFUNCTION(BlueprintPure, Category = "Date and Time")
        static int32 SecondsBetweenDateTimes(FDateTime time1, FDateTime time2);
```

And then the simple C++ implementation:

```
int32 UDateTime::SecondsBetweenDateTimes(FDateTime time1, FDateTime time2)
{
        return time2.ToUnixTimestamp() - time1.ToUnixTimestamp();
}
```

So, in the C++, we use a type that isn't allowed to be used directly in a blueprint, but this works across all modern C++ compilers. Of course, if the dates are very far apart, you could lose some data in this calculation/truncation, but so long as it can be assumed that there is no case where dates would be near that level of separation, it is an easy solution to an int64 calculation that can now be accessed from anywhere in blueprints.

Right before the list of drawbacks mentioned previously, it was stated that these issues overall are very minor, but keep in mind that this was in the context of the power blueprint gives you. For example, you can set up a multiplayer game session, have other players search for and connect to it, and begin playing a match together, all from just a few existing blueprint nodes UE4 provides to you. This is incredibly powerful and could take a programmer who's unfamiliar with that workflow days or even weeks to get correct using `FAsyncTask` tasks and `OnlineSubsystem` calls, all triggered from the right events in the `GameMode`, or the like. So is this the way to go 100%, and let's forget this whole C++ business for your project? That's what we'll finally discuss next.

Blueprint-only games – is this right for you?

We have established that blueprints are required at some level for any game, and blueprint scripting is a very powerful tool that can save a ton of time when implementing systems or reusable pieces that would otherwise be written with dozens, hundreds, or potentially many thousands of lines of C++ code. We have now also discussed the risks and drawbacks to using blueprint scripting, but now keep in mind that in a project that is blueprint only, you are stuck with these choices. As soon as you hit a problem that seemingly can't be solved and have to add as much as one new C++ class to your project, well, you might as well have started with a basic C++ project from day one in hindsight, and that is a very common outcome. Teams that are very experienced with blueprint scripting and its limitations when starting a project can navigate these things in their design up-front. If you're unsure whether you can do all of what needs to be done for your game's design at the start of your project, make it C++ and then you can use as much from blueprint and C++ as your team's bandwidth and developers prefer, but converting a very large blueprint-only project to C++ will be a great deal more work later in a project's workflow. Adding C++ builds may be very disruptive and distracting to a team used to never having to do them if you are farther along in development, so again, when in doubt, just start with C++ capabilities in your flow and balance your workload between the two systems in whichever way is optimal. A team with very little C++ code that changes or is added over time will find their workflow then to mostly be the same quick iterations as a blueprint-only project anyway, but have all the infrastructure available and workflow established to add C++ as needed.

iOS developers! There is a huge reason for you to consider staying blueprint-only for a long time, if not for a whole project, depending on its scope: UE4 can package, run, and test on iOS device builds from a Windows PC, *if* they are blueprint only. This can be a huge advantage to proving out an iOS concept quickly, or to massively reduce build times when iterating quickly on gameplay ideas. You will still eventually need at least a Mac that can run a version of Xcode, and an Apple Developer License, to ultimately submit to Apple, but blueprint-only is a great way to quickly prove what your game can do on an iPhone or iPad.

As a rule of thumb, there are generally two types of teams that will want to go blueprint-only:

- Those with no one available to handle difficult C++ development, problems, or set up the workflow
- Those with a very simple design, or a very experienced set of blueprint-developers who know its limits

Often indie-teams fall into a bit of each of these, and again, there is nothing wrong with prototyping a game quickly in blueprint only and if you find you must switch later, it can be done. For those with some experience on a few different teams, though, always weigh the preceding topics and decide wisely before starting, if at all possible.

Going *back* to a blueprint-only game after some (even not so significant/major) C++ work has been done can be a very difficult to downright-impractical process. It's also another good rule of thumb to just accept once you open the C++ box, do not have any expectation you will shut it again.

Blueprint scripting and performance

So you may be thinking at this point: we sure have talked a lot about the benefits and drawbacks of blueprint scripting and blueprint-only problems, but we still haven't just sat down and *made* any to see how it goes and how we can profile its performance. Let's do so now, and get a real-world game system built that we can investigate with: in this case, a game's classic moving platform.

Blueprint scripting example – moving platform and elevator

As I'm sure you can imagine after all of this talk, this class, and the work implementing its gameplay, will be done almost exclusively in the editor (there are ways you can always hook C++ to blueprint, which will be discussed near the end). So, start off by opening the editor and going in the content **browser tab** to our **Content** | **FirstPersonCPP** | **Blueprints** and right-click, like we have done before, to make a new class:

Click **Actor** as the parent class for the blueprint, and name it MovingPlatform. Now, we have a completely bare-bones actor we could place in our world, but it doesn't even have any geometry, of course. Let's quickly fix this. Panning around the level, you'll see two gray rectangular boxes (not the white boxes, but those actually work fine too): click one and then right-click on it and select **Browse to Asset** (*Ctrl + B*) (note, you can also find this when editing most assets from the menu bar under **Asset**), and you should be in **Content** | **Geometry** | **Meshes** now with **1M_Cube** selected. So, now that we know how to find this simple piece of geometry, let's go back to our **MovingPlatform** and double-click it. You may notice, since we made this as a blueprint class from the start, you get the full blueprint editor automatically, and not the minimal interface it normally starts with for native classes that don't use scripting, as we often had before. For our platform object, we now need to add a component. Note that you could just add a simple cube or plane as a static mesh component. It is great that these things are available, again, especially for quick prototyping. Just to get used to the workflow, however, which is more typical of professional games, we will use the static mesh cube we were just looking at. So, type to filter or just scroll for **Static Mesh** in the components drop-down and add one. Now notice in the hierarchy how this is added under the default scene component (named **DefaultSceneRoot**). Once we have an actor component in our case, that can *be* the root component of our actor object here, the default is really just a placeholder. So, rename the mesh component to **Platform** and drag it on top of the scene component to replace it.

Now we'll do two more quick moves to get this platform looking right, click the mesh component and on the right in its properties, under **Static Mesh | Static Mesh**, select **1M_Cube**, which we found earlier, and click the unlock icon to the right of **Transsform | Scale** and things should be coming together:

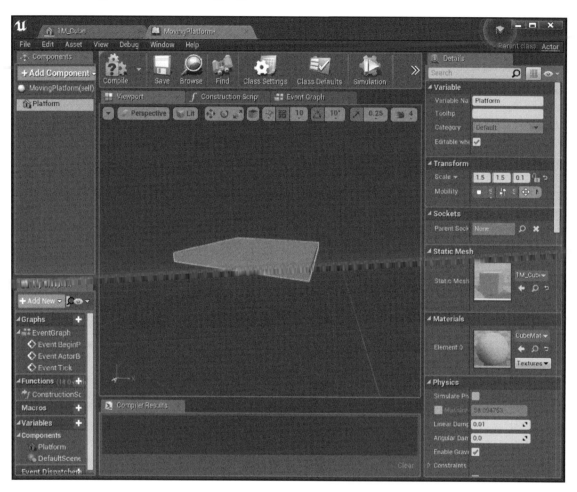

We can now drag these into our scene, but of course, it won't do anything other than block our player, as the step-height is too high for its collision to handle. You will also notice it need to compile and save, good steps any time you are making progress on a blueprint, though if its scripting is not ready to successfully compile, obviously hold off until it is. You can save and use blueprints with broken scripting, but their warning messages can be very distracting and allow people to not notice other broken blueprint issues that may be critical.

Before we can really use and script this platform, however, we need to add one more component. Unreal keeps blocking (hit) and overlap (touch) collisions separate, and in this case we need a bit of both. So, click **Add Component**, and this time we simply will add a cube from its list. Notice it should be parented to **Platform** and because of this, its size is the same since the scale from **Platform** propagates to our new cube. Now, raise it up a few centimeters by either dragging in the viewport along the Z axis or typing in a value in its transform until you can see it is above but is still basically touching our original platform (I found a Z value of 50 worked for 5 cm since our Z scale is 0.1). Now, scroll down until you see the **Collision** flyout and make sure **Generate Overlap Events** is checked. Click in the drop-down for preset to **OverlapOnlyPawn**, and down in the **Rendering** flyout, uncheck **Visible** as we don't want to see this piece because it is only there to detect our character walking on it. In the **Platform** component's collision events, you can leave this as **BlockAllDynamic**, and note that generating overlap events is irrelevant as hit events supersede overlap, so you will receive events when projectiles or the player hit the platform, but we would never get the overlap events we need with these filters.

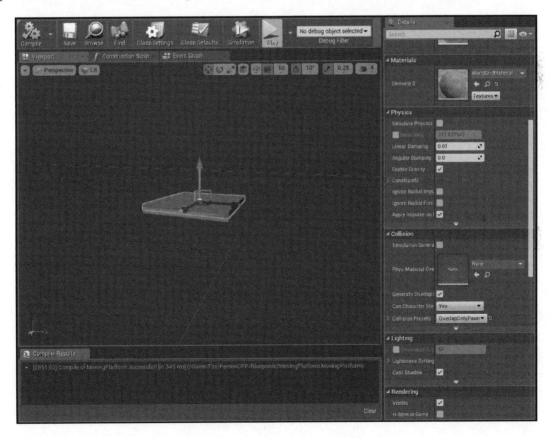

This is how everything should look right before clicking the Visible box at the bottom of this screenshot.

And finally, to some blueprint scripting! Click over to the Event Graph tab and you'll see the existing events are grayed out with notes about how to enable them. In our case, we want the overlap box. Click and drag from the blue **Other Actor** pin (from here on, we'll just call this a *pull* from the pin), and you will see a list of many things we can add that are context-sorted (so long as the checkbox remains checked) to things that take an actor as input, the way that pin from the event is supplying it as an output. Filter for GetClass, and you see it has been added now. For those familiar with blueprint scripting, just check out the following screenshot for the progress. Here are the steps (after adding GetClass) to have that in place:

1. Pull the return value for **Get Class**, and find **Is Child Of** in the list. These should now be wired. In the **Is Child Of** box, in its dropdown, select our **MasteringCharacter** class as the type so only our player gives a true result here.
2. Pull the red result pin from is child of and filter or find **Branch**, then wire this from the white triangle output pin of the actor begin overlap event, and in to the input white pin of the **Branch.**
3. Pull the white output (which points right) pin from the branch's **True** result and filter and add a **MoveComponentTo** block.
4. Pull left from the **MoveComponentTo** block's blue component pin and type to filter for **GetPlatform** (a reference to our root component).
5. Pull left from the **TargetRelativeLocation** yellow pin and type + or otherwise filter/scroll for **vector + vector** in the list.
6. Pull from its top left pin and type/filter for **GetActorLocation**, and you can leave the input pin on that node as self (that's what we want).
7. Set the bottom vector's destination to what you want. In my test case, a Z value of 300 puts us up even with these other large gray blocks around the map.

The **TargetRelativeLocation** variable seems a bit poorly named, as what it wants for a proper motion is a world location. And lastly, on that **MoveToLocation** node, set the time to whatever you like: 4 seconds as here is a little slow and boring, but great for demonstrating that this all works:

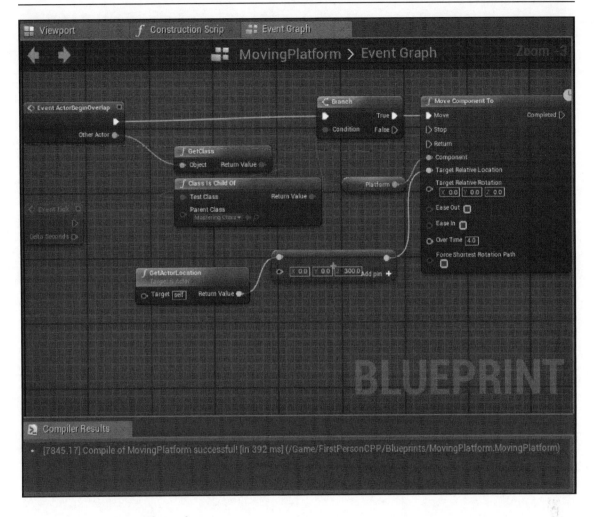

Don't forget to compile and save.

Note that running the game in play-in-editor mode will always try to compile any edited blueprints before running (and give errors to the output log if there are any), but it will *not* save those assets! You still have to do this with a save-all or Ctrl + S on your blueprints and level editing windows! If you shut down your editor directly via Visual Studio, you won't even get prompted to save any unsaved levels or assets, so it's usually best when working in editor to close via its window 's X button.

Now all that's left to show this off is to drag one of our Moving it into the world on the floor somewhere, and walk over and step on it. Off you go in the air! Note that if you step on it again by hopping off and on, it takes you up further. We'll make this thing a bit better shortly, but right now, this is a good checkpoint for the GitHub version of the project. Here you can see where it is placed in the book's project's map (again, by dragging the **MovingPlatform** blueprint icon into the main level window itself):

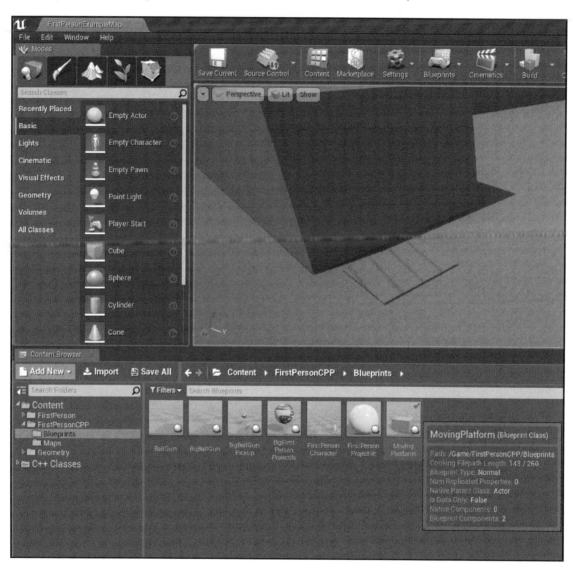

There are many, many more options that we could do with something like this now. It's possible to add all kinds of logic, including other components, allowing this platform to do pathfinding navigation, or adding a spline to the world that in the level blueprint for the platform uses (from the main editor window, click **Blueprints | Open Editor Blueprint** to access individual blueprints that can reference each other in the level). There is a massive amount of very valuable work that can be done in these areas. For now, we will make the platform head back to its start point when the player steps off, and the same when it reaches the top of its movement:

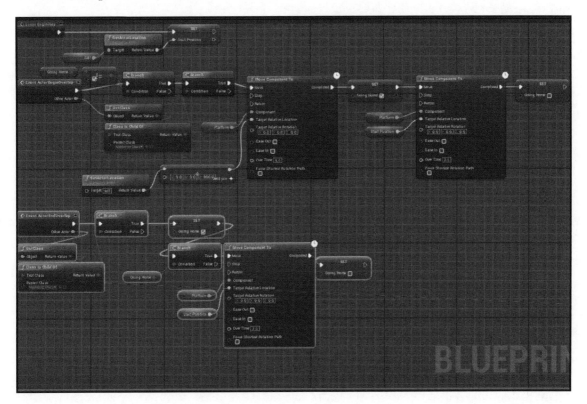

Note that this uses a couple of blueprint variables added to the class, too, a short reference to which is added in the *Further reading* section. The short version is under the **My Blueprint** tab on the left. There is **Add New**, and under that is **Variable**. Once you add one, you can change the type and default value. Here, we added one we renamed under **My Blueprint | Variables** as **StartPosition**, and on the right under details, set its type to vector, and also add **GoingHome** as a **boolean**. You can always then access these types, like C++ exposed variables too, in get/set blocks in blueprint scripting windows. Note, though, that unless you make a specific accessor (and here is an example that is *not* used, but you could implement) these variables cannot be accessed in C++:

```
UFUNCTION(BlueprintImplementableEvent)
FVector GetStartPosition();
```

Making this a blueprint-implementable event that means for a hybrid C++/blueprint class you could add this as an event type function in blueprint and then simply have it return **StartPosition**. This way, a variable that is only defined in blueprint could be accessed by C++. Similarly, to make native functions in C++ that can do work as we have before, be sure to keep in mind BlueprintCallable as a UFUNCTION keyword, as these can be accessed *by* blueprint any time you are in or using an instance of the class that implements it. Spoiler alert: we will be doing this quite a bit in the next chapter, Chapter 4, *U.I. Necessities: Menus, HUD, and Load/Save*, similar to this:

```
UFUNCTION(BlueprintCallable, Category="Appearance")
void SetColorAndOpacity(FSlateColor InColorAndOpacity);
```

These functions do work in C++, but can be directly called by blueprint. Note also that these calls from C++ to blueprint and vice versa have a fairly significant call-stack overhead. On previous hardware this was a major performance issue, but to save you time here and now, on most platforms these days, the overhead really is minimal. Keep this in mind that if you switch between the two frequently, but there is no longer the same level of stress that was caused in UE3's similar systems.

OK, so these asides about how to call back and forth from C++ to blueprint notwithstanding, let's get back to our quick logic to get this elevator in a finished state. As you can see, there are several steps, and once again for brevity, let's just add them here in an ordered list:

1. First, we need our two new variables, so as noted earlier, in the **My Blueprint** tab, click add new twice and pick **variable** from the list for each.
2. For the first one, rename it **GoingHome**, and its type can remain as-is, as a **boolean.**

3. For the second, also as noted, name it **StartPosition** and give it the type of a **vector.**

4. Now, pull from the event for BeginPlay in the scripting window and filter to **Set Start Position.**

5. Pull left from its vector and pick **GetActorLocation** like we did earlier, again leaving self as the object. Now, when we begin playing, this platform will mark its initial location and save it in a blueprint-only variable we just made.

6. Now pull from our existing **MoveComponentTo** node and filter to **Set Going Home**, and check its box to true.

7. Pull from that node, and make a new **MoveComponentTo** node similar to how we did before. Use **Platform** again as the input component, but as the **TargetRelativeLocation**, drag from it and filter to **GetStartPosition**.

8. Pull from the new **MoveComponentTo** node's output and filter to **SetGoingHome**, making sure this time the node is unchecked so it's set to false.

9. We need a new event: right-click anywhere and filter to **ActorEndOverlap.**

10. Drag from its output and add another branch. Pull that branch's condition and do the same logic we did before, pulling the end-overlap's **OtherActor** to a `GetClass` node, then that return to a **ClassIsChildOf MasteringCharacter**, or just copy and paste those nodes with a multi or shift/control select from the begin-overlap and save yourself some trouble.

11. When that branch is true (this means our player's character is no longer on the platform), pull from the true, filter to **SetGoingHome**, and check its box.

12. Pull from that to a branch, pull from its condition to and filter to **GetGoingHome.**

13. Pull from the branch's true and add the same set of logic as before with **MoveComponentTo** (to **StartPosition**, clearing **GoingHome** to false after completion).

What you should have now should match both the preceding screenshot and the final check-in for GitHub in the `chapter 3` branch. This elevator pad should now reliably get you up to the next floor, but also return to its start once it arrives there or is abandoned. Ideally there should probably be a timer when reaching the top before it auto-returns, and there's no reason most games could not generally just rely on the end-overlap path to reset the platform. Again, this is just showing a hint of what blueprint can do for you and is a great starting point for further experimentation!

Blueprint tips, tricks, and performance hits

The last real question with blueprints is how to see where your performance problems may arise and what can make life easier. As has already been noted, you can use the built-in UE4 profiling tools. This is always a good place to start. Also listed at the end of this section in additional reading is a Stack Overflow discussion of profiling tools. I highly recommend VTune from Intel, and if you have a hardware device that's compatible, the NVIDIA Visual Profiler is also an excellent tool. However, note that these items will show you in C++ classes what the hot-spots are. When you see K2 classes (or for older types, classes with *Kismet* in the name) from C++, you can be assured those are things spending time in blueprint doing work, but other things such as pathfinding, physics, or collisions may be less obvious. You may then have to work backwards to find what these mean in blueprint. A faster but cruder way to test performance with blueprints is simply to unhook (make pieces of blueprint not be called) and compare previous profiling with current profiling (or even just look at your frames per second!). There may be obvious areas of blueprint that are causing you performance pain, and fixing them or changing them will mitigate the problem. Keep especially in mind, though, like in the example of what's possible: pathfinding, or modifying the NavMesh, is entirely possible from blueprint objects. If our elevator platform modifies the NavMesh (this is a fairly simple setting, but beyond the scope of this chapter), it can be a significant performance hit as it moves! Know your tools and use what works best, but always have an eye on performance. Every game has to run smoothly on your target platforms to be a success.

One last rule of thumb for this chapter: if you *can* do it in blueprint, *do* it in blueprint first. Prove a mechanic works and is fun there in short order. Get players joining and starting multiplayer games together with blueprint nodes and not huge amounts of new C++ code. Use what is there, and find when it finally hits the limits of your requirements before you write your own C++ versions. Blueprint can't do everything, but it can do a huge amount of things quite well, with very minimal effort for those who know it.

Summary

In this chapter, we've learned to do some blueprint scripting, seen some examples thereof, and some of the limitations and performance problems that it brings. It's vastly powerful and easy to learn compared to writing C++ code, but using it late in a complex project it can be a big headache. Know your team, know your options, and know your limitations: these are the keys to making the right decisions when it comes to blueprint and your project. Additionally, this blueprint knowledge will be invaluable when doing even basic UI work as we will in the next chapter. UMG (the editing interface primarily used by UE4) is heavily ingrained in blueprint work, and blueprint has a relatively easy time integrating from the game back into that UI. These are, like most things in UE4, not specifically required to have to work together, but now that there is a solid foundation and understanding of the strengths of blueprint, the benefits reaped in getting UI working quickly and to desired specifications will be easy to see!

Questions

1. What two systems from UE3 did blueprint grow from, giving in the K2_ prefix for most of its C++ classes?
2. What is a huge advantage of having source control integration in the editor?
3. Why are UFUNCTIONS and UPROPERTIES so valuable?
4. What is a good estimate of the time it would take to add session joining via C++?
5. What are some tools to use to profile the performance of work done in blueprint?
6. What are some drawbacks to building gameplay in blueprint and not C++?
7. Why is blueprint at some level absolutely required for any UE4 project?
8. What do you also need to do if you let running the PIE game compile your blueprints?

Further reading

Git integration in UE4 editor:

```
https://wiki.unrealengine.com/Git_source_control_(Tutorial)
```

Quick overview of blueprint online session nodes. Be sure to read the link about online subsystems if you're unfamiliar with them:

```
https://docs.unrealengine.com/en-us/Engine/Blueprints/UserGuide/OnlineNodes
```

Blueprint variables overview:

```
https://docs.unrealengine.com/en-us/Engine/Blueprints/UserGuide/Variables
```

C++ profiling tools:

```
https://stackoverflow.com/questions/67554/whats-the-best-free-c-profiler-for-windows
```

U.I. Necessities, Menus, HUD, and Load/Save

4

Introduction

In this chapter, we will get to work on another fundamental necessity of any game: our UI, and as a typical example of it, we'll add loading and saving of our game state to our game. Unreal provides some great tools for these two things, especially UMG for creating UIs, which we will explore here. When it comes to loading and saving your game, it is a system almost every game uses in some form, but none in the same way, and the complexity of it will be absolutely driven by your design and desired player experience. We'll first get our inventory showing up in our HUD. In the next section we'll address some strategies for saving based on different game types, and then we'll tackle one of Unreal's most difficult: saving in-map and restoring to an exact point during gameplay. In this chapter, we'll:

- Make inventory icons using an automated screen-capture level
- Integrate the icons into the player's HUD on screen
- Synchronize the inventory with the HUD/U.I.
- Save and load the full game state from anywhere
- Build the U.I. for loading and saving

Technical requirements

As usual, it is recommended to simply begin at the point of progress reached in Chapter 3, *Blueprint Review and When to Use BP Scripting*, as the GitHub project does here:

```
https://github.com/PacktPublishing/Mastering-Game-Development-with-Unreal-
Engine-4-Second-Edition/tree/Chapter-4
```

While the Chapter 3, *Blueprint Review and When to Use BP Scripting*, content is not specifically required, Chapter 2, *Inventory and Weapons for the Player*, will be heavily used and referenced, so those classes should be considered mandatory for the value of this work.

Engine version used: 4.19.0.

Integrating UMG into our player's HUD class

In Chapter 2, *Inventory and Weapons for the Player*, we managed to create an inventory system for our player, a means of picking up new weapons, and an input scheme for switching between them. However, other than visually seeing which projectile was fired, we had no real reference for what we had in hand. So now we will give the player a display so they can see what they are using, and as part of that, we will finally add some new art assets from the free Unreal Marketplace.

Building icons for the inventory with screen captures

To make this exercise more meaningful and a bit more of a real-world scenario, we need more art. As stated before, however, this is not a book about generating art or most UE4 content. That said, as a technical developer trying to prove what can and can't be done, and without requiring you, the reader, to spend money on Marketplace content or outsourced art studios the way a production game typically would, we will use some stand-in art that's free. So the first thing to do is to get to the Epic Games Launcher. As first noted in Chapter 1, *Making a C++ Project for a First-Person Shooter*, it's usually best to just make a shortcut directly to your UE4 editor executable. In case you forgot, here is that sentence where I recommend *"creating a shortcut to your UE4 install folder's* `/Engine/Binaries/Win64/UE4Editor.exe`," or of course you can manually just go and click it to launch it as well.

This launches the editor with no game, brings up a list of game projects you could open, but also in that Unreal Project Browser in the top-right is a **Marketplace** button, so let's head there. At the very top, make sure you select **Unreal Engine**, then on the left, click **Marketplace**. At the top of the content row, you will find what can be a great friend to teams looking to prototype with cool-looking content or make games based on some amazing Epic released assets, the **Free** tab. Scroll down to **Infinity Blade: Weapons** and **Add to Cart** (and then check out with the little shopping cart in the top-right corner):

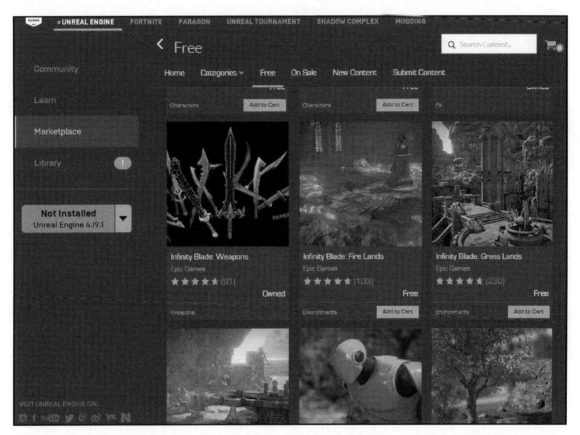

These will now appear when you select the **Library** item on the left, below **Marketplace**. So now, all we need to do is add them to our project to get access to all this great content. Now, glancing at what this package gives you, these are all melee weapons of course, but unfortunately, at the time of writing, there is not a pack of free ranged (gun) weapons, so we'll make do with what we've got. Click **Library** and scroll to the **Vault** section to where you find Infinity Blade: Weapons add click **Add to Project**. From here you will need to click the box for **Show all projects** at the top, and select our **Mastering** project. It will complain these assets are not compatible with Other engine version, so select 4.19 from the dropdown (or whichever is the newest version at or behind the local engine you have been building) and then **Add to Project**. It may then need to download the assets. Wait for this to finish, of course.

Now, opening our project in the editor, if you have your sources panel open, you will see in the Content Browser a new folder, `/Content/InfinityBladeWeapons`, under which there are several which are characters (note that some are static meshes, but as our original gun and pickups expect, we will stick to some of the character weapons). Feel free to open, for example, `/Content/InfinityBladeWeapons/Weapons/Blunt/Blunt_Ravager` and open the `SK_Blunt_Ravager` skeletal mesh to get a look at this interesting spiky hammer weapon. We'll use a few of these to make some new weapons for our game. Since we have already been through this process in `Chapter 2`, *Inventory and Weapons for the Player*, I will quickly list the steps I am using here to create a few new items:

1. In our `/Content/FirstPersonCPP/Blueprints` folder, I'll right-click **BigBallGun** and **Duplicate** it.
2. I'll do the same thing for the pickup (**BigBallGunPickup**).
3. For the ravager weapon, I will now rename these blueprints **RavagerGun** (yes, we're making a gun out of a hammer, but again, the art is just what we have available), and **RavagerGunPickup**, leaving the other items (such as projectile) the same as the **BigBallGun.**
4. Opening the **RavagerGun** in the full BP editor, and selecting its **WeaponMesh** component, I can now set this to the **SK_Blunt_Ravager** we just looked at.
5. Similarly, I set the **BallGunPickup** mesh component to use the same skeletal mesh, and rename the component to **PickupMesh** so that as we duplicate them in the future this has a generic name:

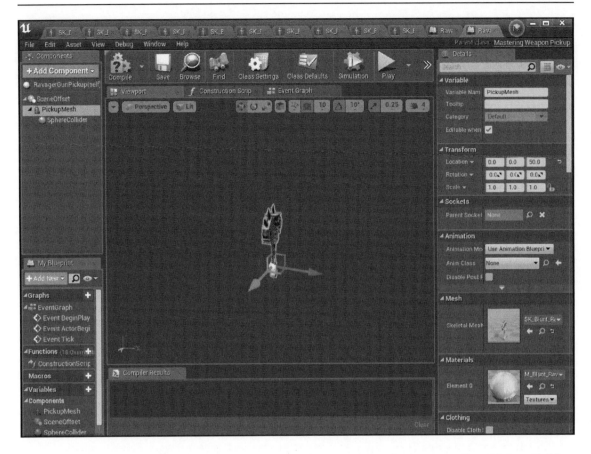

And lastly, to differentiate it, I set the Weapon Power to 2 in the **RavagerGunPickup(self)** details and select the RavagerGun from its Mastering Weapon Pickup fly-out. You can, of course, set the weapon's Projectile to any you'd like, or make a new one, adjust its position in the player's hands, and so on; but for now, we have an axe that shoots!

Adding one of the pick-ups to the level and testing it quickly is a good checkpoint to add the project to GitHub.

> Pulling down the GitHub project from this point will require a bit more time as these assets download (which are larger than the entire rest of the project to this point!), but that delay will only happen the first time they are pulled.

I will repeat this process of adding a weapon and pick-up two more times until there's a total of five weapons at the moment that can be differentiated. For organization purposes now that there are more than a couple of blueprints, I'm moving all of these weapons, projectiles, and pickups to a new `/Content/FirstPersonCPP/Blueprints/Weapons` folder. Our next step is to get some icons built from these models. Some projects will have artists that want to draw these by hand; other games may have no artists and use this technique or simply draw the actors directly into a render target texture to display these items. The render target idea is explored further in the additional reading section, but for now, let's focus on generating icons from screenshots in an automated way.

To accomplish great looking, alpha-masked output icons for high-quality UI use, we will need to do a few things in this order:

1. Make a new Camera Actor that automates our process and takes our screenshots. Implementing this camera will have several parts as well, including placement and orientation of our weapon actors, taking depth-masked screenshots, and importing those back to our actors as textures.
2. Make a new level, add an instance of our new camera to it, and add a SkyLight to it.
3. Hook the imported texture back into our pick-ups to pass to the UI.
4. Make an icon widget in UMG that takes a weapon's texture on creation.
5. Build a list in UMG and add this to the HUD. Hook the inventory class to the list widget and have it update to reflect the player's weapon choice.

With most significant game features such as this, there are a number of steps, and each has various levels of complexity; but if you can order them in such a way to implement and test each of them as we go, as the preceding process is designed to do, it's just a matter of time before you go from A to B and have your finished system. So let's get started with the new camera class. In the editor at the `/Content/Blueprints` level, I'll add a new C++ class and name it **MasteringIconCamera**, and derive it from **CameraActor**. This camera's whole job will be to open weapon pickups and place them in a nice way in front of it and then take screenshots, which we will use as icons.

Here is an opportunity to show where using blueprints can be a real time saver. It's most definitely possible to simply place a camera directly in a level, and with some work, get its viewport to take screenshots. If time permits and someone is determined or is very experienced with these systems in C++, it can be done with effort. Or, you can make a game mode in blueprint, make a new pawn in blueprint, and no C++ native classes are needed. As we have made blueprint classes before, I'll just list the steps taken in this section and, as always, if problems arise, this progress is available in GitHub to check against:

1. In the **Blueprints** folder, create an **IconMaker** folder, and in it create a new blueprint based off **Pawn**, named **IconPawn**.
2. Create a game mode based on **GameModeBase**. Name it **IconGameMode**.
3. In the game mode, uncheck **Allow Tick Before Begin Play** (set false), set **HUD Class** to **None**, and set **Default Pawn Class** to **IconPawn**.
4. In **IconPawn**, under its **DefaultSceneRoot**, add a **ChildActor** component and set its **Child Actor Class** to **MasteringIconCamera**.
5. In that child camera, uncheck **Constrain Aspect Ratio** in **Camera Component's Camera Settings** (this avoids a check from often asserting when using custom depth field screenshots).
6. Optionally set the FOV (for experimental purposes, I set it to 45 as it makes some of the math easier to test later). Any range from very small to 90+ is fine. Normally for this kind of thing I'd want to use an orthographic camera for simplicity, but lighting has had many problems in UE4's orthographic rendering for years. We handle FOV in code, as seen later.

This is it for the blueprint classes. Now we need a new level to use them in. So in the editor, be sure to save your blueprints, then go to **File** > **New Level**, picking the Empty Level template and naming it `IconScreenshotMap`. Drag an Icon Pawn into the level and in the Details pane with it selected, be sure its location and its rotation is set to 0, 0, 0. We can also borrow a trick from the FPS template's example map, and under our in-level pawn's **Pawn** properties, set **Auto Possess Player** to **Player 0**. This way, when the game starts, it puts the local default player right into this pawn rather than making one from a player spawn. Another tip: you can copy all of the lighting objects (or the whole lighting folder) from `FirstPersonExampleMap` and paste them into this map.

In any case, you will certainly need a Sky Light and probably want a Directional Light as in the GitHub version, but this is a bit subjective for changing the look of the weapons as we screenshot them. Tthe GitHub version may be a bit too bright, making the renders a little washed out; but again, this is subjective and not the focus of this chapter.

Now that we have a level and lighting, let's fix up some **World Settings** in the main editor tab for the level. Set the **GameMode Override** to **IconGameMode**, and down in **Physics**, we want to check the **Override World Gravity** box and set it to 0.0 (we don't want our pawn immediately, or ever, falling). For completeness, I added a pickup for the default ball gun and put a scale on the big ball gun pickup to differentiate it later. So now our level and picture-grabbing pawn are all set; all we need now is for the camera in it to actually do something!

We'll begin in its BeginPlay function back in C++. Our header has several member variables and a number of functions that we'll need to automate our screen-grabs:

```cpp
UCLASS()
class MASTERING_API AMasteringIconCamera : public ACameraActor
{
        GENERATED_BODY()
public:
        virtual void BeginPlay() override;

protected:

        virtual void TakeShot();
        virtual void SpawnAndPlaceNextActor();
        virtual FVector ComputeActorLocation();
        virtual void OnFinishedLoadingAssets();

        UPROPERTY(Transient)
        TArray<FSoftObjectPath> WeaponBlueprintSoftRefs;
        UPROPERTY(Transient)
        TArray<class UBlueprint*> WeaponBlueprints;

        UPROPERTY(Transient)
        class UBlueprint* CurrentWeaponBlueprint = nullptr;
        UPROPERTY(Transient)
        class AMasteringWeaponPickup* CurrentWeaponPickup = nullptr;
        UPROPERTY(Transient)
        class UCameraComponent* CameraComp;
        UPROPERTY(Transient)
        bool bInitialied = false;

        UPROPERTY(EditAnywhere, BlueprintReadWrite)
        FString WeaponsPath = "FirstPersonCPP/Blueprints/Weapons";
```

```
UPROPERTY(EditAnywhere, BlueprintReadWrite)
float ShotDelay = 0.4f;
UPROPERTY(EditAnywhere, BlueprintReadWrite)
int ScreenshotResolutionX = 256;
UPROPERTY(EditAnywhere, BlueprintReadWrite)
int ScreenshotResolutionY = 256;

int CurrentWeaponIndex = 0;
};
```

In the interest of brevity when posting progress here, I'm leaving out a lot of the normal spacing and comments that might normally accompany these things in a professional environment. Hopefully, the more traditional and formal examples in the previous chapters have given some good overall guidelines there, but if you notice these things missing here, it's to save space as we have a lot to cover, not out of bad habit. As usual, when there are new concepts, they will be discussed along with the code here. In this case, there's a new UPROPERTY tag, Transient. This tells the engine that these properties are never to be saved with the object: they're used during its lifetime and can be used as any other UPROPERTY can, but changes to them do not "dirty" the object to require saving, and the contents are never serialized in and out with an instance of the object. A brief note on the properties near the bottom: ShotDelay is the amount of time we pause between loading a new weapon pickup in-game and taking its screenshot. This is there primarily to allow some frames for the game to spawn the objects and then update them to be in the proper MIP map level of detail. We will be asynchronously loading in all the blueprints for the weapon pickups, but this delay is still needed because even with assets loaded, objects often still come in at their lowest MIP level and if we take a screenshot right then, the quality is at its worst:

```
void AMasteringIconCamera::BeginPlay()
{
        if (bInitialied)
        {
                return; // BeginPlay will get called multiple times at
                level start
        }

        bInitialied = true;

        CameraComp = GetCameraComponent();

        UWorld* World = GetWorld();
        check(World != nullptr);
        APlayerController* Player = World->GetFirstPlayerController();

        Player->SetCinematicMode(true, true, true, true, true);
```

```
        Player->SetViewTarget(this);

        FString contentPath = FString("/Game/") + WeaponsPath;

        static UObjectLibrary* ObjectLibrary = nullptr;
        ObjectLibrary =
UObjectLibrary::CreateLibrary(AMasteringWeaponPickup::StaticClass(), false,
GIsEditor);
        ObjectLibrary->AddToRoot();
        ObjectLibrary->bHasBlueprintClasses = true;

        ObjectLibrary->LoadBlueprintAssetDataFromPath(contentPath);

        TArray<FAssetData> AssetDatas;
        ObjectLibrary->GetAssetDataList(AssetDatas);

        for (auto itr : AssetDatas)
        {
                FSoftObjectPath assetPath(itr.ObjectPath.ToString());
                WeaponBlueprintSoftRefs.Add(assetPath);
        }

        // Here we stream in the assets found that are weapon pick-ups and
when done, will call the OnFinished function
        FStreamableManager& Streamable =
UAssetManager::GetStreamableManager();
        Streamable.RequestAsyncLoad(WeaponBlueprintSoftRefs,
FStreamableDelegate::CreateUObject(this,
&AMasteringIconCamera::OnFinishedLoadingAssets));
}
```

There are a few interesting things to discuss here. The first is commented at the top that `BeginPlay` can be, and will be, called multiple times on a single object (generally two), and we only need to or want to do the work here once. So first, we set the player into cinematic mode, shutting down movement and HUD and anything else that's not really needed with our super basic pawn, but a good idea in areas such as this in general. We set this camera as the view target and get our path, which is defaulted to where the weapon, pickup, and projectile blueprints were moved: `/Game/FirstPersonCPP/Blueprints/Weapons`. However, this can be edited on an individual icon camera to point to any specific folder as it's an exposed `UPROPERTY` (just like the screenshot resolution and delay mentioned earlier). Next, the `UObjectLibrary` class is used to mass-find our pickup objects in the path. We quickly iterate the list of them, making soft references to those objects. This is not strictly required, but like a few other topics in this chapter, it's meant to be instructive and start building good habits when you're thinking about how to reference objects as you go. On a PC, often you can simply load all the necessary assets all the time for a given level and only free them when you finish playing. On mobile and other platforms, memory can be at a premium, so it's good to have the tools in hand to load assets in the background, not stopping the game, and then also to be sure they will be freed by garbage collection later when they're no longer needed. Once the list of pickups is made, we send that to the `StreamableManager` to batch stream in our blueprints that we need to use. In that request, we add a callback to ourselves using `FStreamableDelegate`'s `CreateUObject` (this creates a callback tied to a `UObject`, in most cases using the `this` pointer). When all these blueprints are loaded into memory, it will call `OnFinishedLoadingAssets`, which we'll look at next.

To speed up testing during work like this (where you simply need to open a level, have it run, and exit), you can right-click the Mastering project in the Solution Explorer and add the map name and `-game` to your Command Arguments line so it looks like this: `"$(SolutionDir)$(ProjectName).uproject"` `IconScreenshotMap -game -skipcompile -debug`. This tells the DebugGame Editor build to launch directly into the game, but as an Editor build. It will still use uncooked content. If you built DebugGame, you will get an error on startup if you are not also cooking your content.

So, once our blueprints are all loaded, we need to spawn one of each of these as actors into the world, take our shot, and then destroy that one and move to the next. We'll do this with a timer and a lambda function (our first, but certainly not last). Look at what we have so far:

```
void AMasteringIconCamera::OnFinishedLoadingAssets()
{
    UWorld* World = GetWorld();
```

```
        for (auto itr = WeaponBlueprintSoftRefs.CreateIterator(); itr;
        ++itr)
        {
                UBlueprint *BPObj =
CastChecked<UBlueprint>((*itr).ResolveObject());
                WeaponBlueprints.Add(BPObj);
        }

        SpawnAndPlaceNextActor(); // this spawns our first pickup and
increments CurrentWeaponIndex to 1

        static FTimerHandle ScreenShotTimer;
        World->GetTimerManager().SetTimer(ScreenShotTimer, [=] {
                        if (CurrentWeaponIndex == 0) // only way we come in
at index 0 is if we're done
                        {
World->GetTimerManager().ClearTimer(ScreenShotTimer);
                                                              if
(APlayerController* Player = UGameplayStatics::GetPlayerController(World,
0))
                                {
Player->ConsoleCommand(TEXT("Exit"), true);
                                        return;
                                }
                        }

                        TakeShot();
                },
                ShotDelay, true, ShotDelay);
}
```

Here, we first convert our soft references (the TArray of FSoftObjectPath items) to hard references (in this case, a simple UPROPERTY TArray of UBlueprint pointers). If you find yourself having trouble with memory leaks or running out of memory, always remember that a UPROPERTY pointer in UE4 will count as a hard reference to the object it points to, preventing it from being freed until you null out that pointer (or point it at another object), or the object with the pointer is destroyed upon which it is also released. You can always walk up the chain of UObject Outer pointers to find out who ultimately owns any other UObject, but right now, we want to force all these blueprints to stay loaded in memory, hence why we convert the soft references to hard ones. After this, we cue up our first pickup to be shot by calling SpawnAndPlaceNextActor, which we will get to shortly.

For most programmers learning C++ in the last 5 or so years, lambda functions are pretty common. For those learning C++ in earlier years this could be something new, but they're incredibly useful and supported by many areas of UE4. We use one here in a simple timer from the game's timer manager: we set an initial delay to our `ShotDelay` member time, as well as the rate the timer will fire at since we set it to looping, and only break this looping when a special condition is hit. `CurrentWeaponIndex` being 0 means we have finished and are out of pickups to capture. The way to stop a looping (or any active non-looping) timer is to have the timer manager clear that timer based on the handle you passed when you set the timer. Now, every `ShotDelay` interval, we'll call `TakeShot`, which also cues up the next shot when it finishes.

As the next thing called is that `TakeShot` function, let's look at it next:

```
void AMasteringIconCamera::TakeShot()
{
        UWorld* World = GetWorld();

        check(CurrentWeaponPickup != nullptr);

        UMeshComponent* Mesh =
Cast<UMeshComponent>(CurrentWeaponPickup->GetComponentByClass(UMeshComponent::StaticClass()));
        check(Mesh != nullptr);

        Mesh->bForceMipStreaming = true;

        Mesh->SetRenderCustomDepth(true);

        GScreenshotResolutionX = ScreenshotResolutionX;
        GScreenshotResolutionY = ScreenshotResolutionY;

        GetHighResScreenshotConfig().SetHDRCapture(true);
        GetHighResScreenshotConfig().bMaskEnabled = true;
        World->GetGameViewport()->Viewport->TakeHighResScreenShot();

        // this timer is here to wait just one frame (hence the tiny time)
and then destroy the current actor
        // and spawn the next one: if you destroy the actor the same frame
as the screenshot it may not appear
        FTimerHandle SpawnNextTimer;
        World->GetTimerManager().SetTimer(SpawnNextTimer, [this] {
                if (CurrentWeaponIndex >= WeaponBlueprints.Num())
                {
                        CurrentWeaponIndex = 0; // we have finished, this
will break our timer loop on its next trigger
                }
                else
```

```
                    {
                            SpawnAndPlaceNextActor();
                    }
            },
            0.001f, false);
    }
```

You'll notice in many of these functions there are `checks` before simply calling functions on those items, such as the Mesh pointer. Given how automated this functionality is, if content creators were having trouble building proper pickups, you would be alerted anywhere important here, but if this were a problem you'd likely want to handle those kinds of setup mistakes in a way that doesn't crash the editor for non-programmers (people hooked into Visual Studio or the like can always skip passed check assertions with **Set Next Statement** or the like). But again, for brevity, and as a minimal safeguard to alert of a problem before a simple crash, these `checks` are at least here. So, getting that Mesh, we then set it up for a proper screenshot, make sure our game's global screenshot resolutions are set to ours, set up our screenshot's properties, and take one using the game viewport. It's by far the easiest one to access, and this is why we take ours from the player pawn's perspective here. We then set an intentionally short timer so the next frame we move to the next actor, or signal to the previous timer that we're done via resetting the weapon index. As noted in the comment, if you destroy an actor (as `SpawnAndPlaceNextActor` will) it is likely that it then will not show up at the time the screenshot is resolved, but if you wait one frame for the shot to finish, there's no problems.

So you've seen it a couple of times now; let's look at `SpawnAndPlaceNextActor`:

```
    void AMasteringIconCamera::SpawnAndPlaceNextActor()
    {
            if (CurrentWeaponPickup != nullptr)
                    CurrentWeaponPickup->Destroy();

            CurrentWeaponBlueprint = WeaponBlueprints[CurrentWeaponIndex];
            check(CurrentWeaponBlueprint != nullptr); // anything not a
    blueprint should never find its way into our list

            UWorld* World = GetWorld();

            FRotator Rot(0.0f);
            FVector Trans(0.0f);

            FTransform Transform(Rot, Trans);
            FActorSpawnParameters ActorSpawnParams;
            ActorSpawnParams.SpawnCollisionHandlingOverride =
    ESpawnActorCollisionHandlingMethod::AlwaysSpawn;
            CurrentWeaponPickup =
```

```
World->SpawnActor<AMasteringWeaponPickup>(CurrentWeaponBlueprint->Generated
Class, Transform, ActorSpawnParams);
        CurrentWeaponPickup->RotationSpeed = 0.0f; // the ones we use for
screenshots we don't want spinning!
        check(CurrentWeaponPickup != nullptr);

        FVector Pos = ComputeActorLocation();
        CurrentWeaponPickup->SetActorLocation(Pos);

        CurrentWeaponIndex++;
}
```

Hopefully, this function is much more straightforward and does not require much attention. We destroy any current existing actor, get the one our index is set to as a blueprint, spawn one of those in the world with the blueprint's GeneratedClass, stop it from spinning, fix its location, and increment our index.

So, how do we fix up that location? By finally using a little bit of basic 3D math:

```
FVector AMasteringIconCamera::ComputeActorLocation()
{
        check(CurrentWeaponPickup != nullptr);
        UMeshComponent* Mesh =
Cast<UMeshComponent>(CurrentWeaponPickup->GetComponentByClass(UMeshComponen
t::StaticClass()));

        FVector InPos;
        FVector BoxExtent;
        CurrentWeaponPickup->GetActorBounds(false, InPos, BoxExtent);

        // uncomment these to view the actor bounding generated for our
pick-ups
        /*FVector CurrentPosition =
CurrentWeaponPickup->GetActorLocation();
    FColor fcRandom(FMath::RandRange(64, 255), FMath::RandRange(64, 255),
FMath::RandRange(64, 255));
    DrawDebugLine(World, CurrentPosition, CurrentPosition + InPos, fcRandom,
false, 20.0f);
    DrawDebugBox(World, CurrentPosition + InPos, 0.5f * BoxExtent,
FQuat(ForceInitToZero), fcRandom, false, 20.0f);*/

        // uncomment these to view the mesh bounding imported with the
assets
        /*FBoxSphereBounds bsMesh = Mesh->Bounds;
    DrawDebugLine(World, CurrentPosition, bsMesh.Origin, fcRandom, false,
20.0f);
    DrawDebugBox(World, bsMesh.Origin, 0.5f * bsMesh.BoxExtent,
FQuat(ForceInitToZero), fcRandom, false, 20.0f);*/
```

```
        const float fX = BoxExtent.X;
        const float fY = BoxExtent.Y;
        const float fZ = BoxExtent.Z;

        if (fX > fY)
        {
                FRotator YawRot(0.0f, 90.0f, 0.0f);
                CurrentWeaponPickup->SetActorRotation(YawRot);
        }

        const float fLongestBoxSide = FMath::Max(fX, FMath::Max(fY,
        fZ));

        // FOV is the whole frustum FOV, to make a right triangle down its
 middle, we use half this angle
        const float FOVhalf = 0.5f * CameraComp->FieldOfView;
        const float FOVradians = FOVhalf * PI / 180.0f;

        const float FOVtan = FMath::Tan(FOVradians);

        float XDistance = fLongestBoxSide / FOVtan;

        FVector Positioning(XDistance, 0.0f, 0.0f);

        return CurrentWeaponPickup->GetActorLocation() + Positioning -
 InPos;
 }
```

If curious about the commented out bounding box/offset drawing chunks, feel free to enable one or both and see what they show you. The reason I used them and left them in was because SkeletalMeshActors primarily get their bounding information at the time the assets are imported from whatever external tool they were built in (3D Studio MAX, Maya, and so on) set by the artists. As I found some of the Infinity Blade weapons' bounding a bit odd, I used this to make sure it was indeed how the assets were made, and there was not a math or other programming error.

In this function, we get the bounding extents of the actor, find its longest dimension (X, Y, or Z) and push it back until that longest side is just at the edge of our view frustum. If it turns out a weapon is more wide than it is long, we rotate the larger side to face our camera too. Figuring out how far away in X to move our actor to best fill/fit the screen before the shot is then just a bit of simple trigonometry. We can get the field of view of the camera frustum, and if we then consider a top-down sort of view of that frustum split down the middle as two right triangles, we know to get that longest side to fit we then use the tangent of half that frustum angle for one of the triangles. By definition, that tangent being the opposite side's length over the adjacent side's length, we divide the long side of our bounding to know how far to push the object out now. We also subtract out the relative position offset (InPos) of the bounding box itself and should have a reasonably centered location to return.

Running our icon map now should generate a screenshot in the **Saved** folder of our project for each pickup. This is a good checkpoint for GitHub, and we'll use those screenshots to finally make some UI elements next.

Using UMG to display inventory icons on screen

After the previous section's significant amount of code, we'll be back working mostly in blueprints and the editor in this section. One quick aside: when moving assets in the editor, it will leave behind a redirector `.uasset` file of the one you moved. All this does is point anything that looks for the old one to the new one. There's a Fix-Up Redirectors commandlet you can run, which searches your content folder for all of these and any objects referencing them, points them properly to the new location, and deletes the redirector. This can also be done manually in the content browser by finding the **Other Filters | Show Redirectors** filter setting, and you can right-click on them in the content browser and select **Fix Up** to get rid of them. I did that at this point to keep things tidy.

So now under **FirstPersonCPP** I next make a **Textures** folder and click the **Import** button in the content browser: browsing to where the screenshots were added (`/Saved/Screenshots/Windows`). Select the generated `.png` files here (five in my case) and let them all import as textures. It's good to have a naming convention for searching blueprints as projects get larger, so for all of these textures I simply name them `T_`(weapon name). Of course, with some effort in UE4's C++ using the `FileManager` we could cleverly automate renaming the `.png` files rather easily, but importing them into game content as textures is a bit more involved—bulk selecting them here and manually renaming is sufficient for us as we get on to the task of drawing them in an inventory UI.

Synchronizing your inventory and HUD

Moving to actually draw our icons and cycle them is the first portion of this book where not all steps of implementation will be fully shown. All of the work as always is available on GitHub, and it is recommended to go look at each change in this Chapter 4 branch submission, but for discussion purposes, the focus will be on new concepts going forward and decision making. This is, after all, a Mastering book, so expect the pace and complexity of work to pick up. First, a bit of housekeeping, as this complexity does ramp up: as a project moves into a more mature state, the sheer number of source files tends to increase and it's best early on to start managing these into logical directories. There are really two main schemes for how you group things in your project hierarchy: by function or by system. Functionally grouping source files is along the lines of (in our current reorganization) things such as all UI widget classes, with maybe subfolders for complex specialized types. Grouping by system would be (as I've done here) more like all things related to inventory. While these may seem like trivial decisions, or it may feel OK with modern IDEs to simply leave every class in one flat hierarchy, project size and developer team size should drive your decisions here. The important part is to make architectural decisions like this early and then stick to them throughout a project for the team's consistency.

OK, on to the fun stuff! The main new class we need to create in C++ is UUserWidget, like so:

```
UCLASS()
class MASTERING_API UMasteringInventoryDisplay : public UUserWidget
{
        GENERATED_BODY()
public:
        virtual void Init(class UMasteringInventory* Inventory);

        UFUNCTION(BlueprintImplementableEvent, Category = Inventory)
        void WeaponSelected(FWeaponProperties Weapon);

        UFUNCTION(BlueprintImplementableEvent, Category = Inventory)
        void WeaponAdded(FWeaponProperties Weapon);

        UFUNCTION(BlueprintImplementableEvent, Category = Inventory)
        void WeaponRemoved(FWeaponProperties Weapon);
};
```

Now, as they're new to this book, note the keyword for `BlueprintImplementableEvent`: these functions are actually not implemented in C++, only declared in the header. Their actual functionality comes in the blueprint events they generate. We'll get to those in a bit, but let's now look at how they are used and then we'll trace that to how they are triggered:

```
void UMasteringInventoryDisplay::Init(class UMasteringInventory* Inventory)
{
        Inventory->OnSelectedWeaponChanged.AddUObject(this,
&UMasteringInventoryDisplay::WeaponSelected);
        Inventory->OnWeaponAdded.AddUObject(this,
&UMasteringInventoryDisplay::WeaponAdded);
        Inventory->OnWeaponRemoved.AddUObject(this,
&UMasteringInventoryDisplay::WeaponRemoved);
}
```

What's happening here is we are hooking into an event in the `Inventory` class that will broadcast to all its listeners (our bindings) when events happen, passing weapon properties into our blueprint implementation. So, how do we do this? First we add these events to our inventory class:

```
DECLARE_EVENT_OneParam(UMasteringInventory, FSelectedWeaponChanged,
FWeaponProperties);
FSelectedWeaponChanged OnSelectedWeaponChanged;

DECLARE_EVENT_OneParam(UMasteringInventory, FWeaponAdded,
FWeaponProperties);
FSelectedWeaponChanged OnWeaponAdded;

DECLARE_EVENT_OneParam(UMasteringInventory, FWeaponRemoved,
FWeaponProperties);
FSelectedWeaponChanged OnWeaponRemoved;
```

And in the `.cpp`, after a good amount of refactoring (and a couple of bug fixes I'm not too ashamed to admit), we have lines like these:

```
void UMasteringInventory::SelectWeapon(FWeaponProperties Weapon)
{
        OnSelectedWeaponChanged.Broadcast(Weapon);

        MyOwner->EquipWeapon(Weapon.WeaponClass);
        CurrentWeapon = Weapon.WeaponClass;
}
```

Similarly added for, well, adding a weapon, and the newly implemented removal of weapons as well (this is done when ammo runs out).

For a game like this, it's important to have a design in mind for how to show the player their inventory and know whether things such as ammo pickups without being a weapon pickup are possible, of course. In this case, if you're out of ammo, you might as well not have the weapon at all, so we remove it from the display. You could, of course, gray it out or the like, but again, make sure at all times your design drives your implementation decisions.

So we're now communicating to our inventory display object key events when the inventory is changed in C++. Let's take a moment than to see what that looks like on the blueprint side of this concept:

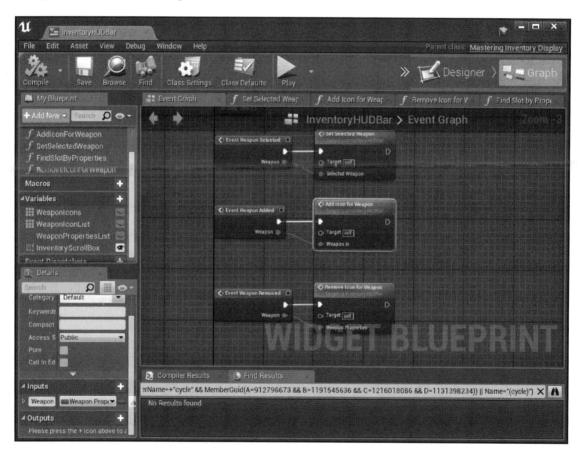

There are several things to note here, but it will be kept brief: notice the functions and variables on the left. These are blueprint-only things added with the + button to make all of this work. This is where a bit of mystery will remain unless you go to GitHub and look at all of the implementations. Hopefully, the functionality of these functions and variables is clear from the naming. As inventory items are added, widgets are added to a **ScrollBox** widget. The layout will follow, but the important concepts are that we'll track weapon classes and icon widgets in parallel arrays so we can map them for selection and removal. That function is demonstrative of why all the functions won't be shown here directly:

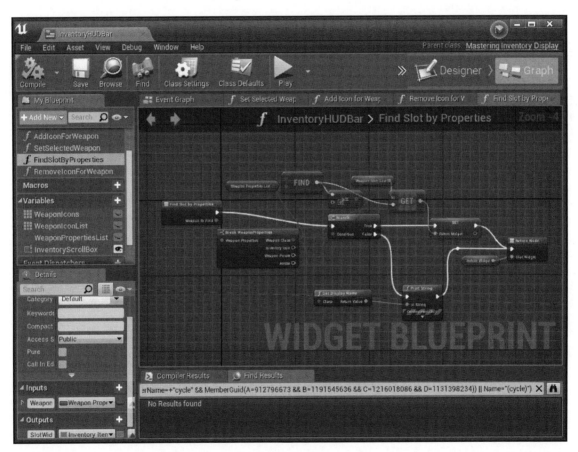

This is not even a particularly complex function, but it's already a bit tight to get into one shot. Notice at the print-string node there's a redirector node. They can be added by dragging from an execution pin (white ones) at any time, and then dragged around to help sometimes with the spaghetti that visual scripting can create. Hopefully, also you're familiar with input and output variables (seen in the bottom left), blueprint functions can be extremely useful for quick implementation, and are all but required when working with UMG widgets. Some UI/UX designers may be comfortable implementing their own functionality, but mostly those roles will be more involved with the **Designer** tab, in the top-right. Let's quickly look at that for this scrolling inventory widget that we'll draw, currently, at the top of the screen:

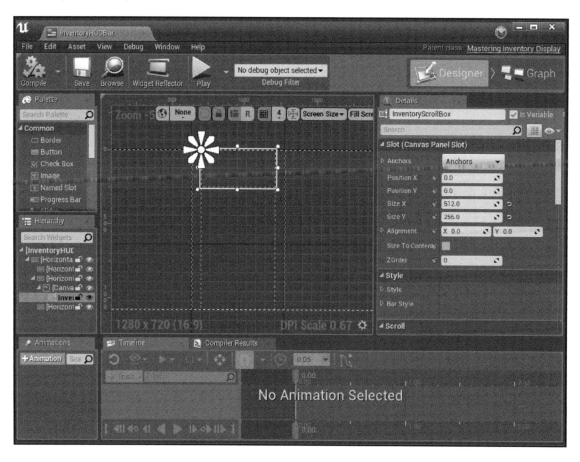

Of note in the top-right is that the **ScrollBox** widget, in this case, is checked to be a variable (you can see it referenced in blueprint scripting) and the slightly odd arrangement of **HorizontalBox** widgets on the left, which basically sandwich our **ScrollBox** into a **Canvas** widget in the middle that is the size we want. There are a **lot** of widget settings to get all this correct, including an **Image**-based widget named **InventoryItem** that can be reviewed in the GitHub project. Looking for what was modified to make things work as they do is always just a search for those little yellow looping arrows (which, as you know if clicked, revert a value to its default) indicating what has been modified.

Now, to make all of this work also requires adding a blueprint for our MasteringGameMode and MasteringHUD so that the former can set the latter as the HUD to use, and World Settings in the main level editing window can be set to use that mode:

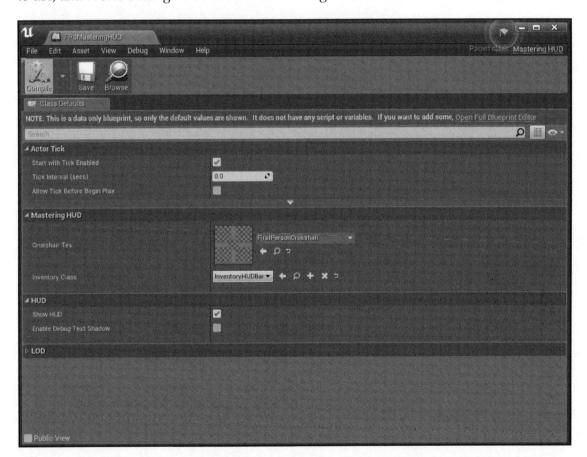

Notice that I un-hardcoded the crosshair texture, but exposing things like this to blueprint means adding extra code to handle if they are not set up properly.

So the net result of this is that we can now scroll through our weapons, see which is selected (as it is the only full-alpha object in our list), and as we cycle what's in-hand, it cycles our **ScrollBox** full of icons, removing any that run out of ammo!

If you find yourself getting errors trying to compile your widgets, be sure to note the change to `Mastering.Build.cs`. This is where you can include source modules your game may find itself needing (and to this point, we did not need UMG):

```
+ PublicDependencyModuleNames.AddRange(new string[] { "Core",
"CoreUObject", "Engine", "InputCore", "HeadMountedDisplay", "UMG" });
```

One last note (which will be well known to experienced GitHub users): I submitted my changes, *then* moved my files to reorganize them. GitHub sees moves as a deletion of the old file and addition of a new file, so you would lose the change history, but that can be seen in the two submissions that go along with this effort.

So now our inventory is synced up and good to go!

Using UMG and game save slots

UE 4.19+ gives us a nice class to actually save and load a chunk of data for objects we want to save. In our case, this will be every actor that can change its state or position, which right now is not a lot. But as a game grows, if in-scene saves are desired, it is incredibly important to start this process as early as possible too. Our biggest challenge will be the one class we implemented in Chapter 3, *Blueprint Review and When to Use BP Scripting*, where almost its entire functionality was implemented on the blueprint side. Creating a solution that works with both native C++ classes and blueprints will be our all-inclusive goal for this section. The UMG UI will be a bit lighter than the last section of this chapter.

Creating a widget for save slots

While the bulk of the work in this section will be actually implementing the loading and saving of various actor classes, we do of course need an interface to display this to players, and that is what we will do first. Our next step then is a UMG widget that we can bring up with buttons to facilitate this. So, back in the editor, we need a widget that has some touch-points back to C++ code so we can do the bulk of the work. To simplify this, we'll make a new C++ class based on `UUserWidget`, call it **MainMenuWidget**, and add the class to the UI folder. Then, like before, we make a new blueprint asset and we will add 4 buttons to that in its design, like so:

Notice we set its initial visibility to **Hidden**, and at the **ButtonBox** level, the anchor is set to center screen with X and Y alignments of 0.5. As always, feel free to reference the version in GitHub for all UMG/blueprint issues not specifically discussed here.

Next, we bind the click events for each of those buttons. Click each button, and at the bottom of its **Details** tab are the events for input with a big green + button. Click that for each button's **OnClicked** event and you'll be taken to the blueprint graph at that event where it's added. We add these functions to the widget class:

```cpp
UCLASS()
class MASTERING_API UMainMenuWidget : public UUserWidget
{
        GENERATED_BODY()
public:
        UFUNCTION(BlueprintCallable)
        void LoadGame(FName SaveFile);

        UFUNCTION(BlueprintCallable)
        void SaveGame();

        UFUNCTION(BlueprintCallable)
        void Open();

        UFUNCTION(BlueprintCallable)
        void Close();
};
```

Wire the save event to the `SaveGame` function, and wire the load event to the `LoadGame` function as well, of course. `Open` is called by an input: we need to bind one in player settings as we have done in the past. I set mine to *F10* as this is common in several games, but of course it can be any key, touch, or gesture desired. In `MasteringCharacter`, I bind this input to a simple pass-through function that gets the HUD like so and calls a function with the same name on that HUD:

```cpp
AMasteringHUD* HUD =
Cast<AMasteringHUD>(CastChecked<APlayerController>(GetController())->GetHUD
());

void AMasteringHUD::ToggleMainMenu()
{
        if (MainMenu != nullptr)
        {
                if (MainMenu->GetVisibility() == ESlateVisibility::Visible)
                        MainMenu->Close();
                else
                        MainMenu->Open();
```

```
                }
        }
```

Back in the widget class, the Open and Close functions are worth looking at, but only open is listed here as close is essentially the same thing in reverse, setting the input mode to FInputModeGameOnly:

```cpp
void UMainMenuWidget::Open()
{
        checkSlow(GetVisibility() == ESlateVisibility::Hidden); // only
want to open from closed
        SetVisibility(ESlateVisibility::Visible);

        UWorld* World = GetWorld();
        if (World != nullptr)
        {
                APlayerController* playerController =
World->GetFirstPlayerController();
                if (playerController)
                {
                        playerController->bShowMouseCursor = true;
                        FInputModeUIOnly InputMode;
                        playerController->SetInputMode(InputMode);
                        UGameplayStatics::SetGamePaused(this, true);
                }
        }
}
```

Now with *F10*, while playing, our main menu comes up, and when the **Return to Game** button is clicked, its event just calls close now on the widget, which unpauses the game and returns mouse control to our normal player input. The last special event, the button labeled **Exit Game**, has a simple blueprint node call to quit playing (and exit standalone), utilizing the **Execute Console Command** node, with the command exit.

Later in the project, this is changed to a **Quit Game** node as this works when console commands may be unavailable (release builds, certain platforms, and so on). The **Quit Game** node is also nice because on mobile platforms it can simply send your app to the background instead of fully ending its execution. Keep in mind that iOS and Android can effectively end the execution of an app that is in the background if the OS decides it needs its resources; but again, at least the **Quit Game** node works across platforms and allows you the choice to try just going to the background.

That's it for the menu side at the moment. Now we need to actually save our game, finally!

Creating a save game file

As noted at the top of this section, our actual game and the state of all our dynamic actors is done in three major steps:

1. Add an interface to all actors that need to save. This involves a few changes to our moving platform, which we'll try to keep straightforward.
2. Serialize all our actors' desired variables to an FArchive by tagging our UPROPERTIES.
3. Write this to a file we can then serialize everything back out from.

For very simple saving (such as player stats and the current level), be sure to check out the USaveGame document link in the *Further reading* section at the end of the chapter. Now, on to our relatively complex version.

First we need an interface that we'll add to all of our actors that we care about saving, this is the first time we need to make a C++ class outside the editor.

 When making new C++ from files, it's often just easiest to right-click the tabs at the top of Visual Studio, open Containing Folder, copy paste a .h and .cpp file up one folder, rename them as needed, copy them back down to the proper folder, then generate project files by right-clicking the .uproject or using the batch file style mentioned in Chapter 1, *Making a C++ Project for a First-Person Shooter*. Of course, the body of the files needs to be replaced.

The header of the .h should look like this:

```
// Fill out your copyright notice in the Description page of Project
Settings.

#pragma once

#include "CoreMinimal.h"
#include "Serialization/ObjectAndNameAsStringProxyArchive.h"
#include "Inventory/MasteringInventory.h"
#include "SavedActorInterface.generated.h"

/**
 *
 */
USTRUCT()
struct FActorSavedData
{
        GENERATED_USTRUCT_BODY()
```

```
        FString MyClass;
        FTransform MyTransform;
        FVector MyVelocity;
        FName MyName;
        TArray<uint8> MyData;

        friend FArchive& operator<<(FArchive& Ar, FActorSavedData&
SavedData)
        {
                Ar << SavedData.MyClass;
                Ar << SavedData.MyTransform;
                Ar << SavedData.MyVelocity;
                Ar << SavedData.MyName;
                Ar << SavedData.MyData;
                return Ar;
        }
};

USTRUCT()
struct FInventoryItemData
{
        GENERATED_USTRUCT_BODY()

        FString WeaponClass;
        int WeaponPower;
        int Ammo;
        FString TextureClass;

        friend FArchive& operator<<(FArchive& Ar, FInventoryItemData&
InvItemData)
        {
                Ar << InvItemData.WeaponClass;
                Ar << InvItemData.WeaponPower;
                Ar << InvItemData.Ammo;
                Ar << InvItemData.TextureClass;
                return Ar;
        }
};

USTRUCT()
struct FInventorySaveData
{
        GENERATED_USTRUCT_BODY()

        FString CurrentWeapon;
        int CurrentWeaponPower = -1;
        TArray<FInventoryItemData> WeaponsArray;
```

```
                friend FArchive& operator<<(FArchive& Ar, FInventorySaveData&
InvData)
        {
                Ar << InvData.CurrentWeapon;
                Ar << InvData.CurrentWeaponPower;
                Ar << InvData.WeaponsArray;
                return Ar;
        }
};

USTRUCT()
struct FGameSavedData
{
        GENERATED_USTRUCT_BODY()

        FDateTime Timestamp;
        FName MapName;
        FInventorySaveData InventoryData;
        TArray<FActorSavedData> SavedActors;

        friend FArchive& operator<<(FArchive& Ar, FGameSavedData& GameData)
        {
                Ar << GameData.MapName;
                Ar << GameData.Timestamp;
                Ar << GameData.InventoryData;
                Ar << GameData.SavedActors;
                return Ar;
        }
};

struct FSaveGameArchive : public FObjectAndNameAsStringProxyArchive
{
        FSaveGameArchive(FArchive& InInnerArchive)
                : FObjectAndNameAsStringProxyArchive(InInnerArchive, true)
        {
                ArIsSaveGame = true;
        }
};

UINTERFACE(BlueprintType)
class USavedActorInterface : public UInterface
{
        GENERATED_UINTERFACE_BODY()
};

class ISavedActorInterface
{
        GENERATED_IINTERFACE_BODY()
```

```
public:
        UFUNCTION(BlueprintNativeEvent, BlueprintCallable, Category =
"Load-Save")
        void ActorLoaded();
};
```

And what is nice about **BlueprintNativeEvent** is that we can fire these from C++, but have them executed in blueprint. The class we have some new work to do for is our moving platform, which again, exists and is defined solely in blueprint. Making the interface `BlueprintType` means we can add this easily to our platform blueprint-only class. So, heading to that class, here are the steps we need to get it saving properly to the archive. Open the moving platform class, click **Class Settings** at the top main menu bar, and on the right, you'll see **Implemented Interfaces**, and we can click **Add** and select **Saved Actor Interface** to add this functionality on the blueprint side. Once we compile the blueprint, we can add an event then for when the actor is loaded. To properly set it in the right state, we need to click on its two variables in the **My Blueprint** tab on the left, and in their **Details** tab, click the down arrow to expose the rest of its options and check the box for **SaveGame** for both the **GoingHome** and **StartPosition** blueprint variables. Now, when we serialize a platform to an archive, these will be saved and loaded and while ideally we would "lasso" select a set of nodes and right-click and select **Collapse to Function**, we can't do this here because asynchronous nodes such as **MoveComponentTo** have to stay in the **Event Graph** layer. But let's add an event for the interface's **Actor Loaded** and then just copy paste some of the movement nodes, making sure that if the platform needs to be moving it goes the right way (based on the **Going Home** variable). There's no harm telling a platform to go where it already is, so we'll set it on the case it has **Going Home** set to move to its **Start Position**. Also fixed slightly is the on-actor-overlap event from before. It will go to **Start Position** + 300 in Z, rather than its current position. So that fixes arguably our hardest case, the blueprint-only class of the group. Let's add the interface to our other classes, and give them a general save functionality as well as a couple of specific ones (such as our `MasteringCharacter`).

MyData will consist of all the UPROPERTY items we tag with SaveGame. Right now, the only one of these we would really need to add is the player's inventory; but because that has class references and an array of structs that also directly reference a texture and class, we'll custom handle inventory.

Saving class and asset references directly does *not* work if you tag those UPROPERTIES. If an object references another object that will be created when the level is loaded, this may work, or to be safe you can look up placed-in-world actors by name in a fix-up pass. Most times, you save the class as a string, then respawn whatever object that is, as we will do extensively here as well as with our inventory special case saving.

If we had other basic types (such as the blueprint variables on our moving platform), simply add UPROPERTY(SaveGame) to their definition and they automatically serialize in and out with the actor data. To make inventory load and save properly, we need a couple of new structs and its own serialization to and from them, which we will demonstrate in the next section. Since it is not an actor class, it is a little annoying to put its structs in the same place as those actor saving ones, but this still seems at this level of complexity to be the best place. So now, how do we use this menu, some new UI, and a lot of saving and loading code to save everything that can change in our levels at any moment and load right back? Let's dive into that now!

Save and load from our menu

Saving our data is relatively straightforward, but as with all load/save systems, is mirrored with a little more difficulty on the load side. This functionality is almost exclusively implemented in the MainMenuWidget class, though I can see that the class might grow, moving it to the SavedActorInterface or the like; but let's now go forward with what is done:

```
UCLASS()
class MASTERING_API UMainMenuWidget : public UUserWidget
{
        GENERATED_BODY()
public:
        UFUNCTION(BlueprintCallable)
        void LoadGame(FString SaveFile);

        UFUNCTION(BlueprintCallable)
        void SaveGame();

        UFUNCTION(BlueprintCallable)
        void Open();

        UFUNCTION(BlueprintCallable)
        void Close();

        UFUNCTION(BlueprintCallable)
```

```
        void PopulateSaveFiles();

        void OnGameLoadedFixup(UWorld* World);
        static TArray<uint8> BinaryData;

protected:
        UPROPERTY(BlueprintReadOnly)
        TArray<FString> SaveFileNames;
};
```

For saving there is a fair bit going on here, some of which is just basic file I/O, but other parts may be unintuitive and are discussed here:

```
void UMainMenuWidget::SaveGame()
{
        FGameSavedData SaveGameData;

        SaveGameData.Timestamp = FDateTime::Now();

        UWorld *World = GetWorld();
        checkSlow(World != nullptr);

        FString mapName = World->GetMapName();

        mapName.Split("_", nullptr, &mapName, ESearchCase::IgnoreCase,
ESearchDir::FromEnd);

        SaveGameData.MapName = *mapName;

        TArray<AActor*> Actors;
        UGameplayStatics::GetAllActorsWithInterface(GetWorld(),
USavedActorInterface::StaticClass(), Actors);

        TArray<FActorSavedData> SavedActors;
        for (auto Actor : Actors)
        {
                FActorSavedData ActorRecord;
                ActorRecord.MyName = FName(*Actor->GetName());
                ActorRecord.MyClass = Actor->GetClass()->GetPathName();
                ActorRecord.MyTransform = Actor->GetTransform();
                ActorRecord.MyVelocity = Actor->GetVelocity();

                FMemoryWriter MemoryWriter(ActorRecord.MyData, true);
                FSaveGameArchive Ar(MemoryWriter);
                AMasteringCharacter* Mast =
Cast<AMasteringCharacter>(Actor);

                Actor->Serialize(Ar);
```

```
                    if (Mast != nullptr)
                    {
                            UMasteringInventory* Inv = Mast->GetInventory();
                            SaveGameData.InventoryData.CurrentWeapon =
Inv->GetCurrentWeapon()->GetPathName();
                            SaveGameData.InventoryData.CurrentWeaponPower =
Inv->GetCurrentWeaponPower();
                            for (FWeaponProperties weapon :
Inv->GetWeaponsArray())
                            {
                                    FInventoryItemData data;
                                    data.WeaponClass =
weapon.WeaponClass->GetPathName();
                                    data.WeaponPower = weapon.WeaponPower;
                                    data.Ammo = weapon.Ammo;
                                    data.TextureClass =
weapon.InventoryIcon->GetPathName();

SaveGameData.InventoryData.WeaponsArray.Add(data);
                            }
                    }

                    SavedActors.Add(ActorRecord);
            }

        FBufferArchive BinaryData;

        SaveGameData.SavedActors = SavedActors;

        BinaryData << SaveGameData;

        FString outPath = FPaths::ProjectSavedDir() +
SaveGameData.Timestamp.ToString() + TEXT(".sav");

        FFileHelper::SaveArrayToFile(BinaryData, *outPath);

        BinaryData.FlushCache();
        BinaryData.Empty();

        APlayerController* playerController =
World->GetFirstPlayerController();
        if (playerController)
        {
                playerController->bShowMouseCursor = false;
                FInputModeGameOnly InputMode;
                playerController->SetInputMode(InputMode);
                UGameplayStatics::SetGamePaused(this, false);
        }
```

```
        Close();
    }
```

We save the timestamp and then split the map name with the _ character. This is a bit of a risk because you'd, of course, want to make it very clear to level designers not to add this character to their map names. In this case, when we're playing and testing in PIE, it appends a couple of things to the left of the map name that end with _ and so splitting from the end gets us, for example, `FirstPersonExampleMap` without the PIE prefixes that wind up there when playing in the editor. We then get a list of all actors that implement our save interface and iterate them. We then always save out the relevant actor transient data, but also look to see whether we've found our mastering character to do a bit of inventory work. As noted earlier, our inventory saving (and loading) needs to be done with the `FInventoryItemData` struct and not the `FWeaponProperties` struct inventory uses directly, because the latter references a class and texture directly (we need them saved by their path/name to properly serialize and then be reloaded from them).

We set all the relevant information, then serialize to a binary for output and save the file, giving it the name of the timestamp we used. You could of course let the user pick the name, or save it otherwise, but this at least shows clearly when loading what time this save was from.

After we have saved, we set the mouse cursor back to hidden, unpause the game, and close the main menu.

When loading, we first have to add some more UI to allow the player to pick the save that they want to load (or cancel):

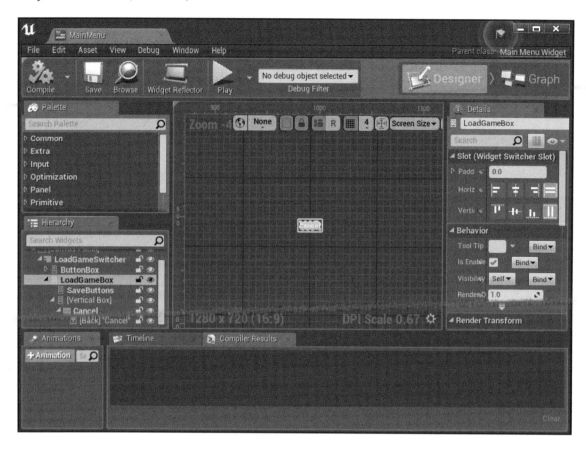

Notice the switcher UMG item. This lets us basically switch (of course) what is shown by the widget from that hierarchy down. We set this from nodes in the main menu blueprint, like when we open the loading portion here in a new function from the load-button's on clicked event:

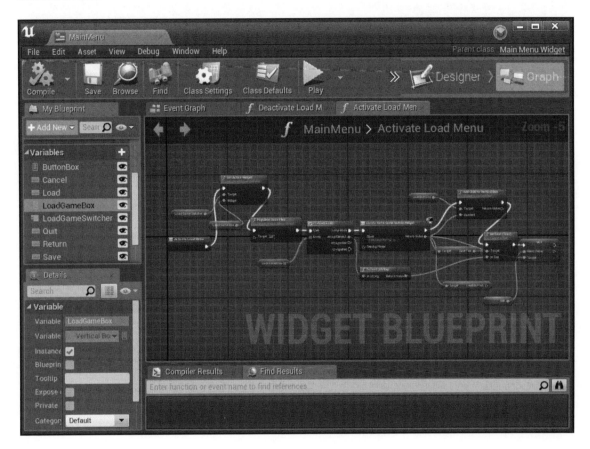

We then call the native function to get all the save files:

```cpp
void UMainMenuWidget::PopulateSaveFiles()
{
        FString dir = FPaths::ProjectSavedDir();
        FString fileExt = TEXT("sav");

        IFileManager::Get().FindFiles(SaveFileNames, *dir, *fileExt);
}
```

And then we create and add a button for each of them (with the main menu as a member) to the load game list. We make a quick UserWidget blueprint that has a simple button and text layout like so, that has one job to do when clicked:

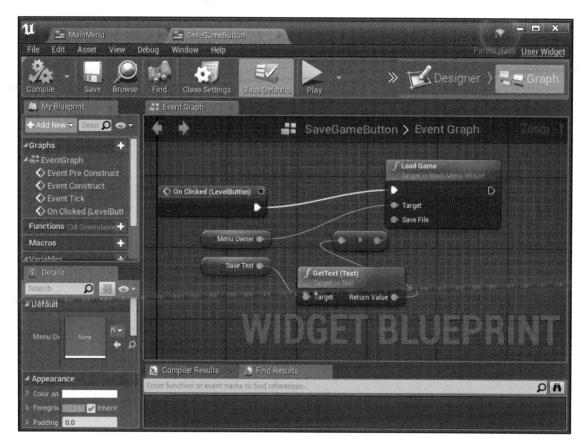

For those looking closely, there are a couple of points that could be handled differently. We will be addressing them later in the book. I would call out that we load (or restart) the map for the save, loading its data, and then, storing it in a static member variable that survives the map re-loading and is then triggered by the HUD's `BeginPlay`. We'll be exploring ways to switch from level to level and pass data between them in `Chapter 6`, *Changing Levels, Streaming, and Retaining Your Data*, so fear not if you still have questions there. Also, at the moment, the only way to delete save files is to go to your content folder, but with all the work we've done here, adding a delete to your menus should not be an issue. And one last note: it's also possible in a number of ways to hook one widget to another. In this case, I simply pass the menu to the button when the menu makes it. There's nothing wrong with using clever techniques, just keep in mind that going with the simplest solution sometimes saves time, which every game ends up needing as it gets closer to being ready for the public.

So that's it, we made it! Checking GitHub, there's a new level with some changes in it, but that's really just there for now to prove out load-save from level to level and back again. Have fun testing that out.

Summary

This chapter really ramps up the complexity level of work closer to the mastering level. After some warm-up work, it's definitely time to dig into this level of detail and start to really learn the tips and tricks that can make or break a game in development. The work here should give a solid base to a number of levels of UI work: we made a bunch of new weapons, used our pick-ups to generate screenshot icons of them, added these back to the pick-ups and our inventory, utilized that inventory to build and sync up a scroll bar of weapons, and made menus and an entire save-anywhere system for all of our objects, whew! The project is finally starting to look more like a real game compared to the bare-bones template we began with, but one thing is missing: enemies to fight. But fear not, we'll have those by the end of the next chapter.

Questions

1. Why is it important to commit any changes to files to GitHub before moving them to a new folder location?
2. What are the steps needed to make a pawn that won't move or fall upon starting an empty level?
3. What are the two ways of cleaning up redirectors in UE4, and why is it important to do so from time to time?
4. What UMG child widgets can be used for placing and spacing other widgets within a parent?
5. What is the advantage of using `BlueprintImplementableEvents` in communicating from C++ to UMG?
6. Which types of `UPROPERTIES` must absolutely not be attempted to serialize when saving class variables?
7. What alternative to saving those properties was used here to save and restore those special types?
8. Which system was used to implement in only a few lines the building of a list of files matching an extension?

Further reading

Simple saves with `USaveGame`:

`https://docs.unrealengine.com/en-US/Gameplay/SaveGame/Code`

5
Adding Enemies!

Introduction

For most games involving combat, there are typically **non-player characters** (**NPCs**) in one form or another. NPCs give a feeling of realism and interaction to games, and the AI that controls them makes them believable (or not!), so it is very important to get it right. Making the most of UE4s BehaviorTree is a very important step to making games efficiently with compelling enemies and friends. In this chapter, we will make a basic melee enemy that will use bits of information from the world to update its choices in its BehaviorTree and react to the player appropriately. We'll also delve into a bit of debugging the tree and its data. Our main goals here will be:

- Importing a new character and skeletal mesh to the game
- Creating a new AIController class
- Building a basic Behavior Tree brain
- Add sensing via C++
- Hook up behavior to the Animation Blueprint

Technical requirements

As always, it's recommended to follow the progress in all the preceding chapters; however, the bulk of this chapter will work as a standalone project as well, with a few exceptions.

The chapter's GitHub branch is, as usual, here:

https://github.com/PacktPublishing/Mastering-Game-Development-with-Unreal-Engine-4-Second-Edition/tree/Chapter-5

Engine version used: 4.19.2.

Creating an AI controller and a basic brain

Much like adding new weapons in the last chapter, we're going to want some interesting new visuals for our AI enemies, so let's head back to the marketplace and see what is freely available. The Paragon project (which was canceled) yielded a huge amount of assets released for free by Epic, so let's import one or more of their characters that we can use for our enemies. Then we give them a controller, spawn them in our level, and see how their brain makes decisions and ultimately becomes a challenging opponent for our player to fight!

Proving out the basics

In the marketplace, to prove out our concept, the GitHub project will begin by importing the Paragon: Countess assets the same way we did at the beginning of Chapter 4, *UI Necessities – Menus, HUD, and Load/Save*. Note that to save approximately 200 MB of the approximately 2 GB download of such a high-detail character, the Tier 2 skins were removed from GitHub, but of course you're welcome to use any of the many amazingly detailed characters that were released from the Paragon project. Once the character is added to the project, there are three main steps to getting it doing anything meaningful in the game:

1. Create a new `AIController` class and make a blueprint instance of it (here, it's called `MeleeAIController`).
2. Add an **AnimationBlueprint** for and hook it to a new **Character**.
3. Add a **BehaviorTree** to the controller with some nodes to get it to start, well, behaving.

Getting some basic functionality from the behavior tree takes a little bit of additional basics, but let's go through these quickly one step at a time to get a basic functioning pawn in the game.

Upon creating the AI controller, for now just add one variable:

```
public:
        UPROPERTY(EditAnywhere, BlueprintReadWrite, Category = "Targeting")
        float HearingRadius = 300.0f;
```

Make a blueprint instance of this in **FirstPersonCPP/AI** and name it **CountessController**.

In **ParagonCountess** | **Characters** | **Global**, make a new **Animation** | **Animation Blueprint** class. When you do this, it will ask for a parent class and a skeleton: use **AnimInstance** and **S_Countess_Skeleton** respectively. Once created, name it ABP_Countess and double-click that to bring up its editor. If you click the **AnimGraph** tab, you can see one simple node, drag from its input and filter to **StateMachine**, and add a new one and double-click it. Drag from **Entry** and add a state. Name it Idle and double-click it and we will be done with a very temporary animation blueprint with one quick node, like so:

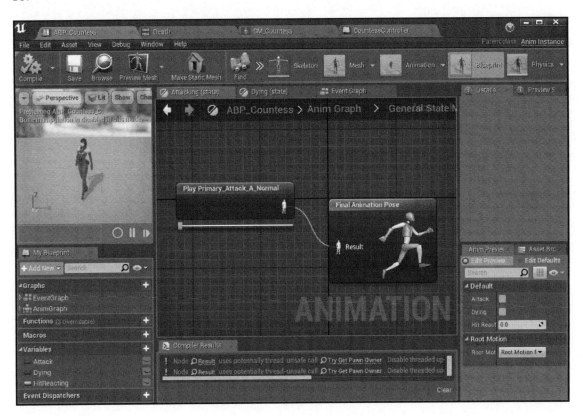

To use and test our character at all, first make a new **Blueprint Class** in
FirstPersonCPP/AI based on **Character**, and name it BP_Countess. We will set it up to
look like so:

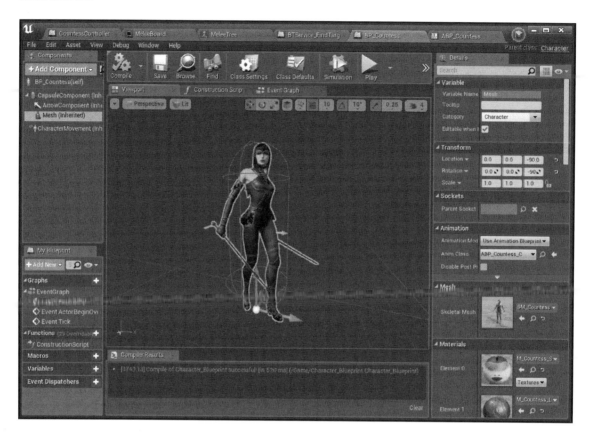

Note the capsule root component for collision purposes, and the mesh's position and
rotation offsets to get things looking right on the ground in game. Also, click the **(self)**
component at the top and set **AIController** to **CountessController**.

Now for the most relevant part, but note that this is also going to be in a very bare-bones state for the moment as we simply get all our classes and requirements blocked out. As noted previously, whenever it's possible to get things working at a basic level and checked in to source control as a checkpoint, this is a great idea even if the overall work changes (or classes are even deleted) as the task progresses. This gives a safe fallback point if anything goes wrong, and when you're working in a team it allows for easy sharing of the state of your work, so we'll do that once our basic tree is in. In our **AI** folder, right-click and under **Artificial Intelligence** and add a **Behavior Tree** and a **Blackboard**. Name them **MeleeTree** and **MeleeBoard** respectively. Opening the blackboard, we will add two keys by using the add button in the top left. Make one an object type and the other a vector, and we'll name them **Target** and **TargetLocation** respectively on the right side of the editor in their properties. Opening the behavior tree next, we first click the button near the top to add a new service. This will create it for you at the same folder level in the content browser. Rename it `BTService_FindTarget` and double-click it. This service works as a piece of blueprint scripting you can use in various places in a behavior tree. It's the only complicated portion of what we'll currently check-in, and building its graph looks like so:

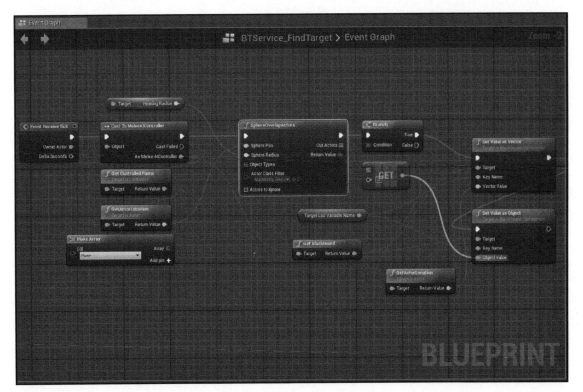

Hopefully, by now this is fairly straightforward: the owning actor of any behavior tree service is the AI controller. We then get our hearing radius from that and do a sphere sweep for any **MasteringCharacter** pawns and, assuming we find one, we set the target and target location variables (by name!) to update to our player location. Blackboards, as the name implies, are a place to post data from various outside locations that can then be directly accessed internally by a behavior tree. Just think of them as variable holders using key/value pairs.

Now that we have that done, we can make a super-simple behavior tree. First, confirm its blackboard in the root's details is set to **MeleeBoard**. Next, in its main editing area, drag down on the behavior tree's root and add a selector node. The quickest way to think about selectors and sequencers is that both do a set of tasks (which can, of course, have child selectors and sequencers), but selectors run from left to right through their children until one succeeds (and then it returns control back up the tree). A selector runs left to right until one of its children fails. On this selector, right-click its node and click **Add Service**. Of course, we'll select our find target service and click it so that in its properties in its details window, we can just remove the random time interval (set to 0.0) so it runs every half second. And lastly, dragging from the selector, pick a task and use **MoveTo**, and set its blackboard key to **TargetLocation** in its details window, and set its **Acceptable Radius** to 100.0 so she doesn't get too close for comfort:

Note on navigation: to generate a nav-mesh used by the behavior here, we need to add a NavMesh volume to the level and have it encompass everywhere you want AI to be able to traverse. Going forward, adding one of these volumes (or many in finer detailed areas) should be standard practice. A quick link about NavMesh volumes will be added to the *Further reading* section at the end.

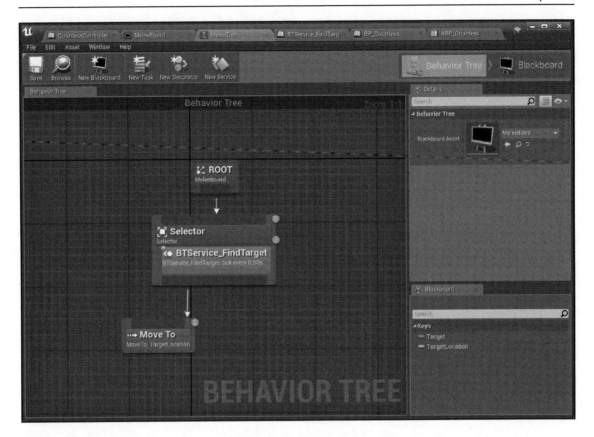

That's it! Place a BP_Countess directly into your level by dragging it in and without properly animating or smoothly turning, she should follow you around the map! We've reached a major checkpoint in this work, and this will be reflected in the GitHub project.

Adding C++ decision making to the behavior tree

The next process involves taking some of the logic and sensing out of blueprints and into C++. This can be valuable for a number of reasons. While the blackboard concept works just fine, it can be difficult to manage and even more difficult at times to debug than even typical blueprint debugging. If a variable is suddenly not what you expected it to be, there isn't always an obvious way to track down why. So, having as much logic as is reasonable and possible in C++ is always a help. In this instance, we're effectively removing the hearing detection and target setting from the preceding task into C++.

There are always advantages and disadvantages to this. For example, we won't really get new functionality out of this work here, but we gain a more scalable performance and easier debugging as complexity later increases. If no further complexity is needed, it's probably best to stop where we did in the last section and call it a day. One major issue arises in synchronizing the two layers, which you must. For an example of iterative development, my first instinct was to use the `OnTargetChange` blueprint event to simply set our blackboard variable and then let the blackboard decorator pull the actor's location from the target object. I remember once encountering a problem when I did this: as the time play begins, the blackboard is told to start and, in the same tick, the sphere now added to the player will do its initial collision query. When trying to use the edge-driven event to set the target, it fails on the first frame as there is no blackboard to set a variable on, and it will never correct itself until the player leaves the hearing sphere radius and re-enters. So a more pull-driven mixed solution was ultimately implemented here as seen here:

```
public:
        AMeleeAIController(const FObjectInitializer& ObjectInitializer =
FObjectInitializer::Get());

        UFUNCTION(BlueprintImplementableEvent)
        void OnTargetChange(class AMasteringCharacter* Target);

        UFUNCTION(BlueprintCallable)
        class AMasteringCharacter* GetTarget();

        virtual void BeginPlay() override;

        UPROPERTY(EditAnywhere, BlueprintReadWrite, Category = "Targeting")
        class USphereComponent* HearingSphere;

        UPROPERTY(EditAnywhere, BlueprintReadWrite, Category = "Targeting")
        float HearingRadius = 1000.0f;

protected:
    UFUNCTION()
    void OnHearingOverlap(UPrimitiveComponent* OverlappedComp, AActor*
Other, UPrimitiveComponent* OtherComp, int32 OtherBodyIndex, bool
bFromSweep, const FHitResult& SweepResult);

    UPROPERTY()
    AMasteringCharacter* CurrentTarget = nullptr;

AMeleeAIController::AMeleeAIController(const FObjectInitializer&
ObjectInitializer)
        : Super(ObjectInitializer)
{
        HearingSphere =
```

```
CreateDefaultSubobject<USphereComponent>(TEXT("HearingSphere"));
        HearingSphere->InitSphereRadius(HearingRadius);
        HearingSphere->SetCollisionObjectType(ECC_Pawn);
        HearingSphere->SetCollisionProfileName("Trigger");

        HearingSphere->OnComponentBeginOverlap.AddDynamic(this,
&AMeleeAIController::OnHearingOverlap);

        bAttachToPawn = true;
}

class AMasteringCharacter* AMeleeAIController::GetTarget()
{
        return CurrentTarget;
}

void AMeleeAIController::BeginPlay()
{
        Super::BeginPlay();

        HearingSphere->AttachComponentTo(GetRootComponent(),
FAttachmentTransformRules::SnapToTargetNotIncludingScale);
}

void AMeleeAIController::OnHearingOverlap(UPrimitiveComponent*
OverlappedComp, AActor* Other, UPrimitiveComponent* OtherComp, int32
OtherBodyIndex, bool bFromSweep, const FHitResult& SweepResult)
{
        AMasteringCharacter *Target = Cast<AMasteringCharacter>(Other);
        if (Target != nullptr && CurrentTarget != Target)
        {
                CurrentTarget = Target;
                OnTargetChange(CurrentTarget);
        }
}
```

Now the other advantage to this work is that our blueprint **FindTarget** service simplifies significantly, so we can call it every 0 . 1 seconds (or every frame, if desired):

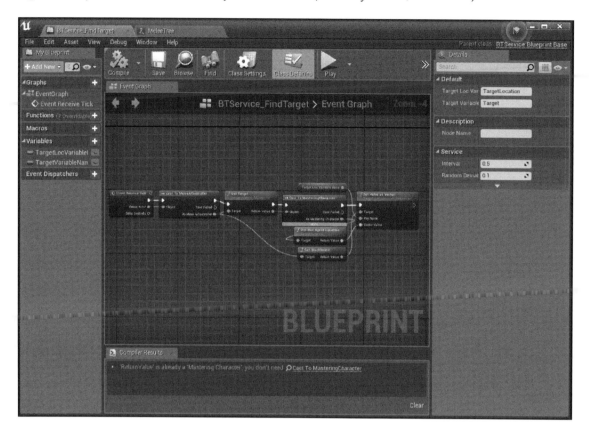

Now you can see this service is just a pass-through, taking the controller's target, and note that it uses the **Nav Agent Location** now too as this is much more accurate for navigating too (it typically puts the target location on the same plane as the agent trying to navigate there, so *close enough* distances are now in 2D rather than a 3D measurement, which is much more intuitive).

While this was all a relatively simple change, setting such a precedent early can be a huge time saver later. Also, note that changing the **Hearing Radius** value in the **CountessController** blueprint won't immediately change the value of the hearing sphere in the blueprint, but when a new one is spawned, the constructor will indeed use that new value for the new instance and have the right radius for you. For a quick test in the default level, the one existing countess was moved to the far right and is now only alerted to the player when she's 6 m away.

Attacking the player

This section sounds deceptively simple, but you'll need several missing pieces when you step through the design process:

- A fleshed out animation blueprint that can switch the enemy's state while moving and attacking
- The enemy's ability to be damaged and killed
- A decision on how and where attack success is resolved (weapon bounding, a one-frame cone-test in front of the enemy, that is, how realistic does hitting the player need to be?)

The second step typically involves a bit more of our UI section's work, and the player should similarly be able to be killed and respawned, but these should be do-able after all the other lessons to this point and won't be covered in depth here. For things such as healthbars to display over the enemy's heads, see the link on 3D widgets in the *Further reading* section at the end of the chapter. The third step is fairly subjective to game complexity: will this be a player taking on many enemies at once, or NPCs that fight each other, or is it more of a 1-3 enemies at a time versus the player scenario and giving the player the absolute feeling of realism is key?

So, as an incremental check-in for this overall work as the next submission to GitHub, there are several points to notice here to set the stage for our final version: the countess' animation blueprint is now set to have her run while moving, she moves up to an attack radius and will tether back to her start location now if she's dragged away too long without reaching her target, and new modes of sensing have been added for vision and a much-reduced hearing radius for stealth characters:

```
void AMeleeAIController::OnHearingOverlap(UPrimitiveComponent*
OverlappedComp, AActor* Other, UPrimitiveComponent* OtherComp, int32
OtherBodyIndex, bool bFromSweep, const FHitResult& SweepResult)
{
        AStealthCharacter* StealthChar = Cast<AStealthCharacter>(Other);
```

```
            if (StealthChar != nullptr)
            {
                    if (StealthChar->IsStealthed())
                    {
                            return; // we let the stealthed sphere deal with
these
                    }
            }

            SetPotentialTarget(Other);
}

void AMeleeAIController::OnStealthHearingOverlap(UPrimitiveComponent*
OverlappedComp, AActor* Other, UPrimitiveComponent* OtherComp, int32
OtherBodyIndex, bool bFromSweep, const FHitResult& SweepResult)
{
            SetPotentialTarget(Other);
}

void AMeleeAIController::OnSightOverlap(UPrimitiveComponent*
OverlappedComp, AActor* Other, UPrimitiveComponent* OtherComp, int32
OtherBodyIndex, bool bFromSweep, const FHitResult& SweepResult)
{
            APawn* Owner = GetPawn();

            if (Owner == Other)
            {
                    return;
            }

            FVector ToTarget = Other->GetActorLocation() -
Owner->GetActorLocation();
            FVector Facing = GetPawn()->GetActorForwardVector();

            if (SightAngle > 90.0f)
            {
                    UE_LOG(LogTemp, Error, TEXT("Sight Angles of 90+ degrees
not supported, please use hearing for this detection!"));
                    SightAngle = 90.0f;
            }

            if (FVector::DotProduct(ToTarget, Facing) < 0.0f)
            {
                    return;
            }

            float DotToTarget = FVector::DotProduct(ToTarget.GetSafeNormal(),
Facing.GetSafeNormal());
```

```
        float RadiansToTarget = FMath::Acos(DotToTarget);
        float AngToTarget = RadiansToTarget * 180.0f / PI;

        if (AngToTarget < SightAngle)
        {
                SetPotentialTarget(Other);
        }
}

void AMeleeAIController::SetPotentialTarget(AActor* Other)
{
        AMasteringCharacter* Target = Cast<AMasteringCharacter>(Other);
        if (Target != nullptr && CurrentTarget != Target)
        {
                CurrentTarget = Target;
                OnTargetChange(CurrentTarget);
        }
}
```

One potential improvement could be doing a line-of-sight test to the player too. This is not a hard task, but one that players would expect or might notice as a bug if we didn't add it down the road. Note also this change:

```
void AMeleeAIController::BeginPlay()
{
        Super::BeginPlay();

        HomeLocation = GetPawn()->GetNavAgentLocation();

    HearingSphere->AttachToComponent(GetRootComponent(),
FAttachmentTransformRules::SnapToTargetNotIncludingScale);
    StealthHearingSphere->AttachToComponent(GetRootComponent(),
FAttachmentTransformRules::SnapToTargetNotIncludingScale);
    SightSphere->AttachToComponent(GetRootComponent(),
FAttachmentTransformRules::SnapToTargetNotIncludingScale);

        OnReturnedHome();
}
```

`OnReturnedHome` sets all the radii of the spheres to their set variable lengths, and in the constructor, `SetReturningHome` is called, which reduces them all to zero. I noticed during testing that on the first frame of the game, you got a collision with the spheres still at the world origin if you let them perform collision before the `Attach` calls in `BeginPlay` are made. Those two functions are also used in a new behavior tree task:

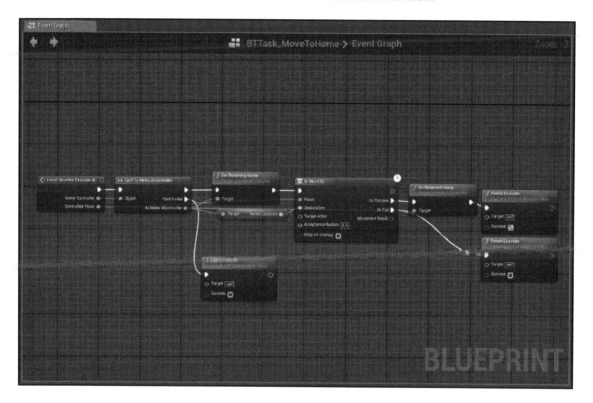

And there is a very similar new task added for moving to the target so we no longer need to worry about the blueprint or updating it (and can remove the old find task service entirely at this point), as seen in our new tree with the 5-second kiting flow built in:

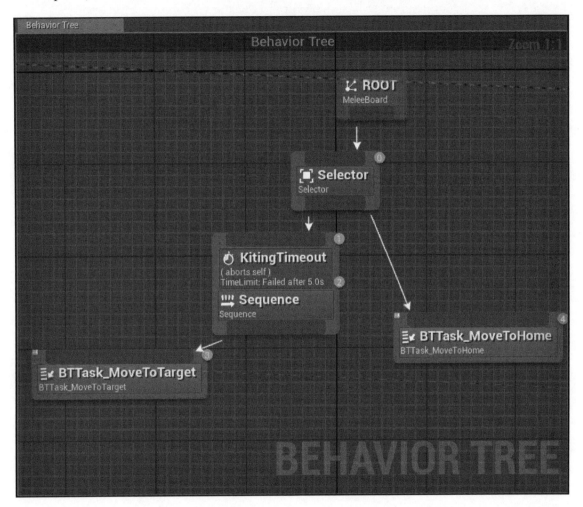

The easiest way in the default map to test the kiting-timeout is to go get the countless enemy's attention, run to the moving platform previously added, and stay on top of the box after that. Once 5 seconds without reaching the player pass (you can do this too by running from one side of the map to the other if you're careful), you'll see the flow kick over to move to home!

The last pieces needed now are a means of switching the countess into an attack state and dealing damage to the player, even if the results of that damage aren't yet handled. To accomplish this, we need to add a variable to our animation instance and set that variable from a task in the behavior tree. We also need a way to say the countess can attack, which we will make a wait node in the behavior tree. The last thing needed is a quick means of dealing that damage, so we'll add an event to the attack animation she uses and when that fires off, we check whether the player is in front of her, and she'll hit the player if so.

The most straightforward way of synchronizing a C++ class with our desired state is to put an enum in the controller class and have it have a reference to the animation instance and set variables on it. There are drawbacks to this, namely, these update on separate threads. And those updates aren't even deterministic, so you might have a C++ controller update, the animation instance update, the animation instance update again, then the C++ controller again, and vice versa. So if you choose to have C++ logic dictating the animation blueprint's state, beware that there can be up to a 2-frame delay between one desiring a change, and the other recognizing it. If you have logic directly from your animation blueprint updating that state too, make sure to always have one point of update, typically the controller, and it is highly recommended to make this a queue that synchronizes between frames and then proceeds to the next queue entry.

So since our AI is fairly simple, we'll add an Attack boolean variable in its blueprint, then we need a new behavior tree task as before, which looks like this:

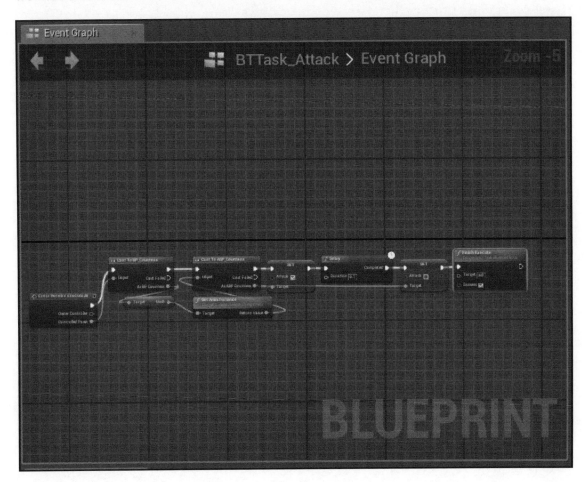

Note that it simply sets us into the attack state of our animation blueprint, waits for a short time, and then clears that (so we don't immediately re-enter again when it finishes). And there's an update to the tree that is quite simple, like so:

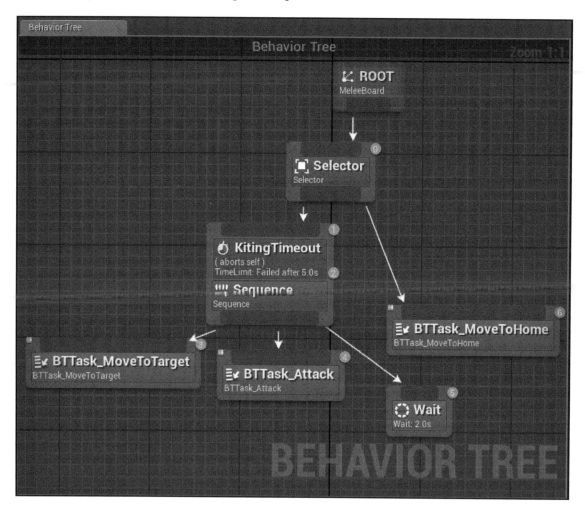

The wait after the attack is our cooldown, and so you'll see our countess waits for that time between attacking the player when in range or defers to moving after the player if she's not in range from the move-to-target node.

And, of course, the animation blueprint must reflect these, so again, add an Attack boolean blueprint variable, and make the transitions look like this (we wait for the attack animation to be near the end to go back to idle, and from idle or moving, we enter attack if the behavior tree sets our Attack variable):

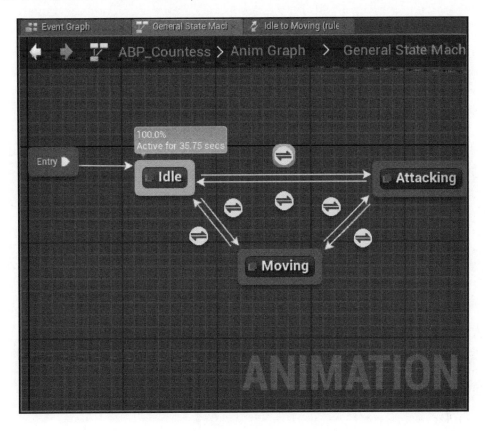

So, the remaining piece to AI attacking is just seeing whether we hit the character. And once again, player death and UI for this are not covered here for brevity but should be fairly trivial after the rest of this work. All we need now is an animation notify event on the attack animation, an event in the animation blueprint that handles this, and a little logic on the controller, all in blueprint here. So, first go to the controller and add this blueprint function:

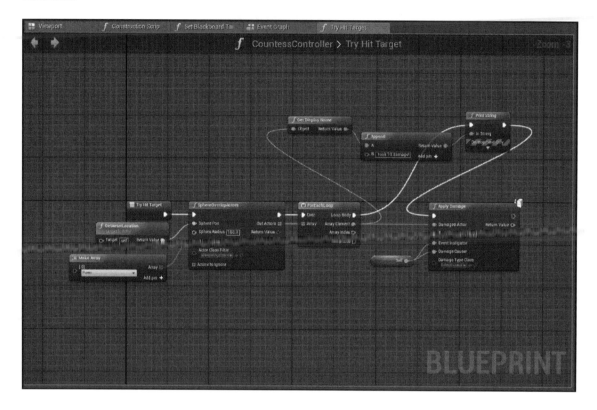

As you can see, this will display to the screen when the player was 1.5 m or closer in front of the countess, was therefore hit, and for how much damage. Again, translating this into gameplay to kill and then respawn the player should be fairly trivial at this point. Next, head to the animation (`Primary_Attack_A_Normal` is what is set in the attack node in the animation blueprint) and add this notification by right-clicking in the timeline, clicking **Add New Notify** at the bottom, and naming it:

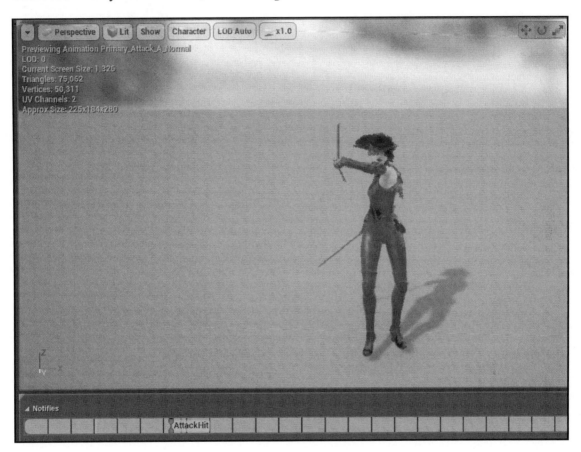

Then go to the animation blueprint's event graph and right-click to add an event for that notify:

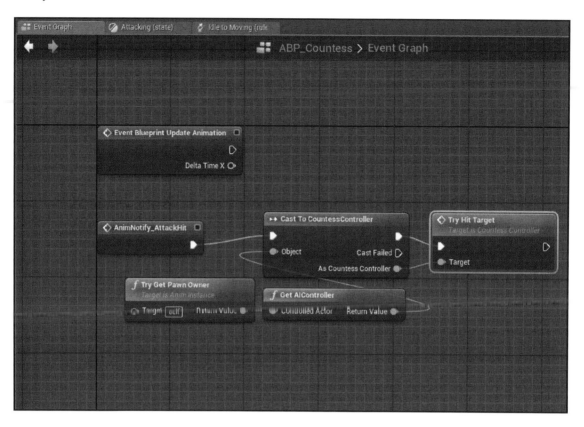

And thus having our AI chase the player, attack on an interval, run home when kited, and transmit damage has been taken when hit is completed. Congratulations, we have a fully functional AI enemy (with some improvements to add in the next section)! And as usual, these latest changes are all in GitHub, so feel free to examine all of them in detail in the submissions there.

More polished combat – spawn points, hit reactions, and dying

So now we have an AI that likes to chase down our player and try to hurt them, great. But at this stage, our player can do almost no interaction with that enemy. We'll want to make things a bit more professional by spawning the enemies from a spawn point actor rather than placing them directly in the level (so we can spawn multiple enemies, wait until they are triggered, and so on), have them react when they're shot (which should not interrupt their other activities, but simply layer on top of them with a blended animation), and of course, be able to kill them (and have all of this reflected when loading/saving).

Spawn points for enemy placement

Spawn points are a valuable tool when working with most shooter games. Players in multiplayer games use them when respawning, and AI often rush forth from them in waves or in a fixed number as a challenge for the player. Here, we will make a quick and simple spawn point, drop an instance in the default level, and test that all is well. First, in the AI folder, right-click and make a new blueprint class of the **Trigger Box** type, here named **Countess Spawner**.

The logic here is that when the player overlaps the box, an instance of our countess is spawned where we want by using a simple scene component with a billboard attached (which is set to editor only and hidden in game). Then we have a bit of logic to spawn **BP_Countess** types and keep an array of those that have been spawned, which is updated when they die, and they will only spawn if the array is below a concurrent count variable:

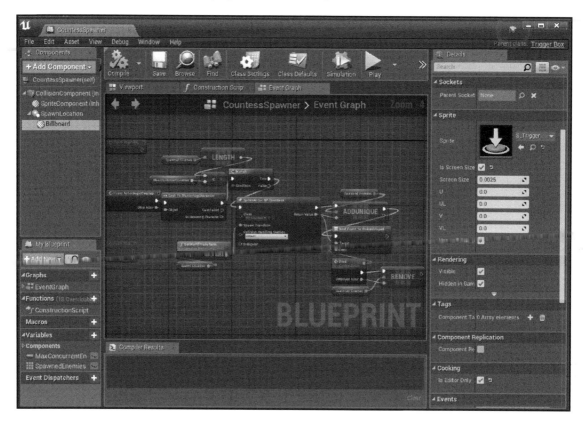

As can be seen in the map, a scaled version of this was placed between some boxes, and its spawn location moved to the corner of the map so that when the player crosses those boxes a countess appears in the corner, but only up to three until one is killed, and then another is allowed. Note that to do this, there are some critical changes to our controller that must be made. First, remove the `BeginPlay` function and replace it with `Possess(APawn* InPawn)` (keeping the contents the same).

This is because `BeginPlay` can (and will) be called potentially before the process of possessing a spawned pawn has occurred. There's also a null check added in `OnSightOverlap` for the same reason (the component may be testing hits before the owner pawn is set). Next, in **BP_Countess** itself, set its **AutoPossess** property to **Placed in World or Spawned** so the AI controller actually runs. Note also that there is a specific **Spawn AI From Class** blueprint node like spawn actor, but it does things slightly differently and since most of our work is done by our controller already, autoprocessing was the best option here.

This should be it for our spawn points. Of course, they can always be made more complex with wave spawning, or random spawn locations, or timers, or whatever logic makes sense and is fun for the game. But the important part is that this can now be reused anywhere to theoretically generate tons of interesting encounters with various AI down the road.

Hit reactions and dying

So far you can shoot our countess as much as you want and nothing interesting happens. We'll fix this with a few code changes to our projectile, and some significant logic we can bundle up in the melee controller. Quickly going through this, we'll add a health parameter to the melee controller like so:

```
UPROPERTY(EditAnywhere, BlueprintReadWrite, SaveGame, Category = "Health")
float Health = 100.0f;
```

Then modify the projectile's on hit to look like so:

```
void AMasteringProjectile::OnHit(UPrimitiveComponent* HitComp, AActor*
OtherActor, UPrimitiveComponent* OtherComp, FVector NormalImpulse, const
FHitResult& Hit)
{
        // Only add impulse and destroy projectile if we hit a physics
        if ((OtherActor != NULL) && (OtherActor != this) && (OtherComp !=
NULL))
        {
                AController* controller = GetInstigatorController();
                AActor* damager = GetInstigator();
                FDamageEvent DamEvt;

                OtherActor->TakeDamage(DamageAmount, DamEvt, controller,
damager != nullptr ? damager : this);

                        if (OtherComp->IsSimulatingPhysics())
                        {
                                OtherComp->AddImpulseAtLocation(GetVelocity() *
```

```
100.0f, GetActorLocation());
                }
                else if (Cast<APawn>(OtherActor) != nullptr)
                {
                        Destroy();
                }
        }
}
```

And in the weapon when we spawn the projectile, add this line:

```
ActorSpawnParams.Instigator = Cast<APawn>(GetOwner());
```

Then to get our countess to react to the hit and die, we'll need a couple of things in the controller blueprint and animation blueprint. First, let's do the controller:

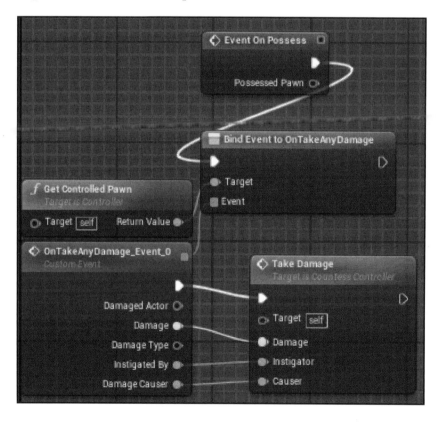

This way, when the pawn is hit and takes damage, the controller is notified, the take damage function (which was created by making the logic, then right-clicking all those logic nodes and selecting **Collapse to Function**) looks like so:

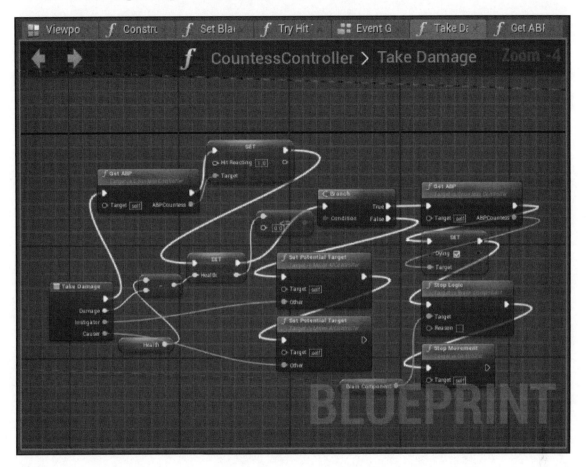

The **Get ABP** function just gets our controlled pawn, casts to a **BP_Countess**, gets its animation instance, and casts that to an **ABP_Countess** in an Output (return) node. The **Hit Reacting** (float) and **Dying** (bool) variables were also simply added directly to the **ABP_Countess** and used in two ways, as seen here:

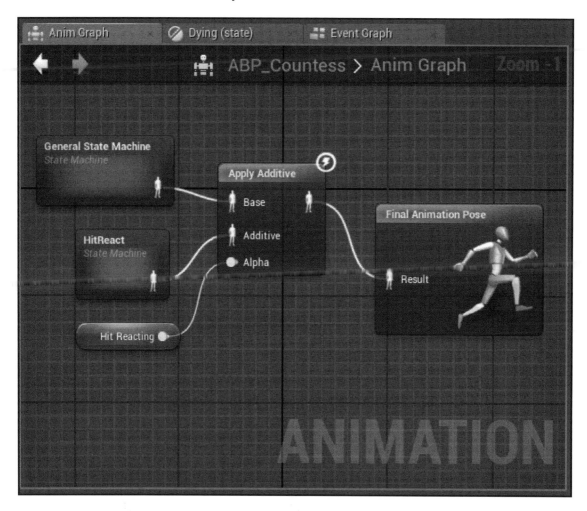

The HitReact state machine only has one state, and all it does is play the countess' **Hit React (fwd)** animation. Inserting the APply Additive blend in our root graph with this variable as the weight blends it in. This was built as an additive animation, so you can see at this stage when she takes damage, her head jerks back, but her other animations continue as normal, perfect. Near the end of the animation, a new notification is added, and an event in the event graph for this clears the blend to 0.0.

And dying:

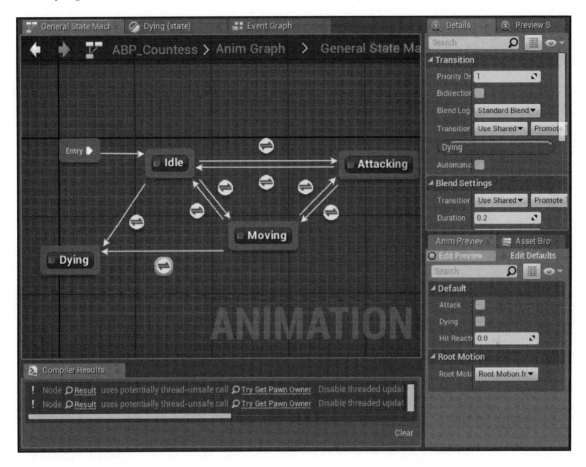

Note the one-way transition – there's no coming back from dying. This node in the main graph only plays the countess' **Death** animation, and near its end has another notify added. In the event graph when that event is triggered, the **Try Get Owner Pawn** is destroyed. Now, the countess takes damage, reacts, and dies, most of what we hope for out of an AI!

Notes on load/save

Loading and saving the AI, in this case, is not a trivial choice. In this instance, I've moved all of the logic for the most part to the spawner, so saving damaged AI (for example) won't work if they're placed directly in the level anymore. You can reverse this by setting the actor save interface in the **BP_Countess**, but then, there's no way to properly fix up the spawners to have links to the AI they've spawned.

As a general rule, as done here, if you can have your AI regenerate its state from where it is spawned in the world, you're far better off than trying to save every aspect of exactly where it was at save time. Granted, this can lead to exploits (for example, an AI about to hit with a very powerful attack when saved, then when loaded, is back to idle and starts a normal attack), but as AI complexity grows, load/save complexity can become a nightmare. If at all possible, spawn the AI into the world and let it figure out what it should be doing from there, as is done here with our spawner class.

Our countess spawner adds two new variables, an array of locations, and an array of health values. These are stored on save, and set to SaveGame variables in the spawner's blueprint the way we did for the state of the moving platform earlier, and respawned and restored on load. This does require adding the actor save interface to the spawner (again, like we did for the platform), and marking up those two variables, but also adding a new native event to the saved actor interface:

```
UFUNCTION(BlueprintNativeEvent, BlueprintCallable, Category = "Load-Save")
void ActorSaved();
```

Then we'd call it when we save, like we do for the load version, currently in the
`MainMenuWidget.cpp`'s `SaveGame` function around line 82:

```
ISavedActorInterface::Execute_ActorSaved(Actor);
```

Now in the countess spawner, triggered from these events (after the interface is added in
class settings as before), we can add two new functions, one for loading its countesses and
one for saving. First, let's look at saving:

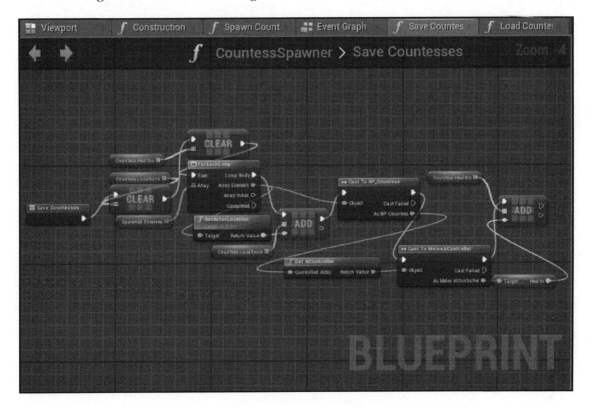

And then we have the load event:

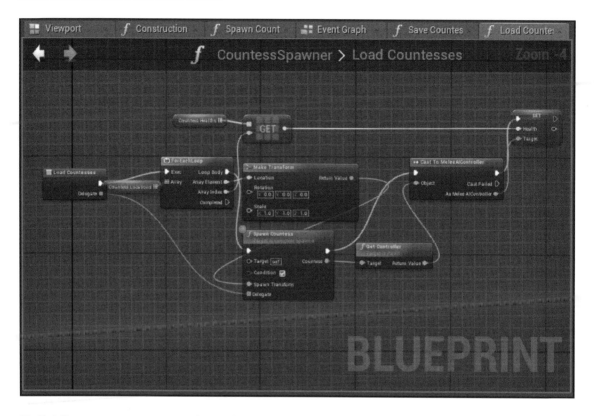

Voila! Our countesses are in the right place, with the right health, but they may not be in the exact step of their AI we saved them at, but they will quickly adjust. One known issue here is that if an AI is saved while it's dying, it will need to be damaged again to start dying again, but with some special work this could be fixed too. But overall, we now have a fully functional AI that chases down the player, hurts the player, can be hurt and react to hits, dies, and be loaded and saved reasonably professionally.

Summary

So this was another whirlwind chapter packed full of many, many changes and a lot of new content. From where we were before, we now have a full functioning enemy who looks great, performs as we might expect in a polished game, and saves with our progress to boot. This is another quantum leap in making a serious game. One last point some may be asking after all of this: doesn't Epic have a built-in senses system for AI? And yes, they do, which you're more than welcome to explore; but in most instances, a custom and debuggable version is typically needed, which we've now made here in solid detail. If the built-in senses and their events are perfect for your project, though, definitely do consider them. But in the overall work-effort of making an AI, making your own sensing code is probably one of the less demanding (and honestly more fun!) portions to write. So, now that we have the core of a solid game going, how do we strategize progressing from level to level or through a large world with a much more significant amount of content than these test levels? Well, that's next!

Questions

1. What are the three major classes needed to make a proper AI in UE4?
2. What purpose does the blackboard serve in AI logic?
3. How was target selection brought from C++ into our behavior tree?
4. What is the difference between a sequencer and selector in a behavior tree?
5. How was the behavior tree informed it should attack and stop moving towards the player?
6. As blueprint logic complexity grows, what's a good trick to compartmentalize sections of logic?
7. What advantages do AI spawners bring to a game's design?
8. What are the trade-offs of perfect AI state load/save versus a simple load/save and logic recovering state?

Further reading

Nav-mesh information:

```
https://docs.unrealengine.com/en-us/Resources/ContentExamples/NavMesh
```

3D widgets:

```
https://docs.unrealengine.com/en-us/Engine/UMG/HowTo/InWorldWidgetInteraction
```

6
Changing Levels, Streaming, and Retaining Data

Introduction

Switching levels in UE4 comes in two varieties. One is very simple: unload the old level, load in the new one, done (if that's all you need, this chapter may be a very short one!). The second method of streaming levels in and out continuously has many more challenges, but can be a much more rewarding user experience too. And in both cases, the question remains: what game elements or player data stay with you as these levels load? Having that data persist can be a real challenge with a couple of solutions we'll explore here too so that whichever methods are chosen, in the end, your player can have a continuous experience that hopefully is not too much of a strain on those working on level design! Our goals here are:

- Cover the basics of map-switching in UE4
- Adding a new level to transition to
- Adapting the load/save system to persist state across map-transitions
- Create a practical example of level streaming from a persistent level

Technical requirements

As usual, it is recommended to pick up from the end of Chapter 5, *Adding Enemies!*, for continuity, but it is by no means required. All lessons here should be able to be applied to any UE4 project at any stage of development.

The GitHub project corresponding to it is found here:

```
https://github.com/PacktPublishing/Mastering-Game-Development-with-Unreal-
Engine-4-Second-Edition/tree/Chapter-6
```

Engine version used: 4.19.2.

Traditional level loading

Changing levels (maps) has been an inherent system of the Unreal Engine since its inception. So, naturally, there are several tools and options that have evolved with it over the years. That said, we already have all the tools needed for basic level changing, but it's still instructive to walk through them, and we'll update our loading and saving in this section to keep our progress and game state during those switches. First, a quick review of the foundations of level changing in UE4.

The basics

Blueprint and C++ both have a built-in way to change levels. In a quick blueprint example we'll use here, it's the **Open Level** node accessible from most places you could ever want to use it in blueprint. In C++, we already used it during load/save (though note that for a server-based game, you would normally pass the desired level as the first parameter; here, we simply use it to restart the existing level with the `"?Restart"` special string):

```
if (mapName == currentMapName)
{
        World->ServerTravel("?Restart", true);
}
else
{
        UGameplayStatics::OpenLevel(World, *mapName, true);
}
```

So, triggering one of these in the game is about as simple as it can get. In our default **FirstPersonExampleMap**, I've added a few blocks to resemble a portal that is at the top of the moving platform we added some time ago.

If you check GitHub, there is a Stash for this chapter on fixing the moving platforms because they can squish pawns (player or NPCs) out of the level when moving back down. It's not a perfect fix, but it simply disables collision as the platform moves back down and re-enables it once it reaches the bottom (and some other minor logic was fixed in the platforms). As this is not a specific goal of this chapter, however, it was stashed instead of checked directly into the GitHub project.

In the middle of this, I added a simple trigger volume from the **Volumes** set on the left (no new blueprint class or instance is even needed):

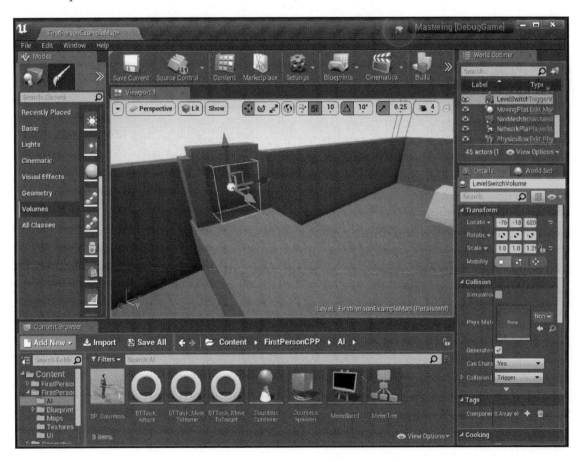

With this selected, open the level blueprint by clicking **Blueprints** button at the top on the main menu bar, and selecting **Open Level Blueprint**. In there, while the volume is selected and you right-click, at the very top you have access to options specific to that specific object in the level. We'll use its overlap event, check whether it's the player, and if so, open **MasteringTestLevel**, as seen here:

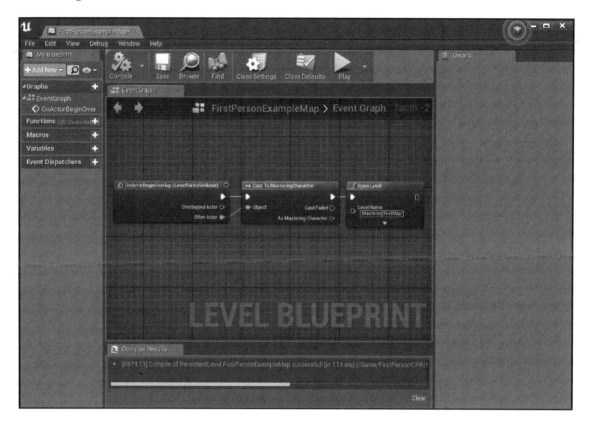

That's it. Really. Just walk into the trigger and we'll be launched in the other level. If this is all your project needs, then it's best to stop here and keep life simple!

Using load/save to transition

Most games, especially those with a story-based single player mode or the like, though, will want the player's status after leaving, as well as the state of the level itself, to be persistent across this transition. If we make a simple portal back to `FirstPersonExampleMap` just like we did in the preceding section, you'll notice when switching back and forth that our player, the items, NPCs, and so on in those levels are as if we had opened them anew, rather than the state they were in when we left, and the player's inventory is loaded anew as well. So now really we need two distinct things:

- Keeping the player's data intact across any level load
- Loading and saving the state of that level and its dynamic objects when switching

Fortunately, we have already implemented dynamic any-time loading and saving, so we'll just modify that and take advantage of it for the level state. But then we need something new for persisting data across map changes. There are several options to this (some definitely safer or more clean than others) but for our game, we'll make a new `UGameInstance` C++ class and use it like a singleton to hold data and information that will persist throughout the entire lifetime of the game being run.

 Any time static or global data is introduced, you must be extremely careful as it can have unforeseen effects on things such as play in editor, where even though you stop playing, so long as the editor is not closed and re-opened, any of that static data persists and so you cannot count on the same behavior starting and restarting PIE versus a standalone version of the game, say, on a device or other platform. We'll put in some safeguards here for our example, but use caution and minimize dangerous data storage whenever possible!

We'll name the new game instance `MasteringGameInstance` and give it some singleton-like functionality:

```
UCLASS()
class MASTERING_API UMasteringGameInstance : public UGameInstance
{
        GENERATED_BODY()

public:
        UFUNCTION(BlueprintCallable, Category = "Mastering Game Instance")
        static UMasteringGameInstance* GetInstance();

        virtual void Init() override;
        virtual void BeginDestroy() override;
```

```
        virtual void FinishDestroy() override;

        bool ShouldPersistInventory() const
        {
                return bPersistPlayerInventory;
        }

        void SetPersistInventory(const bool bPersist = true)
        {
                bPersistPlayerInventory = bPersist;
        }

        void SetPlayerInventory(class UMasteringInventory* Inv);

        FORCEINLINE class UMasteringInventory* GetInventory() const
        {
                return PlayerInv;
        }

        void SetPlayerSafeLocation(const FVector& InLoc)
        {
                PlayerSafeLocation = InLoc;
        }

        FORCEINLINE FVector GetPlayerSafeLocation() const
        {
                return PlayerSafeLocation;
        }

        void ClearData();

protected:

        UPROPERTY()
        class UMasteringInventory* PlayerInv;

        bool bPersistPlayerInventory;
        FVector PlayerSafeLocation;
};
```

As you can see above, this gives us a few pieces of persistent data that we'd like to survive loading and saving cycles.

Next, some helper functions to get all of this working, and to make setting the player's inventory and cleaning up our own state in the game instance simple:

```
static UMasteringGameInstance* Instance = nullptr;

UMasteringGameInstance* UMasteringGameInstance::GetInstance()
{
        checkf(Instance != nullptr, TEXT("Someone is trying to use the game
instance before it has initialized!"));

        return Instance;
}

void UMasteringGameInstance::Init()
{
        Super::Init();

        Instance = this;

        AddToRoot();
}

void UMasteringGameInstance::BeginDestroy()
{
        ClearData();
        Super::BeginDestroy();
}

void UMasteringGameInstance::FinishDestroy()
{
        Super::FinishDestroy();
}

void UMasteringGameInstance::SetPlayerInventory(class UMasteringInventory*
Inv)
{
        if (PlayerInv == nullptr)
        {
                PlayerInv = NewObject<UMasteringInventory>(this,
TEXT("PlayerInventory"));
        }

        PlayerInv->CopyFromOther(Inv);
}

void UMasteringGameInstance::ClearData()
{
        bPersistPlayerInventory = false;
```

```
        PlayerInv = nullptr;
        PlayerSafeLocation = FVector::ZeroVector;
    }
```

At this point, `BeginDestroy` and `FinishDestroy` probably won't need to both be here for us; but it's usually a good idea with static data holders such as this to have both. In `FinishDestroy`, if nothing else, you can put in safeguards to make sure no code after a session uses this same instance of the `GameInstance` without calling `Init` first, and clean up any remaining issues (you can even set `Instance` back to `nullptr` if you want to be extra safe). `BeginDestroy` for reference is the place to immediately clear out any data that any other classes might look to and make use of. We'll have a couple of those once we start this load/save task in earnest (for example you definitely don't want to be in the middle of a load/save cycle, quit the game, and then upon restarting it have your variables set to what they were set to by that load/save starting). Be sure this point to go to Settings, Project Settings, and in Maps and Modes, set your game instance to `MasteringGameInstance`.

Next, to consolidate and abstract our game loading code a bit, we'll make a new Blueprint Function Library C++ class (which almost by definition is a collection of static functions, which is just what we need here, even if it's not necessarily ever called from blueprint):

```cpp
class MASTERING_API LoadSaveLibrary
{
public:
        LoadSaveLibrary();
        ~LoadSaveLibrary();

        UFUNCTION(BlueprintCallable)
        static void LoadGameFile(FString SaveFile, UWorld* World);

        UFUNCTION(BlueprintCallable)
        static void SaveGameFile(FString SaveFile, UWorld* World);

        static void OnGameLoadedFixup(UWorld* World);

        static void FixupPlayer(UWorld* World, class AMasteringCharacter* Char);

protected:
        static TArray<uint8> BinaryData;
};
```

And refactor the `MainMenuWidget` class to move huge swathes of code here where it's more appropriate going forward, making that UI class much more focused and specific. Also, we now have some extra fix-up code that adjusts our player's position and accounts for persisting the current inventory through a load cycle, like we want when returning to a level we previously visited:

```
TArray<uint8> LoadSaveLibrary::BinaryData;

LoadSaveLibrary::LoadSaveLibrary()
{
}

LoadSaveLibrary::~LoadSaveLibrary()
{
}

void LoadSaveLibrary::LoadGameFile(FString SaveFile, UWorld* World)
{
        FString outPath = FPaths::ProjectSavedDir() + SaveFile;
        if (!FFileHelper::LoadFileToArray(BinaryData, *outPath))
        {
                UE_LOG(LogTemp, Warning, TEXT("%s"), *(FString("Game Load
Failed: ") + outPath));
                return;
        }

        checkSlow(World != nullptr);
        FMemoryReader FromBinary = FMemoryReader(BinaryData, true);
        FromBinary.Seek(0);

        FGameSavedData SaveGameData;
        FromBinary << SaveGameData;

        FromBinary.FlushCache();
        FromBinary.Close();

        UMasteringGameInstance* gameInst =
UMasteringGameInstance::GetInstance();
        FVector playerSafeLoc = SaveGameData.PlayerSafeLocation;
        gameInst->SetPlayerSafeLocation(playerSafeLoc);

        FString mapName = SaveGameData.MapName.ToString();

        FString currentMapName = World->GetMapName();

        currentMapName.Split("UEDPIE_0_", nullptr, &currentMapName);
```

```
            if (mapName == currentMapName)
            {
                    World->ServerTravel("?Restart", true);
            }
            else
            {
                    UGameplayStatics::OpenLevel(World, *mapName);
            }
    }
```

Above you can see the method of loading, if we're going to the same world we're already on, we tell the world to restart essentially, otherwise, we open the new level. We also save out the player's current position as "safe" as we can be confident it is a valid position for the player to occupy and we might need it if we're transitioning back to this level later.

```
    void LoadSaveLibrary::SaveGameFile(FString SaveFile, UWorld* World)
    {
            checkSlow(World != nullptr);
            FGameSavedData SaveGameData;
            FString outPath = FPaths::ProjectSavedDir() + SaveFile;

            SaveGameData.Timestamp = FDateTime::Now();

            FString mapName = World->GetMapName();

            mapName.Split("UEDPIE_0_", nullptr, &mapName);

            SaveGameData.MapName = *mapName;

            UMasteringGameInstance* gameInst =
    UMasteringGameInstance::GetInstance();
            SaveGameData.PlayerSafeLocation =
    gameInst->GetPlayerSafeLocation();
            gameInst->SetPlayerSafeLocation(FVector::ZeroVector); // so this
    will not be valid in future saves unless set again

            TArray<AActor*> Actors;
            UGameplayStatics::GetAllActorsWithInterface(World,
    USavedActorInterface::StaticClass(), Actors);

            TArray<FActorSavedData> SavedActors;
            for (auto Actor : Actors)
            {
                    FActorSavedData ActorRecord;
                    ActorRecord.MyName = FName(*Actor->GetName());
                    ActorRecord.MyClass = Actor->GetClass()->GetPathName();
                    ActorRecord.MyTransform = Actor->GetTransform();
                    ActorRecord.MyVelocity = Actor->GetVelocity();
```

```
                FMemoryWriter MemoryWriter(ActorRecord.MyData, true);
                FSaveGameArchive Ar(MemoryWriter);
                AMasteringCharacter* Mast =
Cast<AMasteringCharacter>(Actor);

                ISavedActorInterface::Execute_ActorSaved(Actor);

                Actor->Serialize(Ar);

                if (Mast != nullptr)
                {
                        UMasteringInventory* Inv = Mast->GetInventory();
                        SaveGameData.InventoryData.CurrentWeapon =
Inv->GetCurrentWeapon()->GetPathName();
                        SaveGameData.InventoryData.CurrentWeaponPower =
Inv->GetCurrentWeaponPower();
                        for (FWeaponProperties weapon :
Inv->GetWeaponsArray())
                        {
                                FInventoryItemData data;
                                data.WeaponClass =
weapon.WeaponClass->GetPathName();
                                data.WeaponPower = weapon.WeaponPower;
                                data.Ammo = weapon.Ammo;
                                data.TextureClass =
weapon.InventoryIcon->GetPathName();

SaveGameData.InventoryData.WeaponsArray.Add(data);
                        }
                }

                SavedActors.Add(ActorRecord);
        }

        FBufferArchive SaveData;

        SaveGameData.SavedActors = SavedActors;

        SaveData << SaveGameData;

        FFileHelper::SaveArrayToFile(SaveData, *outPath);

        SaveData.FlushCache();
        SaveData.Empty();
}
```

Saving is where the real work is done, and following the flow can be a bit tricky; but if you collapse the implementation of the actor loop above, the rest is pretty straight-forward, get the safe-location, clear out the safe-location (for clarity), then iterate those actors, serialize to our output, and save that as a file.

```
void LoadSaveLibrary::FixupPlayer(UWorld* World, class AMasteringCharacter*
Char)
{
        UMasteringGameInstance* gameInst =
UMasteringGameInstance::GetInstance();

        // Assuming we found our player character and saved out some
inventory, this is where we do its custom serialization and fix-up
        if (Char != nullptr)
        {
                if (!gameInst->GetPlayerSafeLocation().IsZero())
                {
Char->SetActorLocation(gameInst->GetPlayerSafeLocation());
                }

                if (gameInst->ShouldPersistInventory())
                {
                        UMasteringInventory* NewInv =
NewObject<UMasteringInventory>(Char, TEXT("PlayerInventory"),
RF_Transient);

                        checkf(gameInst->GetInventory() != nullptr,
TEXT("Game Instance is trying to persist inventory with no inventory
setup!"));
                        NewInv->CopyFromOther(gameInst->GetInventory(),
Char);

                        Char->SetInventory(NewInv);
                        NewInv->SetupToCurrent();
                }
                else if (BinaryData.Num() > 0)
                {
                        FMemoryReader FromBinary =
FMemoryReader(BinaryData, true);
                        FromBinary.Seek(0);

                        FGameSavedData SaveGameData;
                        FromBinary << SaveGameData;

                        UMasteringInventory* NewInv =
NewObject<UMasteringInventory>(Char, TEXT("PlayerInventory"),
RF_Transient);
```

```
            Char->SetInventory(NewInv);

            FWeaponProperties propsEquipped;
            for (FInventoryItemData ItemData :
SaveGameData.InventoryData.WeaponsArray)
                {
                        FWeaponProperties props;
                        props.WeaponClass =
FindObject<UClass>(ANY_PACKAGE, *ItemData.WeaponClass);
                        props.InventoryIcon =
FindObject<UTexture2D>(ANY_PACKAGE, *ItemData.TextureClass);
                        props.WeaponPower = ItemData.WeaponPower;
                        props.Ammo = ItemData.Ammo;

                        if (ItemData.WeaponClass ==
SaveGameData.InventoryData.CurrentWeapon)
                                propsEquipped = props;

                        NewInv->AddWeapon(props);
                }

            Char->GetInventory()->SelectWeapon(propsEquipped);
        }
    }
}
```

Fixing up the player is a special case that takes a lot of delicate work so is included here in its full form. It's quite tricky to get all of the properties of the player put back to where we wanted them at the time of saving, but take the time to go through (and step through in your IDE with breakpoints!) the above code a couple of times. Getting this right, and starting the precedent of it *being* right from the start of a load/save system like this is critical. Take the time to understand it and when implementing it, to get it right, and test, test, test!

The changes needed to the menu widget class should be self-evident, but this can be seen in a checkpoint in the GitHub project if necessary. This allows us to take advantage of the loading and saving code from essentially anywhere C++ (or even blueprint).

So now, really our only missing piece is a new trigger box type that has a little bit of special C++ code, adjusting our load/save process to ignore loading the inventory saved at save time, and restoring inventory at level-switch time. So, two quick steps: make a new trigger box subclass, and add the player inventory and volume's safe position to the game instance. So, naming our new volume LevelTransitionVolume and giving it some functionality with added variables and functions to the game instance, we can now transition with our player's inventory and the rest loaded from the save game of where we are going, and if we're just switching levels, we keep the player's current inventory (and if necessary, any other information). If we're doing a full load, of course we need to restore what was saved.

The logic for this volume, in which we'll replace the two volumes in the two levels used previously for testing, looks like this:

```cpp
void ALevelTransitionVolume::NotifyActorBeginOverlap(AActor* OtherActor)
{
        AMasteringCharacter* Mast = Cast<AMasteringCharacter>(OtherActor);
        UWorld* World = GetWorld();

        if (Mast != nullptr)
        {
                UMasteringGameInstance* gameInst =
UMasteringGameInstance::GetInstance();
                gameInst->SetPersistInventory();

                AMasteringCharacter* Char =
Cast<AMasteringCharacter>(World->GetFirstPlayerController()->GetPawn());
                check(Char != nullptr);

                gameInst->SetPlayerInventory(Char->GetInventory());

                FString currentMapName = World->GetMapName();
                currentMapName.Split("UEDPIE_0_", nullptr,
&currentMapName); // strip out PIE prefix if in PIE
                FString toMapName = TransitionLevel;

                FString fromFile = currentMapName + TEXT("_to_") +
toMapName + TEXT(".sav");
                FString toFile = toMapName + TEXT("_to_") + currentMapName
+ TEXT(".sav");

                gameInst->SetPlayerSafeLocation(GetPlayerSafeLocation());

                // always save on our way out so we can restore the state
on the way back
                LoadSaveLibrary::SaveGameFile(fromFile, World);
```

```
            if (FPaths::FileExists(FPaths::ProjectSavedDir() + toFile))
            {
                    LoadSaveLibrary::LoadGameFile(toFile, World);
            }
            else
            {
                    UGameplayStatics::OpenLevel(World, *toMapName);
            }
        }
}
```

So now we're transitioning to the new level, and have saved where we were at the time we left the current one.

```
void LoadSaveLibrary::OnGameLoadedFixup(UWorld* World)
{
        if (BinaryData.Num() == 0)
        {
                checkSlow(World->GetFirstPlayerController() != nullptr);
                AMasteringCharacter* charPawn =
Cast<AMasteringCharacter>(World->GetFirstPlayerController()->GetPawn());

                FixupPlayer(World, charPawn);
                return;
        }

        FMemoryReader FromBinary = FMemoryReader(BinaryData, true);
        FromBinary.Seek(0);

        FGameSavedData SaveGameData;
        FromBinary << SaveGameData;

        FromBinary.FlushCache();
        BinaryData.Empty();
        FromBinary.Close();

        TArray<AActor*> Actors;
        UGameplayStatics::GetAllActorsWithInterface(World,
USavedActorInterface::StaticClass(), Actors);

        TArray<FActorSavedData> ActorDatas = SaveGameData.SavedActors;

        AMasteringCharacter* Char = nullptr; // if ever more than one,
we'll need an array and a map to their inventory

        // iterate these arrays backwards as we will remove objects as we
go, can also use iterators, but RemoveAt is simpler here for now
        for (int i = Actors.Num() - 1; i >= 0; --i)
```

```
        {
                AActor* Actor = Actors[i];

                for (int j = ActorDatas.Num() - 1; j >= 0; --j)
                {
                        FActorSavedData ActorRecord = ActorDatas[j];

                        // These are actors spawned into the world that we
also found in our save data (TODO: use TArray intersection?)
                        if (ActorRecord.MyName == *Actor->GetName())
                        {
                                FMemoryReader
MemoryReader(ActorRecord.MyData, true);
                                FSaveGameArchive Ar(MemoryReader);

                                AMasteringCharacter* Mast =
Cast<AMasteringCharacter>(Actor);
                                if (Mast != nullptr)
                                {
                                        Char = Mast;
                                }

                                Actor->Serialize(Ar);
Actor->SetActorTransform(ActorRecord.MyTransform);
ISavedActorInterface::Execute_ActorLoaded(Actor);

                                APawn* pawn = Cast<APawn>(Actor);
                                if (pawn != nullptr)
                                {
                                        // controller needs the rotation
too as this may set the pawn's rotation once play starts
                                        AController* controller =
pawn->GetController();
controller->ClientSetRotation(ActorRecord.MyTransform.Rotator());
                                }

                                ActorDatas.RemoveAt(j);
                                Actors.RemoveAt(i);
                                break;
                        }
                }
        }
```

We'll do the player here at this point, then finish off with finding any actors we found saved data for that haven't already respawned (typically projectiles we made, for example):

```
FixupPlayer(World, Char);

    // These are actors in our save data, but not in the world, spawn
them
    for (FActorSavedData ActorRecord : ActorDatas)
    {
        FVector SpawnPos = ActorRecord.MyTransform.GetLocation();
        FRotator SpawnRot = ActorRecord.MyTransform.Rotator();
        FActorSpawnParameters SpawnParams;
        // if we were in a space when saved, we should be able to
spawn there again when loaded, but we could also
        // be overlapping an object that loaded, but will be
subsequently destroyed below as it was there at level start
        // but not there at save time
        SpawnParams.SpawnCollisionHandlingOverride =
ESpawnActorCollisionHandlingMethod::AlwaysSpawn;
        SpawnParams.Name = ActorRecord.MyName;
        UClass* SpawnClass = FindObject<UClass>(ANY_PACKAGE,
*ActorRecord.MyClass);
        if (SpawnClass)
        {
            AActor* NewActor = GWorld->SpawnActor(SpawnClass,
&SpawnPos, &SpawnRot, SpawnParams);
            FMemoryReader MemoryReader(ActorRecord.MyData,
true);
            FSaveGameArchive Ar(MemoryReader);
            NewActor->Serialize(Ar);
NewActor->SetActorTransform(ActorRecord.MyTransform);
ISavedActorInterface::Execute_ActorLoaded(NewActor);
        }
    }

    // These are actors in the world that are not in our save data,
destroy them (for example, a weapon pickup that was, well, picked up)
    for (auto Actor : Actors)
    {
        Actor->Destroy();
    }
}
```

After replacing the old trigger volumes and setting the right **Transition Level** names on the new boxes in the levels, of course we can remove the old logic in the level blueprints too. So, as seen previously, if we already have a save file matching the transition of to/from that we are about to do, load that save file. In any case, we will still preserve the player's inventory because of the lines setting this in the game instance near the top of this function, and save the state in our from/to form before leaving.

To allow our inventory to easily be transferred around, we can add a couple of utility functions. Note: it's also possible to persist UObject instances (other than the game instance) across level loading, but this often has unforeseen consequences with objects that reference other objects, which may be destroyed during a level load. So, in this case, we just make copying of inventory objects simple:

```
void UMasteringInventory::CopyFromOther(UMasteringInventory *Other, class
AMasteringCharacter* ownerOverride /* = nullptr */)
{
        Reset();

        TArray<FWeaponProperties>& otherProps = Other->GetWeaponsArray();
        for (auto prop : otherProps)
        {
                WeaponsArray.Add(prop);
        }

        DefaultWeaponPickup = Other->DefaultWeaponPickup;
        CurrentWeapon = Other->GetCurrentWeapon();
        CurrentWeaponPower = Other->GetCurrentWeaponPower();
        MyOwner = ownerOverride == nullptr ? Other->GetOwningCharacter() :
ownerOverride;
}

void UMasteringInventory::Reset()
{
        WeaponsArray.Empty();
        CurrentWeapon = nullptr;
        CurrentWeaponPower = -1;
        MyOwner = nullptr;
}

void UMasteringInventory::SetupToCurrent()
{
        for (auto WeaponIt = WeaponsArray.CreateConstIterator(); WeaponIt;
++WeaponIt)
        {
                const FWeaponProperties &currentProps = *WeaponIt;
                OnWeaponAdded.Broadcast(currentProps);
```

```
if (currentProps.WeaponClass == CurrentWeapon)
{
        SelectWeapon(currentProps);
}
    }
}
```

Now the last thing to do is to make an actual blueprint of the new trigger box and give it a proper safe-location where we can place the player. If we don't do this, the player will be continually placed at the same spot they saved from (when they intersected the box), and you'll get the player bouncing back and forth between the two levels infinitely. For those looking closely, you'll see in the construction script that collision is initially disabled, and then the timer here re-enables it. This is because we need one tick of the game world to move the player to the updated position, and if we don't briefly disable overlap events, we get the ping-pong behavior mentioned earlier when we do try to do the move:

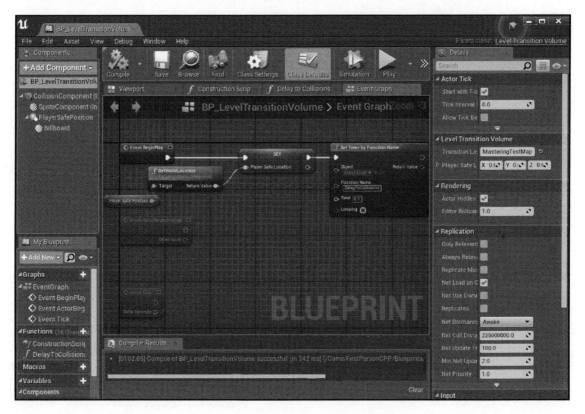

At this point, the player can transition back and forth between our two playable levels, have inventory persist at the current level, be placed at a safe position so they don't immediately go back to the other level, and each level saves and restores the rest of its state like a normal load of a save. The only thing now missing as a general feature would be a spinning icon or fade-to-black and progress bar during the loading itself. UE4 certainly allows for these kinds of things, which update outside of the main game thread tick, but will not be specifically implemented here as we still have another major topic to delve into: streaming levels.

Perchance to stream?

So far we have now used triggering elements to load a specific level. Streaming, as it's commonly known, is another method of loading levels on demand and allows for a much larger playing area without having to have all the encompassing actors loaded at any given time. Unreal allows this in two distinct ways, but they can complement each other: streaming volumes, and world composition. We'll briefly explore these here, but they are great solutions for giving a huge playing area and keeping loaded memory at any given moment at a reasonable level. There are, of course, some drawbacks to this as well

Streaming advantages and disadvantages

The advantages of streaming are probably obvious. As already noted, there's big spaces and manageable memory load. The disadvantages are probably a little less obvious, but are clearly illustrated with our first checkpoint here in the GitHub project: essentially duplicating (minus skybox and lighting) the `MasteringTestMap` into two other levels that are offset from it and streaming those in with streaming volumes. To do this, first go to the main editor **Window** menu and select **Levels**. Two new levels have been added with their offsets and each has a NavMesh volume around it to generate proper meshes. These meshes, when the levels are loaded, will combine.

When a level is streamed out, however, all the actors in it will be destroyed, and when it is streamed back in, they will all be recreated as if loaded anew. So in this example, there are two new levels, MasteringTestMapW1 and W2. MasteringTestMap will be our persistent level. This is the top-most level, which is *always* loaded. All streaming volumes also need to be placed in this level. So, as seen here, in a rough, demonstrative way, when starting MasteringTestMap and turning 90-degrees left and running, you see there is a short overlap of a few meters for the volume that streams in W1, and similarly there is a small overlap of W1's map and the streaming volume for W2. Normally you want these volumes to encompass any time the player can see that area, but in this case, we want to show streaming out: so if you run left, before hitting the edge of MasteringTestMap, W1 streams in. A similar thing will happen if you continue to W2. If you go further into W2 you'll see that W1 then streams out when the player leaves W1's volume, and similarly when heading back through W1 you can watch as W2 quickly streams out. Now come our problems. In W2 there is a volume to spawn more countess enemies. If you go slowly and carefully, they can chase you back into W1, but if you run quickly, W2 streams out and the countesses fall out of the world. Also, when streaming W1 back in, any weapon pickups that were previously collected now return.

Dynamic objects and streaming like this are the biggest issue to reconcile: how do you inform the newly loaded level that it should not respawn weapon pickups placed on the ground? How do the countesses handle their home level streaming out? This utterly breaks their return-home behavior as they literally can't do so (their pathfinding fails). Of course, it's possible to save the state of objects spawned or destroyed in various levels when their streamed level streams out, either in the persistent level in a small way (such as simply storing the actor's position and state) or possibly in the game instance as we with the player's inventory across the level loads in the previous section. However, this is a lot of upkeep, so as with many features like this, if you intend to use streaming be sure to decide early and educate any other team-members on how to properly set these things up so your player feels like it is a seamless world. But first, let's see a quick difference between these two streaming methods and observe the difficulties mentioned.

Example streaming and best practices

To stream these levels, in the **Levels** window, you first have to click the **Levels** drop-down at the top and click on **Add Existing**.

Adding W1 and W2 allows us to select them and then hook their loading state to the volumes shown here:

With those added, and the volumes added like so to **MasteringTestMap**, it should look like this:

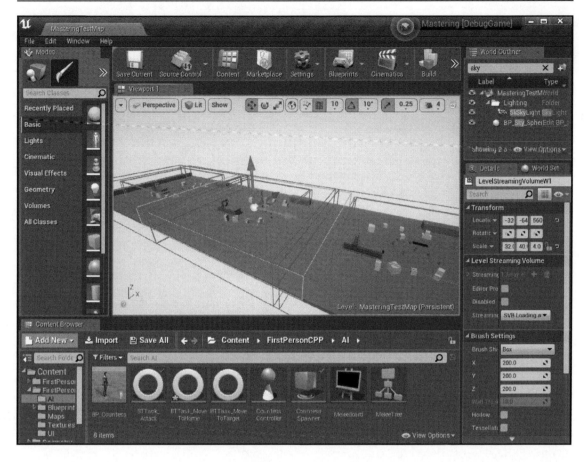

Back in the levels window, clicking the plus button on the volumes array allows us to then use the eye-dropper to drag into the world and select the right volume, or simply use the drop-down and pick the volume we want to associate with this level. Again, note the small overlaps. To avoid players noticing the streaming, it's usually best to make a much larger overlap area and also potentially bring in a fog-distance so the actual loading is not so obvious. For our instructive case, again, we want it to be obvious here. Now, with these pieces in place you can run West and see the levels come in and drop out as the player (actually the camera, to be exact) enters these areas and leaves them. And again, with a couple of test runs, it should be obvious how the drawbacks mentioned are clearly visible if not accounted for as levels stream in and out. Should a countess never leave her home level? Should she disappear when her home level streams out? Should pickups somehow know they've previously been picked up and either not spawn or destroy themselves, like we do with pick-ups picked up when loading a save game? These are all questions each project must decide, weighing the complexity of maintaining such a system versus the player experience and not breaking their immersion.

Using volumes can be a great way to manually control exact levels of detail. For example, you can stream in basic physics and a bit of static mesh geometry with a very large volume to avoid any worries of the falling out of world problems such as the countess has, while then having an additional level with a smaller volume that only loads in when the player is closer, which loads a large number of cosmetic geometry that doesn't impact gameplay. A limitation of volume-based streaming, though, is that levels can only extend from the origin of the persistent level out to WORLD_MAX, which is about 2 km (or from the start, 1 km East/West, 1 km North/South). In most games, this is plenty. For an open world (and don't forget you can still hard-transition to other persistent levels, such as indoor areas!) within this size limitation, we found a brick-like tiling was best for overlapping levels to be loaded. So, when you're in the level in the center, the levels around it in this pattern would be loaded:

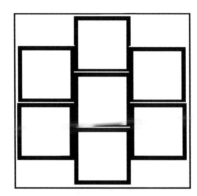

This way you can also work with level designers so that the sum memory of those seven levels is always less than a certain cap. So, for example, you could have some low-detail areas with a very high-detail area in the center, but of course as you move around and this pattern repeats, the sum of any seven loaded levels should be maintained under that agreed-upon cap. And the nice part is that server-based multiplayer games already respect this kind of streaming and have no problems tracking players across these boundaries from their clients. If your world needs a much larger or nearly boundless play space, world composition is worth exploring.

World composition is a great way to create automated, grid-based tiling built into UE4. This is particularly useful for very large worlds where the player can then travel almost endlessly in any given direction, but requires a large effort by artists or level designers typically to make these sections and make them match exactly at their borders. A perfect application for world composition is a single-player open-world game where exploration and a truly vast play area are the goal. As this is a bit niche, and Epic themselves have done a very nice job of documenting the feature, a link will be added to the *Further reading* section.

Summary

From the start of this chapter to its completion, we have now demonstrated how to persist level state and player state independently across traditional level loads, as well as the basics of streaming levels as the player moves around. These are fundamental to almost all conceivable games in UE4 and should now form the basis of whatever strategy works best for a team and project going forward. Always remember: make these decisions early! It can be nearly impossible, for example, to retrofit levels built assuming a hard level-load into a streaming model, but if you adopt that streaming model and help your team stick to its limits from day one, this is one worry that won't haunt you late in a project cycle.

Questions

1. What existing classes or objects can be used in UE4 to implement level loading with no new changes?
2. What are some limitations of using only these methods?
3. What is the scope of the lifetime of the game instance object?
4. How is the game instance used to persist data when opening a new level or loading an existing one's state?
5. What is the purpose of abstracting level load/save code to a blueprint function library?
6. Why is the player's inventory copied rather than scoping a UObject to the game instance?
7. What are the major drawbacks of volume-based streaming?
8. Which types of games should definitely use world composition?

Further reading

World composition in UE4:

https://docs.unrealengine.com/en-US/Engine/LevelStreaming/WorldBrowser

Getting Audio in Your Game

7

Introduction

Audio is an often-overlooked component of games that is often only noticed when it is done poorly. While not as prominent as graphics and gameplay tend to be, given how it can ruin an experience or enhance it, it's definitely best to aim for the latter. Think about an action or horror film with the volume muted, and you get a feel for how important of an impact audio can have! In this chapter we'll cover:

- Fundamental components of UE4 audio
- Triggering audio from an animation
- Material-based audio (including unique impact sounds for projectiles and various player foot-falls)
- Environmental FX (reverb by a volume)

Technical requirements

This chapter will extensively use the audio resources from the countess character assets added back in Chapter 5, *Adding Enemies!*, but with similar assets the lessons can be followed without these specifically.

The GitHub chapter will begin here:

https://github.com/PacktPublishing/Mastering-Game-Development-with-Unreal-Engine-4-Second-Edition/tree/Chapter-7

Engine version used: 4.19.2.

Basic sounds and triggering by animation

We already have, as is obvious to dedicated followers of the book, exactly one sound in our game, it's found here and has been there since Chapter 1, *Making a C++ Project for a First-Person Shooter*, with our FPS template (though it was moved from AMasteringCharacter to AMasteringWeapon in Chapter 2, *Inventory and Weapons for the Player*:

```
// try and play the sound if specified
if (FireSound != nullptr)
{
        UGameplayStatics::PlaySoundAtLocation(this, FireSound,
GetActorLocation());
}
```

That is a great example of the most basic way to play a sound, and from C++ no less, but we'll try to branch out in a few new areas in this section and add material-based sounds in the one that follows. We'll also be adding a professional-looking level from Epic to demonstrate some of these concepts. You can find it from Epic here (**Infinity Blade: Ice Lands**; we'll use the **Ice Cove** in its pack):

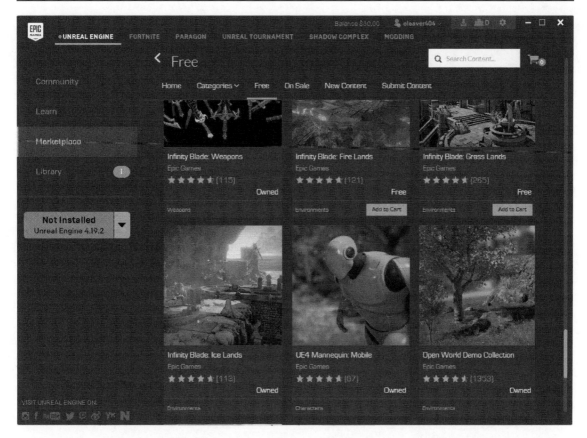

It's a similar size (close to 2 GB) as the countess content was, so if you're keeping up with the GitHub project, it might be best to start downloading it now.

An important note here for GitHub users! The project as of this map being uploaded sets maps to use GitHub LFS (large file system), and if you're unfamiliar, you will now need to not just do a pull from GitHub going forward, but then also a `pull lfs content`. You'll notice the problem if Unreal says the map files are in the wrong format on startup. More information on Git LFS is in additional reading.

Sounds, cues, channels, dialog, FX volumes, and more!

UE4 offers a huge array of audio-based classes that can be as simple as `USoundBase`, or incredibly complex combinations of branching dialog and specially applied FX.

Let's first just walk through the major classes to make sure it's clear what capabilities already exist. If you just right-click to add an asset and hover on the sound fly-out, you'll see a list like this:

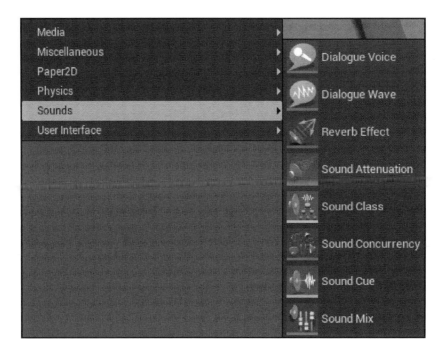

This by itself can be intimidating, so let's just make a quick overview of each of them and their purpose before we start some more practical examples.

Sound Wave: This is the most basic level of a sound in the game. While it is not in the Sounds drop-down menu, this is how sounds are brought into the game from the **Import** button rather than Sounds. You take a raw sound (a .wav file, for example), import it into your project, and have a **Sound Wave**. These can take various properties, or be used to make Sound Cues and take further properties. A summary of all the items to follow can be made like this: all further sound design or audio engineering is really dependent on your game's complexity and needs. **Sound Waves**, though, are your most basic starting point and are required for any audio to be played in UE4.

Dialog Voice: These simply specify a speaker type and a speaker gender. Think of the voice as its name: who is speaking, and what type of voice do they use?

Dialog Wave: These are basically an indicator of how one speaker should interact with another speaker, defined through **DialogContext** objects that you can add from one speaker to another, as well as add on-screen spoken text and subtitle overrides (as well as flagging the content as mature). A quick version of this will be demonstrated with our countess performing a taunt in combat in the next section. The dialog system is great for simple dialog between a couple of interactable characters (the player being one or several), but this really only works well for basic interactions. If that is all that is needed by the design of your game, this is a perfectly good option and should be utilized. More general information on the dialog system is linked in the *Further reading* section.

Reverb Effect: Reverb effects really should be utilized by sound designers, but their function is to add effects based on the environment to the sounds played and heard. They can be used to make a bit of an echo in a cave environment, for example, or the interior of a vehicle, to add a professional and realistic audio effect to your sounds. These are attached to audio volumes in your world that tell the environment how your sound should be heard.

Sound Attenuation: Similar to the Reverb Effect, you can define various attenuation settings. Environmental sounds (which we will address further) can reference one of these objects, or typically be specified individually. Attenuation is really the drop-off properties of a sound: spatially based on the listener's location, how does the sound drop off? For example, in an area with winding corridors, you'll want sound to drop off more quickly the further away it is to reflect the loss of amplitude as the sound travels to the listener. Once again, audio engineers and sound designers are typically very familiar with the concepts here and can apply them to great effect to make atmospheric effects on the sounds being played (a creepy noise from a distance away may play very quietly, but when near the player, is much louder).

Sound Class: This is another nice way to organize your sound types based on how they are meant to be heard and are applied on top of all other properties. Sounds can be set, for example, to ignore reverb, ignore attenuation (set them as a **UISound!**), or otherwise alter properties such as their stereo (left/right channel) output, and be applied in a hierarchy through other sound classes.

Sound Concurrency: Before this object was added, it was possible to limit a sound by Max Count and other properties that will be found as we work. So, for example, you don't have 20 footstep sounds from NPCs playing at the same time, you limit it to 6 even if 20 NPCs are simultaneously walking. **Sound Concurrency** objects give finer control over this based on the sound's player. So, for the previous example, perhaps you want all attack sounds from a certain type of enemy to be played, but you only want a limited set from another type of enemy to be heard at any given time. As with many previous descriptions, this is a great tool for audio designers to have available, but it is really only needed in games or areas of games where sounds can become overwhelming to the player and some should have definite priority over others. These can then be specified like other properties to a **Sound Wave** object.

Sound Cue: These are a bit like a blueprint for playing sounds. You can combine effects and local modifiers to an output. Think of these like taking an actual sound input (a gunshot, a bit of spoken dialog, and so on) and specifying in great detail how it should be combined for the final output. Many of these options at this point surely seem like they have a lot of overlap, but consider many of them as *ways to modify any sound*, and this one as *ways we modify a specific sound*. Sound Cues can often be quite simple and just take your input and put it to an output, though of course, that output itself can still be modified by global environmental FX set (or, again, set for just this sound).

Sound Mix: Sound mixes can be pushed and popped and applied on top of each other as well, but control more global settings such as pitch, EQ (high-end to low-end filtering), and how volume should be applied to, for example, the center-channel in 5.1 or other surround sound options for advanced mixing.

Triggering sounds from animation

By far the most common usage case in games is audio triggered as animations are played. We'll set up several events like this for our countess NPC and, in the next section, some footsetps based on materials for our player (even though our player character model has no feet!). To get started, let's open our **ABP_Countess** animation blueprint and look again at her attack state:

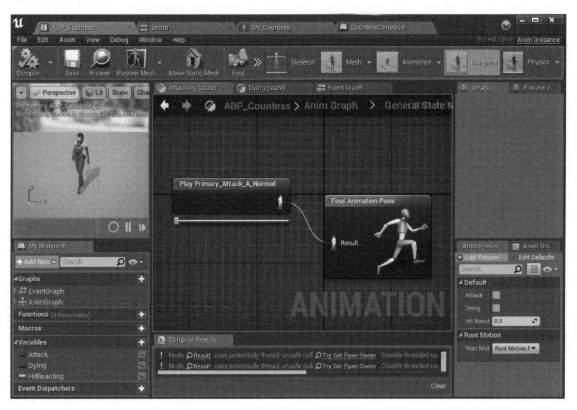

We'll now work on **Primary_Attack_A_Normal** with an event to make her attack not so eerily silent. Double-click the attack anim. node and, like we did earlier for the try-to-hit event, we'll add another event to her animation a bit earlier:

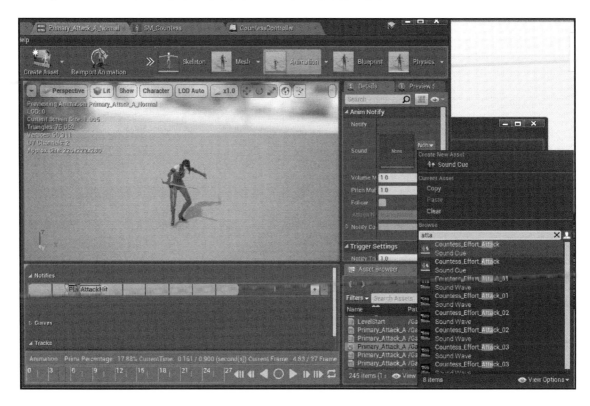

At the bottom on the timeline, we can scrub the little red bar to where we want, then up in the **Notifies** timeline, right-click and add a Play Sound notify. Then over on the right, filter to and pick a **Countess_Effort_Attack** sound that we like. Now, two notes: the sound cues set up for her are invalid because the project doesn't have the whole set of characters from the game, and they rely on dialog players mentioned in the previous section. So they won't play any sound. Second note: the sound wave objects all work individually, of course, but if we wanted to mix them up, we could make a normal animation notify like we did for the attack-hit previously, set up some blueprint logic to pick a sound wave at random, and play that. For now, we've picked attack_01, so we now have her making noise in the game and can test it in our levels.

For those following along, there is some cleanup in the project at this point: renaming to better reflect our assets' current state of things and bringing some of our other classes up to date. If you're syncing at this point, you may also notice the Infinity Blade weapons now have their own projectiles that look like their actual weapons and gives them a bit more of a thrown weapon feel and helps differentiate each further for future work.

If you're curious how the static meshes for the projectiles were made, open the skeletal mesh actor for the mesh of any of these weapons we've made, and at the top is a **Make Static Mesh** button on the main toolbar. It's very convenient when you don't want to import a separate model or don't have access to the original assets but need a static mesh version, like here.

If you play the game at this point, you'll notice our countess' attack noise gets very repetitive and it all still feels a bit basic. Given the huge number of awesome assets this character contains, we'll now randomize her attacks, give each attack its own sound (we could also just randomize the sound each time the same attack is played, however), and give her an occasional taunt piece of dialog directed at our player. Let's start by opening up our **ABP_Countess** animation blueprint. In here, in the Attacking state, we'll change from playing a single animation to playing via a random sequence player. As you can see on the right, you can then add as many animation sequences as you like, weight their relative chance to be picked, turn on shuffle mode, set looping, all kinds of great stuff:

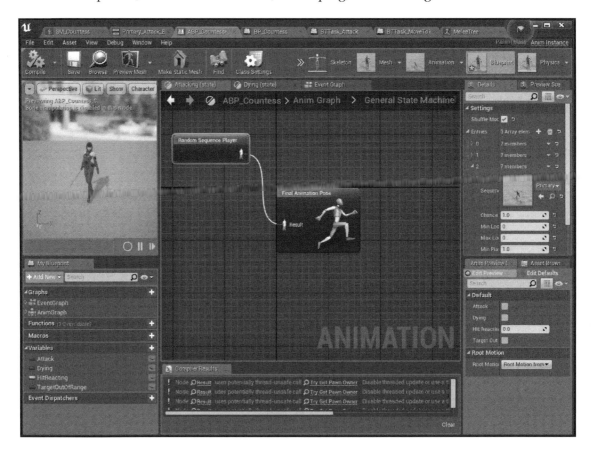

However, once we do this, we can't count on the play time of a given animation as our exit transition anymore and need a new way to transition out of this state. We need a new variable on the bottom-left: **TargetOutOfRange**. This is used here to get us out of this continuing attacking sequence and into moving to chase the player (or run back home if we take too long), like normal:

Setting that requires us to modify the attack behavior tree task, adding this function at the end when our MoveTo succeeds:

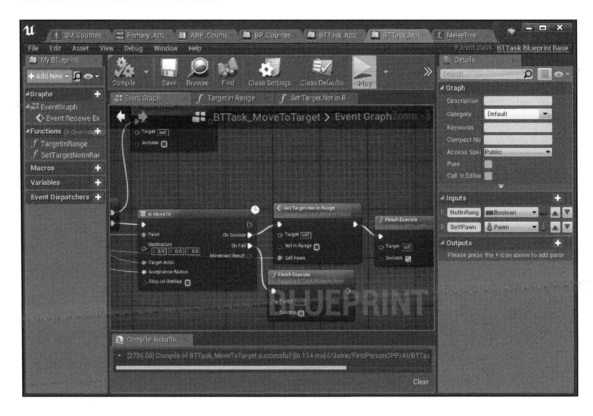

The function called there is rather simple and so is omitted here. It just does all of our casing from pawn, getting the animation blueprint, and then setting its out of range variable to whatever was passed in. And as can be seen in the GitHub project, that variable is marked true every time we enter our move to behavior task, so it is only set to false on each pass through the function where our AI MoveTo succeeds (which is every pass unless the player moves out of the acceptance radius). As an added bonus, you can see in the last of the three animation sequences used that the sound cue chosen here has three dialog entries and picks one randomly. So we have three random attacks, and the third one set up here picks from three random sounds each time it is used. A perfect example of our options.

And lastly, we'll make a quick taunt that plays some percentage of the time. Note that it can play multiple times in a row as-is, but there are plenty of tools available to prevent this. To get her to play a taunt 10% of the time, this dialog setup is added at the end of the attack behavior task (and note that a DialogVoice with default settings was added for our stealth character):

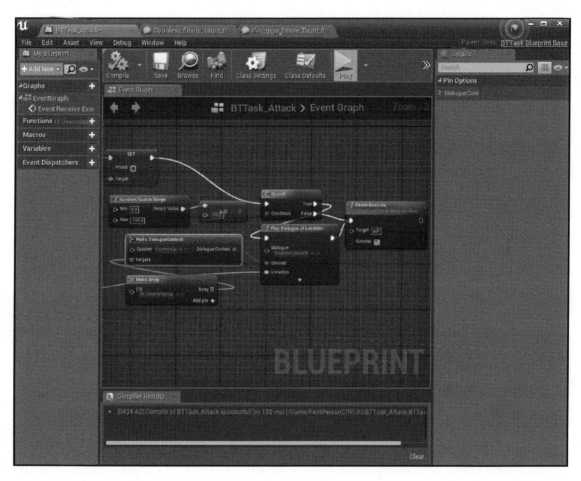

Note that whichever dialog wave is chosen (in this case **Countess_Emote_Taunt_010_Dialogue**) you need to open it and ensure that the speaker is set to the right type (I am using the not Vamp versions) and add the stealth character (specified in the array in the bottom-left) as a listener. And there we have it: random attacks, new sounds, random dialog, and a random taunt!

Environments and sound

Our sounds to this point are indifferent to where or why they are played. We'll quickly now add a sound for a couple of types of things our projectile can hit, as well as some footstep sounds for the player just to prove our physics material approach is working. Unlike some of the amazing visual assets made freely available in the Unreal Marketplace, it's a bit tougher to find similarly freely shared libraries of common sounds, but we'll use what we have to make the most of it and realize that in a full-production game, many sounds will be built by dedicated sound designers, or hopefully some budget is at least set aside to purchase existing commercial libraries.

Hitting different surfaces

Hitting objects with our projectiles is the easiest sound to quickly set up, but then, we need new functionality on our projectile class to make sure each one knows what sound to play as they hit each type of surface. This can be quite a bit of work to maintain as the number of surface types (physical materials) and projectiles with unique sounds begin to multiply, but this is also the kind of detail-oriented work that sets apart a commercially successful game from the less professional demos or indie titles that don't take the time to add these touches.

We'll start with the absolute basics that we need to address in the project: setting up material types. For the work here, we're just going to set up two types, but of course, you could then follow this pattern and create as many as desired for every type. First, open up the project settings, and under **Engine/Physics**, we'll add snow and stone like so:

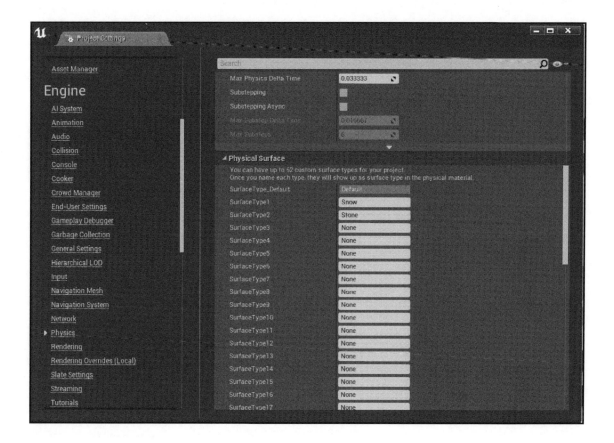

In the **FirstPerson/Audio** section, I added several sound cues, but they're just FX-modified versions of sounds already in the project since, as noted, there are no specific obvious free downloads in the Unreal Marketplace:

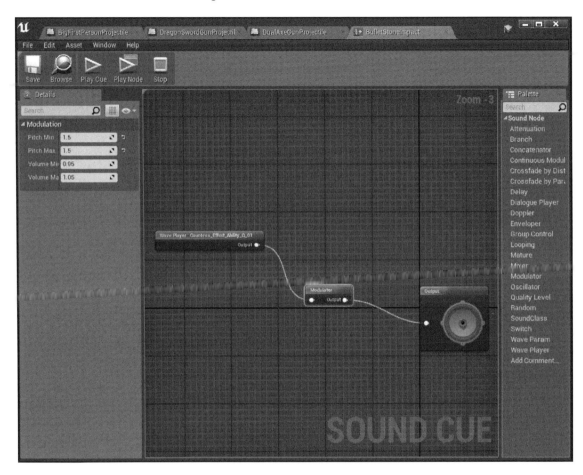

Important note! If at this stage (or any point going forward) these sounds are bothersome (they became so to me!), please go to GitHub and cherry-pick commit 7ff24f7 from this chapter (which will be used going forward in all subsequent versions) for some relatively good percussion sounds for all the impacts in this chapter. Having a synthesizer and pulling in some .wav samples is a big advantage, but remember: in any case where you're not 100% sure, you must check any licensing on any assets like this. Even hardware you own generating sounds can have some set of licensing in commercial products if used directly!

Next, for projectiles we will need a way of matching material types and a surface that was hit. For now, we'll make a struct in our projectile header. We'll add these two properties:

```
USTRUCT(BlueprintType)
struct FPhysSound
{
        GENERATED_USTRUCT_BODY()

        UPROPERTY(EditAnywhere, BlueprintReadWrite)
        TEnumAsByte<EPhysicalSurface> SurfaceType;

        UPROPERTY(EditAnywhere, BlueprintReadWrite)
        class USoundCue* SoundCue;
};
```

And, of course, our projectiles will need an array of these:

```
UPROPERTY(EditAnywhere, BlueprintReadWrite)
TArray<FPhysSound> ImpactSounds;
```

As noted, when the complexity of physics surface types and projectiles gets greater and greater, maintaining a system such as this can get out of hand. And with even the small set here, if decisions made early can mean building in changes as you progress, instead of retro-fitting changes onto a huge number of individual assets, you're always better off making these decisions as early as possible. The level of complexity currently is manageable, but if it were multiplied to a significantly larger number, the work about to be done would be pretty miserable, and the chances for mistakes multiplies. In such a case, I'd recommend perhaps making a DataTable in Unreal and tracking large changes in a .csv spreadsheet or the like. More information on that is provided in the *Further reading* section. For now, though, let's go to each of our projectiles and begin setting default surfaces to default impact noise, thrown projectiles' snow to thrown-snow impacts, and so on:

Once all of this is set up, then it's just a matter of a bit of code in the `OnHit` function for projectiles:

```
#include "Sound/SoundCue.h"
EPhysicalSurface surfType = SurfaceType_Default;
if (OtherComp->GetBodyInstance() != nullptr &&
OtherComp->GetBodyInstance()->GetSimplePhysicalMaterial() != nullptr)
{
        surfType =
OtherComp->GetBodyInstance()->GetSimplePhysicalMaterial()->SurfaceType;
}

USoundCue* cueToPlay = nullptr;
for (auto physSound : ImpactSounds)
{
        if (physSound.SurfaceType == surfType)
        {
                cueToPlay = physSound.SoundCue;
                break;
        }
}

const float minVelocity = 400.0f;
if (cueToPlay != nullptr && GetVelocity().Size() > minVelocity)
{
        UGameplayStatics::PlaySoundAtLocation(this, cueToPlay,
Hit.Location);
}
```

Unfortunately, our `FHitResult` is for us the projectile in this case. Also note the hardcoded minimum velocity: this is to prevent spamming the game with a huge number of very small bounces towards the end of the projectile's velocity/lifetime, but you could of course handle this in a number of other or more flexible ways. If you are in the future looking to play a sound from that perspective, there is a great accessor to make getting the surface type trivial here:

```
UGameplayStatics::GetSurfaceType(Hit);
```

The most obvious facing surface in the default map has been set to a stone type, for testing, and now the different surfaces and different projectiles can be shown, changing their impact sounds! The next section will work briefly in our new (finally visual high quality) map for footfalls and setting reverb based on a sound volume.

Player footfalls and environment FX

Now our player finally gets some footstep sounds of their own. Again, we'll work with what we've got, but we can hopefully find a few types to at least prove out the system so helping teammates in future work should come easily. The footfall work can be done almost identically to the projectile hits, but we'll trigger it from specific moments in the player's (albeit very limited) moving animation. These will simply trigger a ray-cast, we'll get the material, and once we have it, the work will make footsteps work everywhere we go.

First, MasteringCharacter needs the same struct as our projectile just got. In general, assuming more things will use this shared functionality, I'd move the struct and some of this behavior into an actor component but as it's not super informative for our lesson here, we'll just forgive ourselves a little bit of copy/paste for now, first from the top of our .h file:

```
USTRUCT(BlueprintType)
struct FFootstepSounds
{
        GENERATED_USTRUCT_BODY()

        UPROPERTY(EditAnywhere, BlueprintReadWrite)
        TEnumAsByte<EPhysicalSurface> SurfaceType;

        UPROPERTY(EditAnywhere, BlueprintReadWrite)
        class USoundCue* SoundCue;
};

UPROPERTY(EditAnywhere, BlueprintReadWrite)
TArray<FFootstepSounds> FootstepSounds;

UFUNCTION(BlueprintCallable)
void PlayFootstepSound();
```

Next, we'll do this in our .cpp file:

```
#include "Sound/SoundCue.h"
#include "PhysicalMaterials/PhysicalMaterial.h"
```

Snippet

```
void AMasteringCharacter::PlayFootstepSound()
{
        FVector startPos = GetActorLocation();
        FVector endPos = startPos - FVector(0.0f, 0.0f, 200.0f); // 2m down

        FCollisionQueryParams queryParams;
        queryParams.AddIgnoredActor(this);
```

```
        queryParams.bTraceComplex = true;
        queryParams.bReturnPhysicalMaterial = true;
        FHitResult hitOut;

        bool bHit = GetWorld()->LineTraceSingleByProfile(hitOut, startPos,
endPos, TEXT("IgnoreOnlyPawn"));

        if (bHit)
        {
                EPhysicalSurface surfHit = SurfaceType_Default;

                if (hitOut.Component->GetBodyInstance() != nullptr &&
hitOut.Component->GetBodyInstance()->GetSimplePhysicalMaterial() !=
nullptr)
                {
                        surfHit =
hitOut.Component->GetBodyInstance()->GetSimplePhysicalMaterial()->SurfaceTy
pe;
                }

                if (hitOut.PhysMaterial != nullptr)
                {
                        surfHit = hitOut.PhysMaterial->SurfaceType;
                }
                USoundCue* cueToPlay = nullptr;
                for (auto physSound : FootstepSounds)
                {
                        if (physSound.SurfaceType == surfHit)
                        {
                                cueToPlay = physSound.SoundCue;
                                break;
                        }
                }

                if (cueToPlay != nullptr)
                {
                        UGameplayStatics::PlaySoundAtLocation(this,
cueToPlay, hitOut.Location);
                }
        }
}
```

Notice that we'll do our own raytrace to see what's below us and use that for the results of what and where to play. Note also that in my experience, even though we are getting a hit on a static mesh with a physical material, we still have to manually dig it out as even specifying in the query to return a physical material always comes back as `nullptr` in the hit result.

To trigger these, we need a new event in the minimalist first-person running animation:

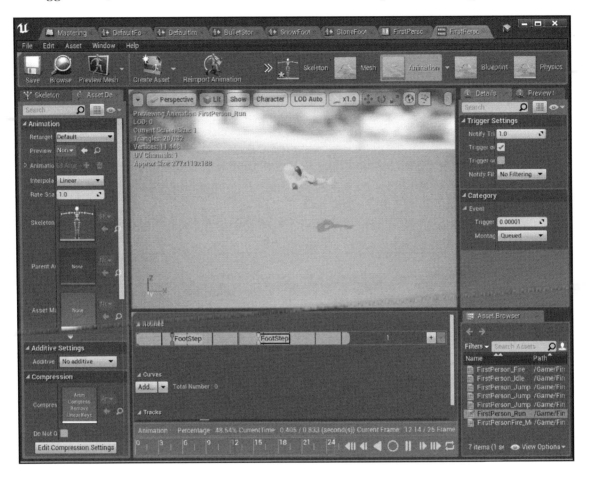

And we'll add a call to our pawn's new function from **FirstPerson_AnimBP**:

Similarly, new footstep sound cues were added in the editor and added to the array on our stealth character, just like with the weapons. Now we have some weird-sounding footstep noises!

Opening the FrozenCove level finally, we'll select several surfaces that look like stone or ice and you can easily jump to their materials from there. You can also see there is an existing stone physical material from the level as downloaded in **InfinityBladeIceLands/Environments/SurfaceTypes**.

Click the materials of those static meshes to open them and we'll set several of their physical materials:

To do this fully, we'll make a new snow physical material duplicating the stone one (which is effectively set to stone as surface type 2, but should be explicitly set to stone now that we added it by name to our project), name it **PhysicalMaterial_Snow**, and we'll set the new one to snow surface type of course in its properties. The whole list of materials changed can be seen in GitHub, but some examples are (all under **InfinityBladeIceLands/Environments/Ice**) **Ice_Fortress/Materials/M_Ice_FortFloor_1_SnowPaint** and **Ice_Castle/Materials/M_IceT3 _Fort_Floor_05**.

And finally, we right-click and add a new **Sounds/Reverb** object in **InfinityBladeIceLands/Effects**, named here **WallReverb**, and it's been given some pretty extreme parameters to make its presence obvious when used. And how is it used? Simple! In the level, on the left in the basic types, under **Volumes** is **AudioVolume**, in this case added to the whole corridor on the left from where the player starts:

Set its reverb object to the one we just created, and you can't miss the change when moving in there and making any sounds. There are a huge number of possibilities with this sort of work to explore, and if you're immediately curious, it is definitely possible to allow whole classes of sounds to ignore effects (and some, if set to the UI type, already do by default).

Summary

While audio is often left as an afterthought to games, the work done here should hopefully show just how much is possible in UE4 and why it's important. Getting sounds right and being able to tell your designers and other team members how to do these things (or even that they're readily possible!) is a huge advantage over many less experienced teams trying to make a similar game. Don't be left out in the cold on this one: your audience will thank you!

Questions

1. What is the absolutely simplest way to quickly play a sound during gameplay?
2. What are the major components of the dialog system?
3. Which situations will the dialog system suffice in, and where will it require a managing system on top of it?
4. How do we play a simple sound from an animation?
5. What is the preferred route to play more complex and varied sounds from animations?
6. How do we find the material hit in a collision, and why is it never as obvious as it appears it should be?
7. Where are surface types defined, and where are they then applied from in game?
8. How can a level or sound designer quickly set up areas in a level to differentiate the audio properties there?

Further reading

Git LFS:

```
https://help.github.com/articles/installing-git-large-file-storage/
```

Unreal Dialog system:

```
https://docs.unrealengine.com/en-us/Engine/Audio/Dialogue
```

Ambient sounds:

`https://docs.unrealengine.com/en-us/Engine/Audio/SoundActors`

DataTables driven and maintained via .csv:

`https://docs.unrealengine.com/en-us/Gameplay/DataDriven`

8
Shader Editing and Optimization Tips

Introduction

Shaders (and the Materials they are built from in UE4) are responsible for all we see in the game. Some are very simple and require no user input whatsoever (such as most UI work), but eventually, any team making a modern day 3D game will likely need some custom solutions, if not a huge number, beyond what comes packaged with the basic game and templates. Knowing how to create and modify them, how to use (and re-use) them efficiently at runtime, and some of the powerful capabilities they provide, is major importance. Thankfully, UE4 makes some of this much easier than other platforms with their Material Editor, saving time and resources for teams, but of course this comes at the risk of improper use, which can be devastating for performance. Throughout this chapter are tips to prevent that, while getting the most out of the system and tools. And keep in mind, our goal here is not to become a specialized expert in every topic but to gain a holistic mastery of the major systems of UE4 and the confidence to guide a team or project to its best effectiveness. Material and shader mastery can (and does!) fill its own books entirely, but after this chapter, you should have the confidence to give grounded answers on the capabilities and limitations of what can be done with materials in UE4. Our main topics will be:

- Basics of creating and editing materials
- Editing material networks and editor-time performance tips
- Runtime tips for optimizing shaders
- Adapting shaders across various platforms

Technical requirements

This chapter will use the project from the following GitHub link. While the lessons can be applied to any project, specific examples will be given using assets directly from the game project, so of course syncing it is recommended:

```
https://github.com/PacktPublishing/Mastering-Game-Development-with-Unreal-
Engine-4-Second-Edition/tree/Chapter-8
```

Engine version used: 4.19.2.

Knowing and building materials

It is assumed most readers are familiar with the concept of shaders: specific rendering code sent at runtime to tell the hardware how we want it to draw a given item to the screen. There are numerous places a novice can begin learning about them, but the assumption here is the reader has at least basic knowledge of how shaders work: compilation, upload to a GPU or software renderer, and execution there. As this is not a graphics primer, we'll skip ahead now to UE4's ubiquitous method of generating and porting shaders across platforms: Materials.

Overview of materials, material instance creation, and use

There's no perfect place to start when it comes to materials. However, the obvious one not everyone even knows is there are engine materials. If you open the editor and go to the content browser, you'll see in the bottom-right a **View Options** drop-down menu. Selecting **Show Engine Content** will make a new folder show up in the sources browser on the left, and selecting this folder, then adding a filter of **Material** and **Material Instance**, as here, from the Filters drop-down menu will show you a huge list of existing built-in materials:

Selecting the Daylight Ambient Cubemap as a quick example will open the material editor and look like this:

For those new to editing materials, you can see it looks a lot like the blueprint editor and other node-based editing in UE4, which helps give a sense of familiarity across the different editor windows offered. Briefly describing what is shown here, the top-left has a preview (always just mapped to a sphere in the middle) of the material's output. The bottom-left is the details of whatever node is selected. The center, of course, is the main editing pane. At the bottom is a summary of the shader's complexity (more on this later!), and to the right is a list of nodes you can drop in (the same as if you right-click in the main pane). Browsing through the engine materials, you'll see many are simply used by the editor itself. You'll also notice (given the filter) several material instances. What's the difference? And what's different about a dynamic material instance? Let's do a quick list here and continue to some more specific examples:

- A material is the most basic type, typically a parent class to material instances, when used, and consists of the basic flow of what the material (and compiled shader) are going to do
- By adding parameter nodes (more on this soon too), material instances can be inherited from a parent master material and given individual properties, so the whole material doesn't have to be remade to change, say, an input texture
- Dynamic material instances are material instances created at runtime that can take real-time parameters and change them in places like blueprints of an actor

We'll go through some examples of each, creating our own as we go, and viewing others already built in the content of our project to date. But it's important to consider the usage of a material before you begin work on it. Is this a material that will be used in a very specific way with no need to derive children? Then it can probably just remain and be directly referenced as a material. Is the intention to have several variants of one core set of shader logic? Then you'll likely want a base material with a set of material instance children of course. Do you want something that takes parameters (think like a function being passed arguments in C++) at runtime with different outcomes based on that? You'll want to make a material, a material instance (at least one) thereof, and then at runtime, create a dynamic material instance (the easiest way is usually in the blueprint constructor of the object), and pass that its parameters either at startup or throughout that object's life. So let's take these one at a time in the next section, see what's involved in each of those cases, and get in the habit of building your materials right the first time to fit their use.

Working on material networks and performance tips at editor time

While we can easily begin a material from scratch (and it's highly recommended to just take some time playing with what can be done if you're unfamiliar), let's begin with an existing material and go through what it does, then begin changing it to something more useful in our test map.

To give a quick example of how we can change a material instance and apply it to the world, let's start with **Content/InfinityBladeIceLands/Environments/Misc/Exo_Deco01/Materials**, and we'll use the **M_Exo_Crate_Open** material as our starting point. Feel free to select it and open it in the material editor now.

To get a demonstration rolling, we'll quickly do a few things to this base material. Drag from the Emissive Color pin and filter for time or the like to get the **TimeWithSpeedVariable** node placed here. Drag from its speed to the left and add a **Constant**. We'll make sure that constant defaults to 0.0, thus not changing the base behavior everywhere else this crate material is used (in the frozen cove level). Lastly, right-click on that constant node, select **Convert to Parameter**, and name it **EmissiveSpeed**, as shown here:

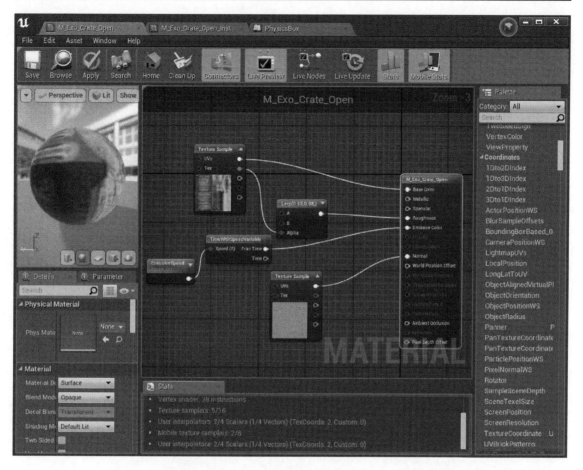

For those paying close attention, you'll notice the **Mobile texture samplers** at the bottom is currently 2/8. As soon as you save the material, its current graph gets applied (both to the material asset, as well as any instances in the level), and you'll see it jump from 2 to 6/8! Granted, tripling our texture sampling at runtime isn't great, but on mobile platforms that magic 8 number can be a very significant limit (more on that later in the chapter). But remember: *save to apply changes fully!*

Once that's all done, back in the content browser, right-click on the crate material, and at the top is the option to Create Material Instance. We'll use that to activate this emissive color in the instance:

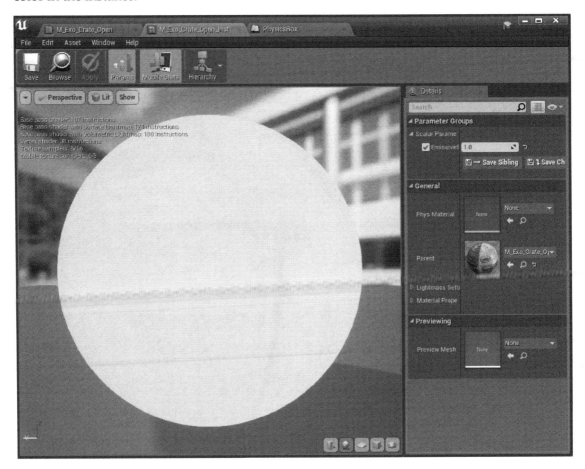

Just like in base materials, it's important to always have whatever stats you need clicked to **on** at the top of these editors as you can immediately see an overview of the complexity of the material: base and vertex instructions and texture samplers. Small changes can make *huge* differences to these numbers, and getting artists and anyone working with materials familiar with what reasonable numbers are for your platform is critical to do early and always enforce!

Notice that while editing a material instance, the logic of the shader is gone. You can't modify it in an instance, but you can modify parameters (that's sort of the whole point of them!). In the top-right, check the box to allow editing of the **EmissiveSpeed**, and we'll set it to 1.0. Now, keep in mind this texture and its corresponding normal map were made for a specific model, not these cubes, but we're again demonstrating concepts here, not making ready-to-ship art. We can now drag this (the instance's icon from the content browser) on to one of the cubes in the level and play it. In the screenshot here, I lowered the direction light's intensity to 0.6 or so, and brought the color of the sky light to a dark gray, but you don't have to do these things. It just makes the lighting-independent nature of this pulsing emissive more obvious:

So while it's not perfect (we'll improve it in just a moment!) you can see now a trick that a lot of games use to highlight items that the player should pick up in a game. They often have a pulsing shine to them that makes them stand out from the static backgrounds near them so the player won't miss those valuable pick-ups. To test its pulsing, you can click **Simulate** from the **Play** button pull-down in the editor, though again for those of you playing along closely in the GitHub project, you'll notice this exposes a check of mine on the player controller being the right type. So, any time a serious bug like that is found, you check in a fix ASAP. But let's view that box now (either by playing the level normally, or syncing commit ce0da7c, or making the following fix locally):

```
void AMasteringCharacter::InitializeInventoryHUD()
{
        APlayerController* player =
Cast<APlayerController>(GetController());

        if (player != nullptr) // function is called with a non-player
controller in simulation in editor
        {
                AMasteringHUD* HUD = Cast<AMasteringHUD>(player->GetHUD());

                if (HUD != nullptr)
                {
                        HUD->InitializeInventory(Inventory);
                }
        }
}
```

And you can now see the results of a few quick changes to the material. Let's improve it a bit quickly, and then move on. First we'll make the pulsing follow a sine output rather than linear, and we'll put a cap on its magnitude, defaulted to 0.5:

Now if you go to the material instance. As the MaxEmissive is also a parameter now, you can see it and set it to something else (say 0.25 to make it all a bit more subtle) and look at our result.

To make a dynamic material instance, we need to edit the blueprint of the **Physics Box** object in the test level, select any of them, and then in its details pane, pick **Edit Blueprint** and open the editor. Here we can add logic such as this, but note: this will change the logic for *all* of the boxes in the level now, and will even overwrite (as we put it in slot 0) the unmodified material instance on the box we were working on before. Add this and check out the result:

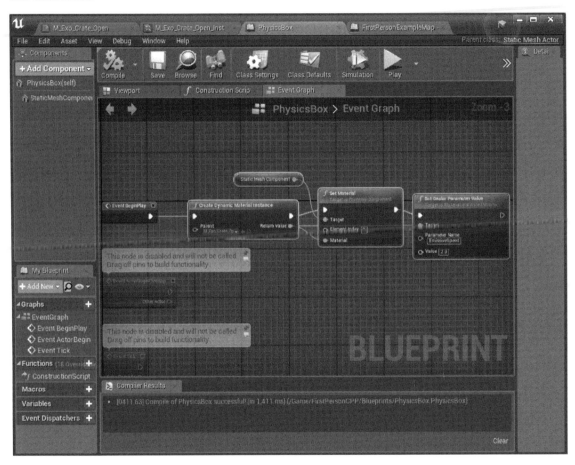

Now we have a really fast pulsing material on all our boxes. If you wanted it on just a select few, it's possible to do this by referencing it in the level blueprint or by making individual box types instead of just the one they all are instances of, but now, hopefully, the value of creating a dynamic instance with parameters that can be set at runtime by blueprint events is evident. You could even change the material back to the default cube material upon being hit. The flexibility here is very powerful! Just keep in mind there are some specific precomputed possibilities that are lost if you replace a material dynamically at runtime, but for most games and projects, real-time lighting and effects are the prominent feature on anything you would give a dynamic material instance to.

Don't forget also that static meshes (and other meshes) can have many materials: just look around at some of the pieces in the map Frozen Cove! All will be applied when rendering the actor. The first material is typically the one used for setting the Physical Material and the most basic/fundamental rendering of the object, but if you pick a static mesh object (including the **1M_Cube** of this test level), you can see its materials are just an array with no hard limit (only practical ones for performance and manageability).

Materials at runtime and various platforms

Now that editing materials is familiar and we briefly noted how one seemingly small change drastically increased one of the stats of a material, it's time to get a bit more in-depth here and understand the tools available for runtime analysis. There are myriad tools for analyzing the graphical performance of your scene, several built into UE4, and others that are free that you can explore. NVIDIA makes a great set of tools, a lifesaver for Android developers, which can be found in the additional reading section. For now, we'll focus on what we can do inside Unreal and the editor first and foremost as our main tool and early testing spot.

Runtime tools and techniques to quickly iterate shaders

One of the most immediately useful tools in your arsenal for shader performance is the **Shader Complexity** viewmode. In any viewport window in the editor, this can be found by clicking the lighting drop-down menu (next to the perspective drop-down menu in the top-left corner of the viewport. In the screenshots, these are typically **Lit** and **Perspective** respectively). In there, under **Optimization Viewmodes** is **Shader Complexity** (*Alt+8* being the shortcut on PC, *Alt+4* to get back to lit). However, in our test level there's not much to look at, so let's quickly go to the frozen cove map, which has a lot more of interest. At runtime, on any platform with the console enabled (~ key on PC, 4-finger tap on most mobile devices), you can access this also via the show ShaderComplexity command, and as that's most interesting here, let's take a look at what we get at the start of frozen cove:

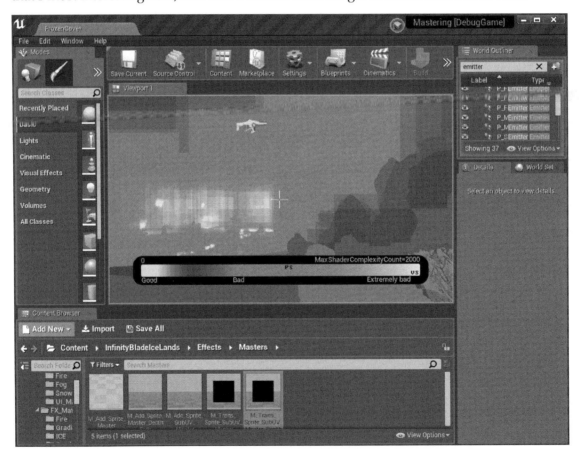

Yikes! As is obvious from the color scale at the bottom, there's something serious going on there in the middle, and of course, it's obvious it's the blowing snow/clouds that drift through the center of the map. What you'll often find on most platforms is your most hated foe from a performance standpoint is overdraw. Most developers are at least familiar with the term, but this is where the GPU is forced to draw then re-draw the same pixel on the screen a number of times. Translucence tends to be the biggest cause of overdraw, as is exactly the case here. We have a ton of giant particles, all with alpha translucence, on top of each other from a rendering standpoint (our camera's perspective). Thus to blend them all, those pixels where they overlap are redrawn a huge number of times, making those bright white spots of shader work. On a decent PC this is all fine and good as the framerate in even a non-optimized build is still 50+ fps for this level, but on other platforms (especially mobile devices), this will quickly become a nightmare scenario, discussed further in the next section.

In the meantime, since we don't have a dedicated chapter in this book on optimization, hopefully an overview of helpful tools and some links to further reading will suffice. First, get to know your stat ... command-line cheats. These can give you huge amounts of real-time data in-game, and being familiar with a number of them is always recommended. That said, the ones I recommend most highly are **stat CPU, stat GPU** (where you can easily see the cost of translucence), **stat Game,** and **stat FPS**, the latter of which should probably be turned on by default in almost every non-release build. Also of note, **stat Memory** is a huge help too, but for memory consumption, not directly performance. Figuring out where your game is bound of course is the key to knowing where to optimize to improve your framerate. Again, this is probably fairly common knowledge among most developers; but this simply means: is your main thread, render thread, or GPU cost the highest each frame. You're only as fast as the slowest member of that group, and the Profiler in the Session Frontend window was discussed very early on. It is a good tool for getting very detailed information about the first two (main/game thread and render thread) to see whether you are using up too much CPU. The `stat GPU` command is the fastest way to check whether that is your bottleneck, but for detailed information such as in the profiler, you can use **stat startfile** and **stat stopfile** to generate detailed information and also open it in the frontend window. On other platforms or for a different perspective, again, see NVIDIA's tools (mentioned earlier) or explore the many options each platform typically supplies to its developers. For a little bit more detail on UE4's options, a couple of links have been added to the *Further reading* section. Of note at this point, you can, even while simulating or running a level, begin editing materials (and remember to save them to propagate changes!) and see the results directly and immediately. So let's now explore a couple of options here with these blending particles as examples of this.

Know Your Platform and How to Adapt Shaders!

Knowing what platform you are developing for is obviously key to any performance optimization, especially in the graphics and shader department. For example, let's say we're aiming to include mid-performance Android phones and tablets as a platform. The fastest way to test what things may look like there is to go to the main editor menu's settings drop-down menu, then **Preview Rendering Level**, **Mobile / HTML5**, and pick **Android Preview**. At this point, you'll probably see this:

We're now having to rebuild something like 8,000+ shaders for this new platform, but as may have been noted, this happened the first time opening this level on PC as well. It simply has to be done once, then smaller changes will cause smaller shader recompilations, but initially, this can be several minutes of serious CPU utilization as it builds all of those shaders. Just know that it won't keep happening in this level once they're cached for this preview mode.

Once that's done, let's play again and show shader complexity again now that we're in OpenGL ES2 emulation in our viewport while playing:

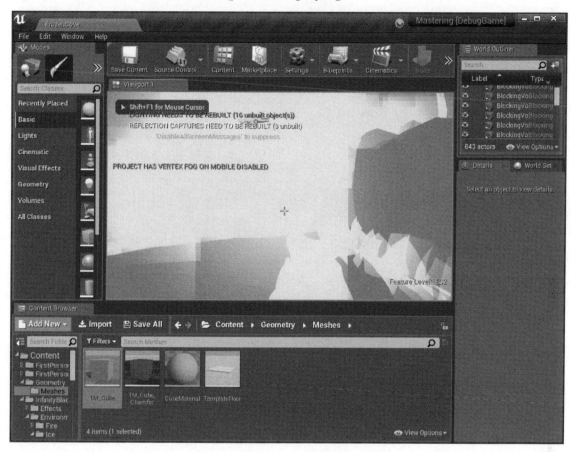

Yikes! Now that overdraw is getting serious. So what can we do?

Well, the most obvious approach, as these are just a cosmetic feature (and other than a bit of visibility, are not there to affect gameplay), we simply tell the particle emitters not to run at certain quality levels. This section is not on particle FX (but there is one coming later!) so we'll just briefly test this theory to prove our ES2 killing overdraw is coming from them specifically. Searching the level for emitters, eventually
P_Snow_BlowingLarge_particulates stands out and is in fact the culprit. Opening it up, we can click on the emitter with the large swirling cloud particles and set its **Detail Mode** to **Medium**, as shown here:

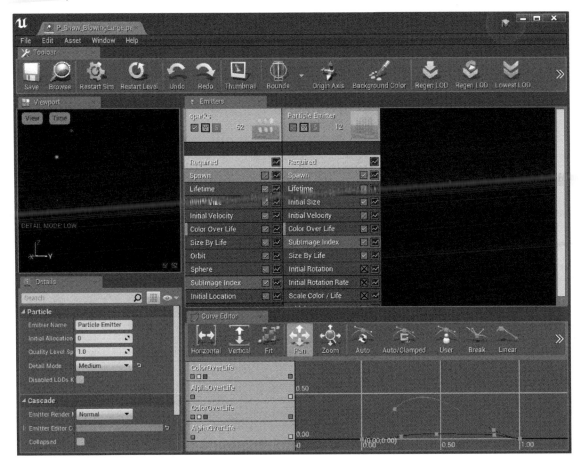

But, of course, nothing changes in our preview until we change the available performance levels there, too. Here, we'll want to modify the scalability settings we're using to preview this in-editor:

So, as shown here, we're going to set our current **Effects** level to **Low**, and voila, no more particles causing our biggest burning overdraw performance hit:

 Don't worry about the lighting rebuild warning here in-game, as you can't build precomputed lighting in the editor under ES2 emulation (which you conveniently can see is on in the bottom-right corner), and it's also saying the vertex fog this level uses won't work at all in this mode. Good information, but *always* be sure to test whenever possible on the actual devices themselves. The emulation is a great way to quickly iterate a few ideas, but until you actually test these changes on a proper device with its library and OS updated to whatever level is appropriate, and it's using its own drivers, you can't be sure your results will match anything like the best emulation you could hope for here.

While there are still plenty of things to worry about if we were to use this level on anything but higher-range Android devices (using ES3+ or other rendering), the biggest offender was just removed. But you may be asking, "*isn't this chapter about modifying materials to suit your needs?*" Yes, it certainly is. Let's find the material used in these particles. Tracing it from the emitters properties, it's a smoke-like material instance whose parent is a translucent material. A typical adjustment from high-end rendering to ES2 OpenGL or lower-end rendering is to turn those translucent materials into masked, and rather than sending a graded alpha in to the translucency channel, you just send a 1-bit mask, like here, in the grass material near the start point in the map:

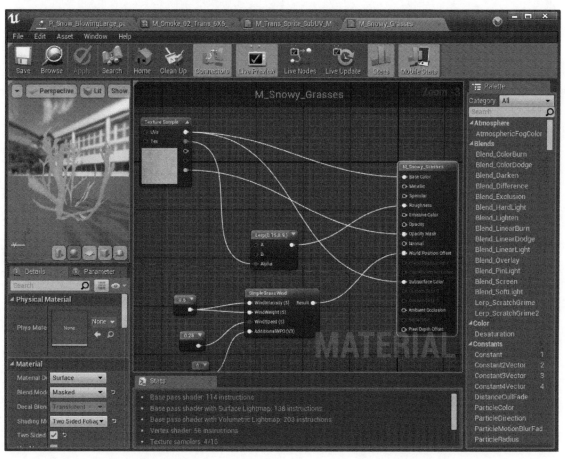

Note the alpha channel of the input texture going to the mask input of the shader (also interesting is the wind node which is used to shift the grass around at runtime, feel free to experiment with it, too). Now, we have some pros and cons to this of course. Pro: there's no overdraw where you see through the texture, because the mask tells the renderer to never draw the pixel in the first place! Con: you get hard edges where the mask falls, not smooth, subtle fading edges. We've all seen this in games before, but take a look here at the grass in our preview window:

This works OK for things such as plants, or literally holes in surfaces, but would look amateurish at best for something like a puff of a snowy cloud like the effect here. So what can be done with materials to address this? Let's get acquainted with by far the most helpful little node for this purpose, the quality switch. Here is the translucent material as it shipped with the level:

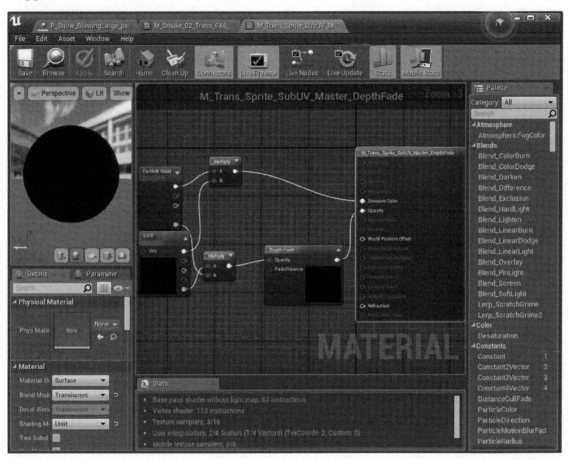

And here's how we can insert the quality node to set low-quality FX to not do this alpha blending business on those devices:

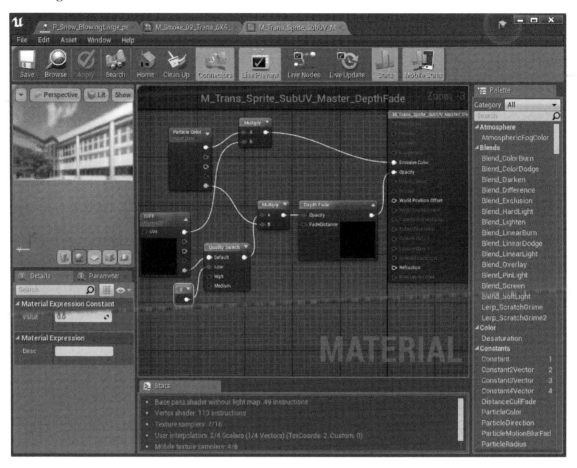

If we now set the particle system back to >= Low detail mode (so it always tries to emit), but keep our editor's scalability setting for effects to Low, the particles will also stop drawing and will not be a drag on our GPU performance anymore. This can be shown real time by playing the level before saving the change (or simply wiring the alpha of **DIFF** directly back into the **A** channel of the multiply node). With it wired up with the quality switch, save the material, and poof: the snowy cloud wisps are gone.

So, one last point here. That's all fine and good in the editor, but how do these things get set per platform, or even per device? Config (.ini) files. Keep in mind that in the Config folder of the project, you can have a subfolder for each relevant platform (so Config/Android, Config/Windows, Config/iOS, and so on), and for each Default... .ini in the base folder, you can create a platform-specific one in its folder (so, for example, DefaultEngine.ini is overridden on Android devices by `Config/Android/AndroidEngine.ini`). Config files are always applied from most specific to least specific, so if a property is in `AndroidEngine.ini`, the game's `Config/DefaultEngine.ini`, *and* the engine's `Config/BaseEngine.ini`, the `AndroidEngine.ini` propery will be the last one applied, and the one used at runtime. That said, if you're working with a significant number of devices, you'll likely want to add these properties at the game's `Config/DefaultDeviceProfiles.ini` level. Here's a quick rundown of what can be done there:

```
[DeviceProfiles]
+DeviceProfileNameAndTypes=Android_Adreno4xx_High,Android
```

Here we define a special named device and its type (Android).

```
[/Script/AndroidDeviceProfileSelector.AndroidDeviceProfileMatchingRules]
+MatchProfile=(Profile="Android_Adreno4xx_High",Match=((SourceType=SRC_GpuF
amily,CompareType=CMP_Regex,MatchString="Adreno \\(TM\\) 4[3-9][0-9]")))
```

This chunk tells the engine how to figure out whether the device it's started on is running that device type (by searching for the GPU type):

```
[Android DeviceProfile]
+CVars=r.BloomQuality=1
+CVars=r.Shadow.MaxResolution=1024
+CVars=r.MaterialQualityLevel=2
```

Here we have a couple of default values for an Android device (all of them unless overridden more specifically after):

```
[Android_High DeviceProfile]
+CVars=r.MaterialQualityLevel=1
+CVars=r.MobileContentScaleFactor=2.0
+CVars=r.ShadowQuality=5
+CVars=r.DetailMode=2
```

This is a profile for high-performance Android properties to use:

```
[Android_Adreno4xx_High DeviceProfile]
DeviceType=Android
BaseProfileName=Android_High
```

And lastly, we simply set the specific Adreno4xx_High type to the Android_High type, but we could at that point set any properties we wanted to different levels as well. For our material, in the profiles we wanted the snowy clouds not to show up, so we'd simply set the following:

```
+r.DetailMode=0
```

In a more general fashion, you can set (Platform)Scalability.ini's sg.EffectsQuality to 0, as is shown in great detail in the scalability reference link from Epic in the *Further reading* section.

One warning: at the end of the GitHub project for this chapter, .uasset file types were added to Git's LFS system because of some very large assets. Jumping back to earlier projects will turn any later changed .uasset pointers back into .uasset data objects and confuse LFS, which may require you to fix your local branch by doing a hard reset to before this LFS change (commit c24d2db), then doing a hard reset to the changelist or branch forward that you wanted to work in if it refuses to let you discard .uasset changes because it says it can't parse the pointer (thinking it should be an LFS pointer, not a binary .uasset). All maintained branches going forward (Chapter-9, master, and the new In-Progress) will be set to have their .uassets tracked properly. It's only an issue when jumping back, but hopefully these tips can get past it for any who do.

Summary

For those already familiar with UE4's material system, hopefully this was a good review and came with some new information or pointers along the way. For those who were previously inexperienced, you should now have a solid foundation to build upon for driving a team and project forward and making the right decisions with the most commonly used powerful tools that Unreal makes available. There is always more to learn, but having a level of competence across areas such as this is mandatory for being able to take a project to a higher level and demonstrate to a team the skills and knowledge needed to manage such a complex and powerful world that UE4's materials offer every project. Finally, as promised, for those familiar with writing HLSL or GLSL directly, and wondering what this looks like for UE4, take a look in the Engine's Shaders/Private folder at things such as VolumetricFog.usf. For those who want to get started down this path or who are new to Unreal's way of compiling shaders themselves, another great link is in the *Further reading* section for just that pursuit.

Questions

1. What is the difference between a material and a material instance?
2. A material instance is only meaningful if adding a very specific node type to a material. What is that type?
3. Simulation from the play drop-down menu can be helpful. What things did it reveal in this chapter?
4. What is the purpose of a dynamic material instance, and where/when can they be made?
5. What is the key tool for finding GPU-killing shaders in an area of a map?
6. Which command-line options are most helpful for profiling any and all performance problems?
7. What node is your best friend when trying to tune materials across various platforms?
8. How can per-platform settings across almost all significant performance factors be set?

Further reading

NVIDIA PerfKit (Android and PC):

```
https://developer.nvidia.com/nvidia-perfkit
```

UE4 CPU profiling:

```
https://docs.unrealengine.com/en-us/Engine/Performance/CPU
```

UE4 GPU profiling:

```
https://docs.unrealengine.com/en-US/Engine/Performance/GPU
```

Unreal scalability reference:

```
https://docs.unrealengine.com/en-us/Engine/Performance/Scalability/
ScalabilityReference
```

Unreal Shader development (.usf, including HLSL/GLSL cross-compiling explained):

```
https://docs.unrealengine.com/en-us/Programming/Rendering/ShaderDevelopment
```

Adding an In-game Cutscene with Sequencer

9

Introduction

Many games made with UE4 are known for having excellent in-engine and in-game cutscenes. Traditionally, these were made with the tool/system known as Matinee. These days, Sequencer is the new-and-improved system for creating these scenes and is being widely adopted in modern UE4 titles. The last section of this chapter will deal a bit with Matinee, namely, why it isn't used anymore. Games going back many years have done just fine with Matinee and it's still a viable tool; but first, let's get to know Sequencer and its capabilities and a bit of what working with it is like.

- Sequencer basics
- Adding a scene
- Track editing
- Sequencer alternatives
- Dialog system, blueprint scripting
- Matinee

Technical requirements

This chapter will use specific assets added over the course of the GitHub project. To follow the practical examples, please start with the Chapter 9 GitHub branch: https://github.com/PacktPublishing/Mastering-Game-Development-with-Unreal-Engine-4-Second-Edition/tree/Chapter-9.

Engine version used: 4.19.2.

Sequencer – UE4's newest cutscene tool

Sequencer was launched around UE4 4.12 to replace (or rather, succeed) Matinee, and if a content developer or team has no experience with Matinee, and even if you do, it's the best place to work. It's similar enough that those with experience with any other sort of keyframe track-based tool can use it, it's easy enough to pick up, and will be the technology that Epic is using and improving going forward. Getting familiar with its capabilities is key for any game hoping to incorporate great-quality cutscenes into their game, whether they're simple arrangements of actors in a level that the player can passively view, or cinematic-quality fully-controlled scenes to help convey narrative and story. So let's take a look at what it can do.

Why use sequencer?

As discussed, sequencer is the technology to use going forward and has a massive amount of options and power for proficient users. As this is designed to help give a holistic knowledge of the engine's capabilities, and not a content-creation specialization course, we'll likely only scratch the surface of what's possible with the tool; but knowing what it can do, and how it can help you, is crucial to making those early decisions in content pipeline and delivering the best experience possible to your audience.

A quick aside, for those following the GitHub project closely, you'll notice some commits in this chapter's beginning, which get it to build and run for HTML5 (tested on PC/Chrome, and Mac/Safari – the latter seems to have some stability issues, but is testable now). Code-side, most of these are simply headers that the build does not otherwise pick up on as the Windows build did, this is fairly common with various platforms, but things like this:

```
#include "Engine/World.h"
```

In `MasteringInventory.cpp` are harmless to the Windows build as it already picked up on the header elsewhere. But back to Sequencer.

While the history of sequencer's addition and its ongoing and future support are reason enough to use it, a quick overview of its capabilities is in order. What does it do? Is there anything it can't do? Let's list a few of its more common features and their uses:

- **Level Sequences**: These are where the bulk of the work is done in Sequencer Cinematics, they can be individual end-to-end scenes, or a hierarchy of subsequences (more level-sequence objects)
- **Master Sequences**: Generally used to manage groups or dynamic-level sequence and shot objects, but can work as a thin wrapper for a standalone level sequence (adding a few options)
- **Shot Track**: This is a track that can be added to a sequence, but is also saved as a standalone asset, it is the most fundamental track, typically controlling camera, focus, and so on
- **Takes**: Upon arranging multiple shots in a shot track, a take object can be made, which is that particular sequence of the shot track, and takes can be swapped with each other to quickly iterate the feel and flow of a shot
- **Actor to Sequencer Track**: These are used to add individual actors from the level to a sequence, this is how things in the world are moved and animated within a sequence

While there are many other components, these are the primary ones we can use to get immediately familiar with Sequencer's basic and most commonly used features. First however, we'll also need to just lay some background changes into our **FirstPersonExampleMap** to get prepared. In the GitHub project, you'll notice several changes without much direct effect at the moment: lighting was brightened back up again, the boxes except for the one special one were made to not use their special flashing (distracting) material, and a "backstage" area was added just under our main floor:

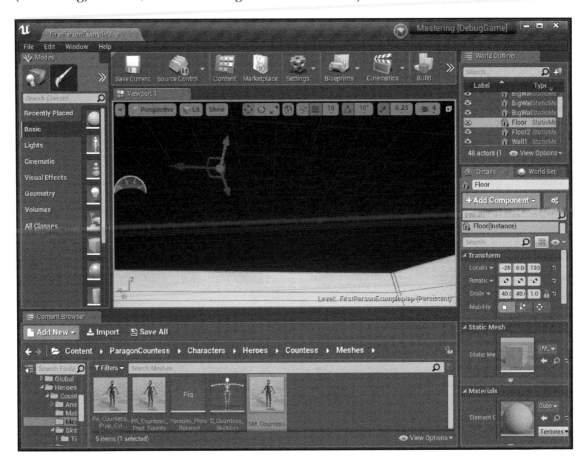

A super convenient way to duplicate an object is just to drag its transform in a direction while holding the *Alt* key (the *command* key on Mac); this will make a copy and move it in the direction you want – in this case, a duplicated floor moving directly below our existing floor.

Once we have a plane to place our scene's actors on, we some new items to make our scene interesting. First, we'll head to the content browser's **Add New** button and at the very top is the option for **Add Feature or Content Pack...**, we'll use this twice. Be sure to first click on the root, Content folder, in the content browser so everything goes to the right level; you're welcome to organize assets as you or your team see fit; but this will make it match what is in GitHub and if you're clever can save the GitHub download time (as this content is already on your computer from getting the full source of the engine, in `Chapter 1`, *Making a C++ Project for a First Person Shooter*, adding it just copies it over from the engine's content folder to your project). We'll add from the **Blueprint Feature** tab the **Third Person** pack, and from the **Content Packs** tab, **Starter Content**:

These have a number of assets that we likely won't use, which adds to the overall size in GitHub; but will *not* add to the game's package size on platforms unless directly referenced in a level by another asset (or the level itself), or added to the force cook list, which will be gone over in great detail in the next chapter!

So now we can add our new assets to the backstage area. Keep two things in mind when making such a backstage area:

- The player should never be able to see it or access it
- It should have similar lighting to where you place the actors there so their lighting doesn't noticeably "pop" when added to another area during a sequence.

Note also, you can make characters in a sequence "spawn" on cue, so they're not visible anyway (we'll demonstrate this); but then you are also potentially paying the cost of a synchronous load (if the character was not otherwise previously loaded) at the time you do, so beware. Here's how our backstage is shaping up:

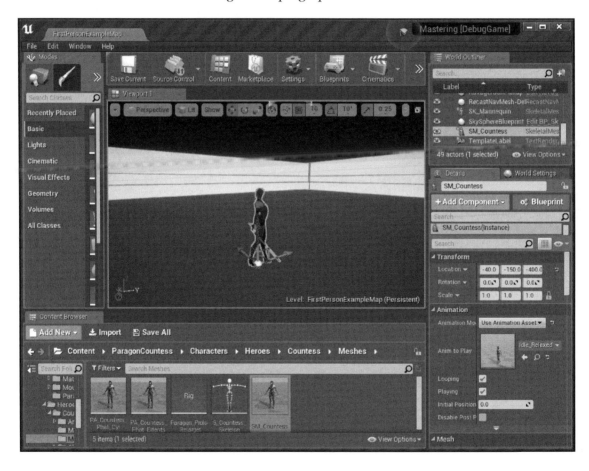

Now notice, this is a plain skeletal mesh, not even a pawn, and importantly, is using as its animation "mode" on the right: **Use Animation Asset** *not* using the Animation Blueprint we made elsewhere as this will override what we try to do animation-wise in our sequence. The mannequin character, which most readers probably know well from Epic's templates, is similarly setup to not use the AnimBP, for our sequence's benefit. You can also see here that we can add that main-level sequence from the **Cinematics** button in the top main menu. I prefer to add these in the content folder, where the map is housed, since they tend to be closely associated; but it's certainly possible and reasonable to make a separate Cinematics folder or something similar:

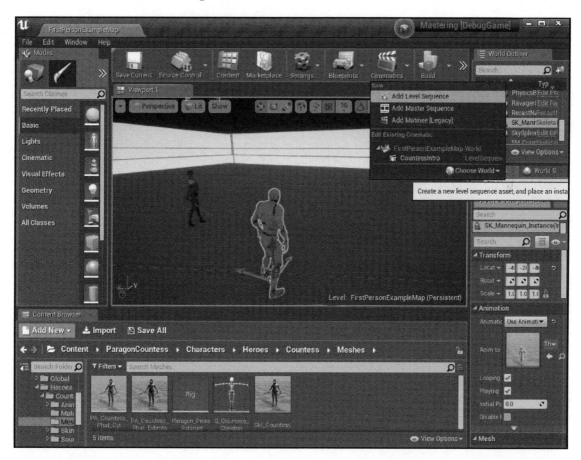

As I had already added the scene when this shot was taken, you can see it in the editable cinematics, where it is named **CountessIntro** and kept in **FirstPersonExampleMap**. From here, we can get on with the fun of actually making and triggering a cutscene!

Adding a scene and triggering it

We've added an empty barebones-level sequence to our map now, but how do we use it? Let's quickly go over the triggering side of things, then we can get to making a fairly basic scene and watching it play. We'll then up the quality and detail it with some interesting options. The very first thing to do when working on a scene such as this, though, is to give yourself a proper view to do it from, so in the viewport drop-down, select the **Two Panes** layout seen here:

 Make sure when using the cinematic preview window that you have your cinematic camera selected, it's easy to forget and that's the one that will be used during the scene of course.

With the left pane selected, set it (in the same drop-down arrow in the top-left) to **Cinematic Preview**. So now with a dedicated cinematic preview pane, it's easy to work quickly on the scene itself. But there's one more step before we get started there – we need a space we can use and a trigger volume:

Also note that in the GitHub project, the platform, which begins up in the air in the scene, is just one of our level's boxes scaled flat, and with **Simulate Physics** and **Enable Gravity** both unchecked in its properties. The trigger volume is set to only detect overlapping pawns and, as will be seen in the level blueprint, destroys itself upon being triggered once by a mastering character:

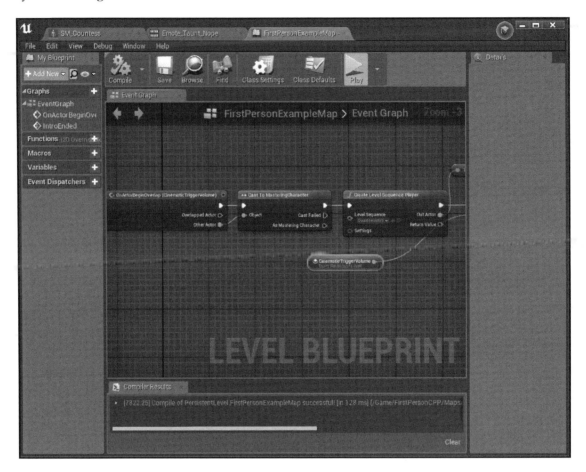

though to show that this blueprint needed to be split to two shots, but you can see the trigger volume is then the immediate actor destroyed, and we have then created a level sequence player and done one other clever thing or two at the end of the scene:

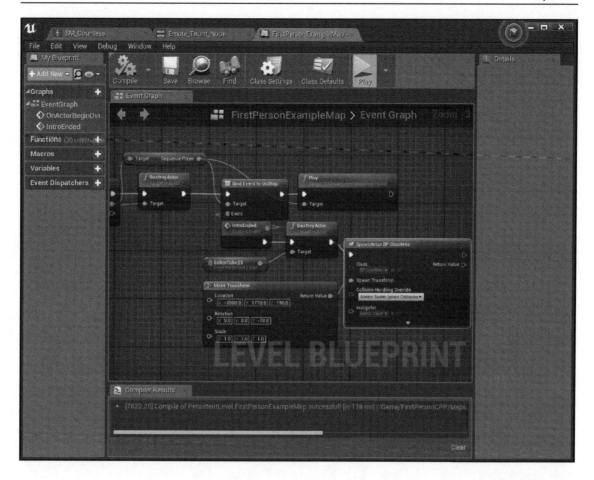

At this point, our sequence actually plays, but until we have it do something, it should just immediately end and destroy the platform and spawn **BP_Countess**. So before we get to the "how" of the scene, let's jump ahead for a second to the "what" of the scene: when the player walks into this corner, the countess rides down to the ground on a platform, playing her turn-in-place animation to face outward, pauses with an idle for a moment at the bottom, then plays a taunt animation in front of her. This is all from, of course, our backstage skeletal mesh countess, so this one can't take damage and has no running AI. At the end of the sequence (noted by the event we bound to that), we destroy the platform she rode in on, the skeletal mesh is automatically returned backstage, and we replace at the same transform (with a 90-degree turn since we have that set in the **BP_Countess** class' mesh) a fully-functional AI version.

Now on to the basic sequence itself:

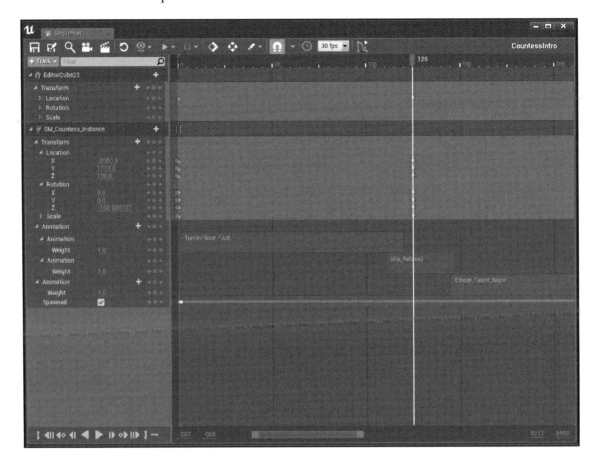

First, we need to add our two actors for this basic scene to the sequence, so double-click the **CountessIntro** to open it up and click the **+Track** button near the top. It's easiest if you already have the actor selected in the world (in this case our platform, and the countess skeletal mesh instance respectively) as they will then appear at the top to add instead of searching. Once added, it's best to add a transform keyframe right where they are currently at (assuming this is the desired start point for each actor). You can do this by clicking the transform as a whole, or like for our platform, you really only need its location selected. When the track is selected and the time slider (red notch at top with the line down the tracks) is at the start (click the <I I looking icon at the bottom to send it there), hit *Enter*, or you can click the tiny + icon between the left and right arrows in the track selector section to add one. Most content developer used to any sort of keyframing interface (animation in the major packages, other cinematic tools) should quickly get the hang of changing transforms and keyframing.

For the simplest example, selecting this platform, scrubbing the time slider forward to 125 , moving the platform down to ground level, and adding another keyframe in the sequence editor, will now let you scrub between, or play from the start, the sequence and see the platform move between the keyframes. You'll notice the keyframe is an orange circle by default; in this case, I right-clicked that starting keyframe and set its interpolation to linear (green triangle) so there's no acceleration on the motion as it moves from the start keyframe to the end keyframe. Similarly, for the countess, you'll see a square at the -1 unit mark, which moves her to be standing on the platform. Along with this, right-click the countess instance name/area itself and set it to **Convert to Spawnable**, this prevents a super-fast, but visible, motion from underground to the top of the platform. There are a number of alternate solutions to this; but since the backstage countess is always spawned at the start of the level, there's no load-time hit for keyframing the spawn. So at time 0, uncheck the **Spawned** box and add a keyframe to the **Spawned** track. At time 1, check it, add another keyframe. See also of course that there is a Constant type keyframe (blue box) of her translation and rotation (simply snaps to these) at time zero. Now she neatly appears there at the start of the scene (you could add a nice effect to this or whatever else makes sense for your design). To have the translation with the platform exactly match, I actually keyframed them, selected together with both of their translation tracks set as I moved the two actors down to the ground and set the first keyframe at time zero, then scrubbed to 125, moved them both down, and set both actors' second keyframes (and again, both to linear motion). I then did a curved rotation from facing away from the inside of the map, to facing in towards it, but in that case only selecting her rotation track as I set the initial rotation at 0, left it defaulted to **Cubic (auto)** transform type, and then at time 125, rotated her to face in the map and set the second keyframe.

If you view it as it stands, you can walk around wherever you like, see the scene play out once it's triggered, and then interact with a "normal" version of the countess upon its completion (which should be based on its vision sense, generally immediately comes after the player). She's currently not animating, so adding from her instance's **Track+** button (to the right of her name, **SM_Countess_Instance**), you'll notice in the screenshot and GitHub, you can add multiple animations to one animation track, or multiple animation tracks. Here, one of each is done, picking her turning animation until down to the ground, putting a bit of overlap on her idle animation so there's not a visible pop between, and then adding a track to play her taunt and scrubbing its start until it also just overlaps the idle a little. In many games, this is exactly the level of "cinematic" experience needed. We'll put some audio on this for a more authentic feel; this is a fairly traditional "in-game" scene, rather than a dedicated "cinematic" cutscene which typically takes away player control and directly manipulates the camera. We'll handle this quickly here with the aforementioned audio.

When working with the vast majority of tracks in Sequencer, double-clicking will size that track in your editor window to the length of the sequence, double-clicking again will bring it back to a typically more zoomed-in level. This is great when you want an overall look at your sequence.

Under **Content/FirstPersonCPP/Maps**, add one more **LevelSequence** object (found under **Animation** if you right-click in the content browser) to it: **IntroShot1**. Opening shot 1, it's not very helpful as it's not "attached" to our sequence, but for rapidly making a number of shots focusing on actors that don't have to keyframe into existence as ours does, this can be a very useful tool, making many level sequences used as shots in a single sequence. For reference, I did use several shots in experimenting with this scene (and again, we're learning the tech and its capabilities, not proving artistic talent here!), but in the end found using a few select keyframe types in a single shot worked best for this scene, so that is the only one checked in to GitHub. However, using multiple shots, combining them into Takes, and quickly swapping those in and out of a single sequence has a very handy link from Epic in the *Further reading* section for those interested. The sheer depth and breadth of what is capable with Sequencer can be overwhelming, but once again: know your project's level of expectations and your team's ability to deliver, and you'll succeed every time where other teams fail.

Now, on to finishing up our screen; in the countess intro sequence, add a track with the + button at the top and select **Shot Track**. Using the + shot button, add our **IntroShot1**. Again just for the sake of learning, it's fair to point out that I did lay out much of this track in the level as its own sequence, before importing, but had to do a bit of tweaking afterwards, which is a bit more difficult as you're manipulating **CineCameraActor** directly in the level in viewports at that point, though you can always dedicate a viewport specifically to that camera actor for keyframing. Looking at the shot, you'll see linear keyframes as we follow the countess descending, a pair of constant keyframes I use as a jump cut (rather than an alternate shot, but that's always an option as noted), and then some more cubic keyframes as the camera pans out:

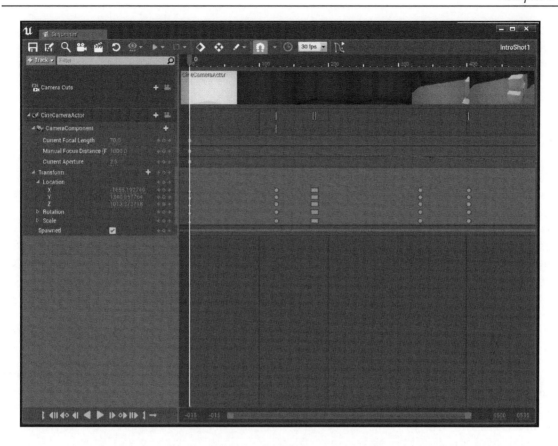

Note: your subtracks only exist for as long as they are set to in their parent sequence! In many cases, you may need to drag their end-time in the parent sequence to snap to the end of itself, to edit that subtrack in the sequence editor. Another is you can right click many tracks to allow the end-result to persist after the cinematic plays, this is very useful for moving entities around and then having them resume the game after the sequence exactly where they were placed, for example.

Back in the intro sequence itself, it's then just a matter of adding an audio track with a taunt at the right time (of course the scene could do with a good deal more audio). Lastly, add the mannequin to the scene to give the player a sense of their own location in perspective, but note that this is a fixed location as we're spawning the skeletal mesh into the cutscene once again, since the player's first-person pawn is even less palatable to look at. If you compare the first version of the scene where the player views it from their perspective against this final version, the differences should be highly obvious – and professional content creators can do even more impressive things once made aware of the tools available!

CineCamera Actors are immensely powerful in and of themselves. Now that we have one in this scene, feel free to explore what it can do, and check out the link from Epic in the *Further reading* section for some more useful info.

Let's do one final bit of cleanup while the camera is in the scene, hide our reticle. Via the triggering and ending blueprint events, we hide the whole HUD, but this is the only visible piece in our game:

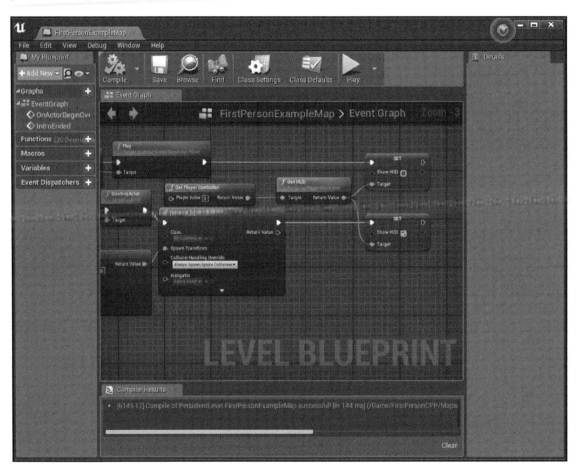

And that's it! Without too much pain, the essentials of getting a cutscene are in and can be built upon for any level of professionalism needed with a little more experimentation and invested time.

> Don't forget that when working with embedded sequences, you will frequently need to save the shot, the sequence the shot is contained in, and the level the sequence is in. Keep the volume of changes and the versioning-control of your levels in mind when creating a workflow. It's entirely possible to create a duplicate level and have cinematic artists work here while level designers work in the "real" level so they don't collide with binary assets you can't merge; but of course that means extra work making sure what each does remains in sync as they both evolve their pieces!

Alternatives to sequencer

The main goal of this chapter is to build familiarity and confidence with Sequencer. That said, if a team doesn't have time (or the need!) to generate such cinematic cutscenes, what else is available? Most games will require some level of scripted scenes to help the story learn the game (tutorials) or give story exposition, immersion, and emotional impact at certain moments. But given all that UE4 has to offer and that we've touched on several of these things, it's worth diving in a bit further to ensure the right tool is being used for the job.

Fast and easy in-game scenes

There are a few important ways to consider in-game scenes without the full Sequencer-based cinematic demonstrated in the last section. Here is a quick list of options and common uses:

- **The Dialog system**: This was discussed in some detail in `Chapter 7`, *Getting Audio in Your Game* with additional reading to help those using it further. Dialog is great for characters interacting with audio (and potentially animations) in the game, with customized localization text and tunable audio between individual character types (so dialog to a male character can differ from female, or friends versus enemies in a scene). That said, the flow of dialog, animations played, and the level of player control is largely up to the designer making these interactions, Dialog is more of an audio and flow-control tool than a full scene-creating device, hence our next possibility.

- **Blueprint**: With enough effort, you can do just about anything you can imagine (including, as noted in `Chapter 3`, *Blueprint Review and When to Use BP Scripting*, creating entire games) in blueprint. It's all just a matter of managing complexity in the end; but taking away player control, setting a specific camera actor, triggering that to play movement along a spline, delayed animations with audio playing, and special FX are all completely doable with blueprint. There is a huge amount of information on any subsection of blueprint you might want to learn more about for this context, too, and great community support if you run into any problems. The biggest drawback is that there is a steep learning curve to using blueprint this fully, and there is a huge amount of risk both for error when used by team members not deeply trained in what should maybe be "off-limits" without a deep level of training, and maintaining these massive graphs of logic can get overwhelming. Constantly reducing reused bits of logic into function libraries and oversight (or content being created) by highly technical people often mitigate these issues, but beware before launching it on unsuspecting artists!

- **Simple Sequences**: Our intro scene from the last section should be entirely manageable in a matter of hours simply going through this lesson even without any familiarity with Sequencer. The simple version in the first half will take a fraction of that time, if merely positioning actors, playing some animations, and maybe putting in a few cool effects is all that's needed, technical and non-technical types should be able to manage these with minimal training.

And what was that way back at the top about Matinee? Read on!

Matinee

As has probably been hammered home enough by now, basically anything Epic's previous tool, which is kept for legacy purposes, could do, Sequencer can also do. That said, there can arise situations where someone has a great deal of experience with Matinee, or maybe an outsourcing group still uses it, and they want to quickly bring that to bear on a project. Other than the already-stated reasons of Sequencer being the supported tool going forward, there's not a specific reason Matinee can't be used still. Matinee has been a classic for having flying cars loop around buildings in smooth parabolic curved circuits. It was the mainstay of cinematic work in any number of classic UE3 and all early UE4 titles. Anyone having just gone through the Sequencer work should immediately recognize a lot of familiar themes opening up the Matinee editor:

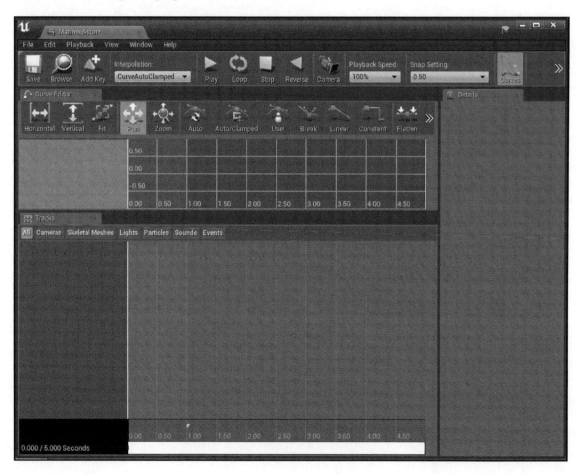

While the main striking difference is the curve-editing tools on the front face of Matinee, fear not, all these controls and some new perks are available in Sequencer (check out the tool button near the top of sequencer to view as a curve, and select a transform or other track with keyframes):

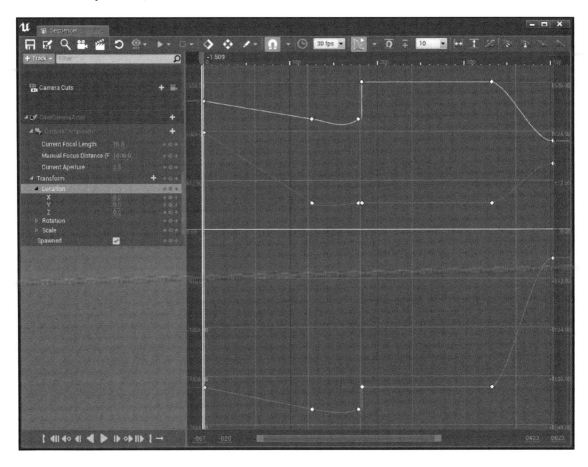

Regardless of what ultimately works best, knowing the options available is the name of the game in making your project a success, and in all likelihood, you'll end up using any number of the options available in some combination; but by now at least the risks and possibilities should be clear from the start.

Summary

Sequencer is an amazing tool, people are literally making cinematic-quality movies in it in realtime these days with the technology Epic has made available, which is a wondrous thing. Like most aspects of UE4, these are deep topics and each of these can (and likely will) have experts in their field; but as a leader and driver of technology in a team, using them all with a level of comfort and knowing how they can and do all interact is held in extremely high value. Sequencer, and other available tools, can enhance any game and get it out the door to eager players hungry for more. Speaking of that, our next chapter will cover how to actually *reach* those players with your project.

Questions

1. What is the main reason to become familiar with Sequencer and use it going forward?
2. What are the most commonly-used tracks added in Sequencer?
3. How do you get an actor into a track?
4. Why not use a pawn with an animation blueprint directly in Sequencer?
5. What is the purpose and benefit of using level-sequence Shots? How do they relate to tracks?
6. What is a major risk of having sequences embedded in your map levels directly?
7. If blueprint scripting can do almost anything a sequence can do, what's the risk of using it for cutscenes?
8. How can you fine-tune the curves of keyframes in Sequencer?

Further reading

Multiple Shots and Takes:

```
https://docs.unrealengine.com/en-US/Engine/Sequencer/HowTo/TracksShot
```

CineCamera Actors:

```
https://docs.unrealengine.com/en-US/Engine/Sequencer/HowTo/CineCameraActors
```

Packaging the Game (PC, Mobile) **10**

Introduction

Getting your game successfully out to an audience is quite possibly the most underrated and absolutely necessary skill in being a user of UE4. In this chapter, we will explore a couple of those avenues. Every team and every project will need to explore their respective platforms, but the process is fairly similar across each, with their own specifics of course. For some it's definitely more complicated to get to an audience than others, but hopefully by the end of this chapter you will have a good idea of the expectations to bring a product to just about any market. In this chapter we'll cover:

- Packaging the game for the PC
- Android and iOS setup
- When and how to make standalone installed versions of the game
- Build and run on Android and iOS
- Compare UE4's play vs. package builds
- Tips to avoid downtime to builds

Technical requirements

Specific examples and references will be made with, and tested in, the Chapter 10 GitHub branch, but as usual, the principles and processes described can be applied to any project. Additionally, the game will be built for and tested on at least two devices: Windows and Visual Studio installed to a Samsung Galaxy Note 8 for Android, and macOS and Xcode used to build and install on an iPad Mini 3 for iOS. While neither of these setups or platforms is required for the lessons here, hopefully they provide valuable insight and information for those who do need it. And lastly, for any number of freely-available browsers (Chrome primarily here on both Mac and PC), an HTML5 build will be created and deployed: `https://github.com/PacktPublishing/Mastering-Game-Development-with-Unreal-Engine-4-Second-Edition/tree/Chapter-10`.

Engine version used: 4.19.2.

Know your platform(s)

Of course, packaging a game is very different on every platform you can put it on. Building, submitting, and launching a game for iOS is a wholly different experience and process from PS4 or PC ,say, via Steam. Obviously the first question to ask is, "What is our audience, and which platforms will we deliver on?" The great part about UE4 is that of any platform you are likely to put out a game, it has a path and it can make a build that runs on that platform. We'll go through a few examples here, though Xbox and PS4 are different creatures as they require more direct involvement of their hosts (Microsoft and Sony, respectively), whereas the platforms here tend to be a little less restrictive.

It's always good to partner up with someone who has experience in the final stages of setting up a project for deployment from a platform. For example, Microsoft has for Xbox and other areas Developer Account Managers (DAMs) who partner up with medium- and large-sized projects, and this is generally left to a studio's production team to establish contacts and facilitate communication with the development team. That said, for independent developers, this may sound obvious, but partner up if you can with other indie devs who have had success on your platform. The communities in these areas are generally quite inclusive and supportive. Everybody needs a little help sometimes, and contributing to, and being a part of, such relationships is another underrepresented advantage to successful game development.

Setting up an installable PC version and general settings

Probably the easiest platform for UE4 to package on is the PC (or Mac): you're already running on one, and most likely the work you've done and tested in PIE will just "work" on PC when you package a build. That said, we'll explore what it takes to prepare to make a version for the most popular mobile platforms of Android (an installable .APK) and iOS (a similar .IPA. Note that for the latter (iOS), to actually build and properly test, *unless making a blueprint only game*, requires an Apple developer license, which as of this writing costs about $99 for a one-year subscription. If this is one of your target platforms, it's usually best to just get that license as early as possible; but for hobbyists and indie developers on a budget, please do note that deploying and testing on Android and HTML5 with the project presented here works just fine and is free.

For specific platform users, please note that a Windows 10 PC and Visual Studio were used to build, test, and deploy Android (which won't work from a Mac), and to build, test, and deploy iOS, a MacBook Pro with Xcode was used (and won't work on a PC without a Mac of some sort, as code changes have been made to our project). It is possible to build iOS builds from a PC with a Mac in the network; but this was often found to be problematic both in a professional mid-sized studio and team, and in home development for this book. If it works easily and reliably for you, congratulations, but the steps to set that up will only be presented in the *Further reading* section.

Before diving into an Android build, here are some general notes for in this case, both mobile platforms discussed here. First, for those curious, the next section will specifically address some of the differences between using the Play button in the editor on a device/platform combination compared to the packaging discussed in the rest of this section, so if that seems missing at this stage, just be patient. Here are some general settings for our project for cooking and packaging all platforms should simply have set, let's look at here under **Project/Packaging**:

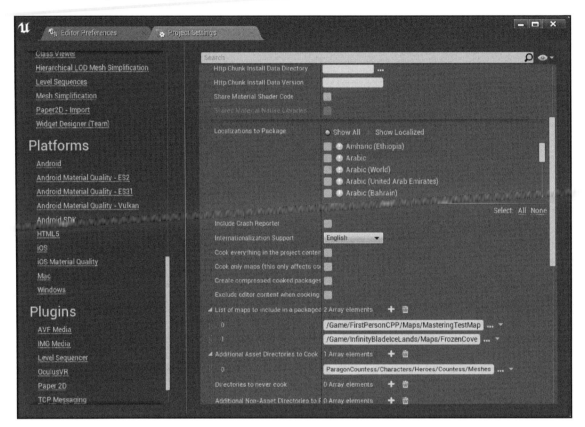

Since FrozenCove, for example, is only referenced "lightly" by name in the level-transition volume of our default map. We add it (and similarly MasteringTestMap) to the always-included list above:

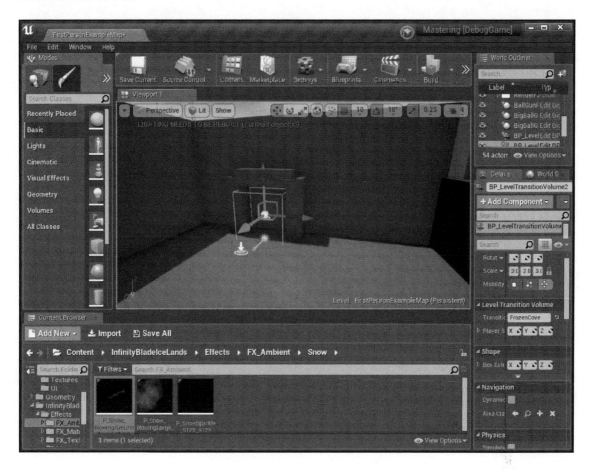

Additionally, since she can be spawned potentially dynamically without a hard reference, we cook in the Countess's Meshes folder (really it's just as an example of what you may need to do when you have assets you may load and use that aren't hard-referenced in maps directly). If you browse around under each platform's options in the platform section of project settings, you'll notice they all have splash-screen textures you can set, and many have resolution or orientation options that your team can (and should) set as appropriate.

Android setup

Those things handled, we move on to building on for Android. First, go to your engine install's `/Extras/AndroidWorks/Win64` folder and launch the executable there. This will automatically take you through what's needed to successfully build a UE4 Android project, and the basic integration for Visual Studio. There are several differences between doing local Android builds and release-to-public Android builds regarding store keys (or an upload key, which I recommend), and what's helpful to avoid me simply copying all these URLs into Further Reading is that Epic integrates links directly to the information you need in the project settings for the Android platform, see here:

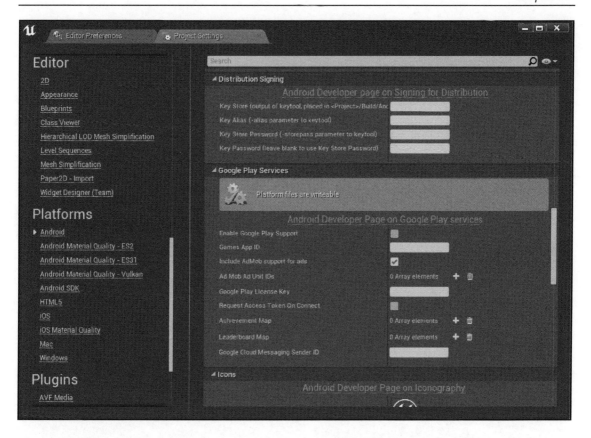

Those blue links should take you to up-to-date Android pages on those topics. There, you can read all about the various methods for singing and submitting your build to the Google Play store, and a link to signing up for a Key Store. As that process is then specific to a given project and the team's choices (the links give good background I don't need to repeat here), here are just a couple of quick general notes that will lead into the more technical next topic: for those who don't know already, in the Play store, you can restrict your title by excluding certain types of hardware, specific phones, or devices, restrict it showing up only to users with a certain Android version (which should match the one you set here in Epic's project settings!), and have a great deal of options on their end for what specifics your game is presented to, or restricted from. Typically, a project manager or other team member dedicated to this will set up those specifics on the Play web interface for your project, but from a technical standpoint, it is critical to know what those options mean, and how they are compatible with the builds you're generating and uploading. Here is a specific example that was obvious to see:

One of the most basic loadouts for Android is building with open GL ES2, and ETC2 compression, the former in Project Settings (more on that in a moment), the latter selected here, with one of those choices being a multi-config you can tune:

Now, ETC2 is a very widely-distributed and supported texture-compression for Android, and ES2 is a base-level Open GL ES version on a huge swath of older phones and tablets. If built with these two settings, the build will fail when trying to compile shaders. If you simply change to a newer compression routine, ASTC, you'll notice things build, but the Countess shows up with the grey-checkered default texture. Her material will not fail the build in ASTC, but it also is not rendered correctly in ES2. The problem is easy to track down if you go check on one of those materials:

ES2 is no good here, the most obvious solution is to change to ES3.1 for our Android builds, as it recommends:

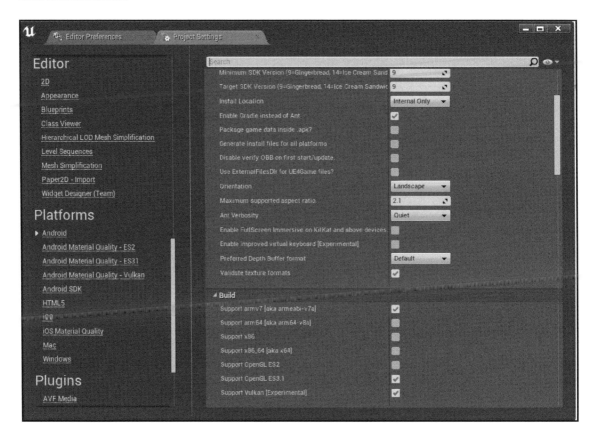

And in this case, our build builds and packages successfully and the Countess looks great on the Galaxy Note 8 used here (but that's a high-end phone as of this writing and rather expensive). So what happens if your team wants the game to run on older devices? Well, that's where the quality switch referenced in `Chapter 8`, *Shader Editing and Optimization Tips* comes in:

If you double-click that node (**MF_CharacterEffects**), you'll notice we're skipping only one specific aspect of the material (death fade); but that's often the case, if you make one project that needs to work across a large array of devices and capabilities. ES2 builds just skip the problematic feature entirely, and now ETC2/ES2 builds are successful and run fine, though this did of course require saving several materials affected and rebuilding a ton of shaders, yet again, so beware of these kinds of risks! Note also, it's perfectly acceptable, and quite common, to have separate "SKUs" (think product model) of a game that can be delivered to different sets of hardware. A game doesn't have to be made to be tolerant of all possible hardware combinations it may be installed to, but it's desirable if you can, especially for multiplayer games. If maintaining this tolerance of high- and low-end potential platforms becomes unreasonable, set up one SKU for high-end, set up another for low-end, and just be ready to double-up (or otherwise multiply) your builds, and their testing time, every time you need to release updates.

One last thing, you'll notice that Android has an option to package assets into .apk – for a very small project this might be ok, but for most projects (including even this small one) it's advisable not to use this. This will generate an .obb file for the project, which the Play store knows how to handle downloading and installing, and makes life much simpler especially if small .apk changes are needed (such as bug fixes) with no asset changes to the project. People can test and run, and you can submit builds much faster if you're not including hundreds of MB or 1+ GB of assets in every build and just working with a typical dozen-MB-sized .apk.

iOS setup

Similar to Android's Play Store Key, Apple has a rather arcane, but well-defined, process of generating keys and signing its .ipa packages to deploy to your iOS devices for testing. In the end, what you're using should look something like this with nice "**Valid**" sections everywhere, for both a development signing Provisioning Profile, and Certificate, as well as various Ad-hoc or other production profile/certificate combinations:

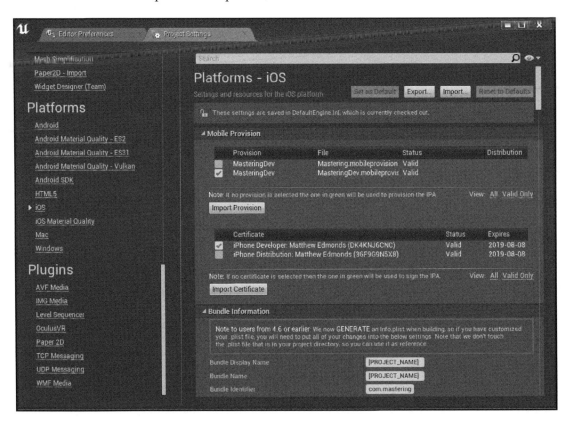

Links for all of Apple's steps for this are listed here, since Epic does not link them directly as it does for Android. Note, you'll need a valid Developer Account with Apple for most of these links.

1. First, you will need an AppID, make sure that *if* you use something such as "com.mastering.*" that in your project settings you don't set it to "com.mastering" or this will not be found, it needs to be "com.mastering.dev" or something for the provisioning profile to match your certificate (more on that from Apple in a moment): `https://developer.apple.com/account/ios/identifier/bundle`

2. Set up at least one device (such as test iPads or iPhones): `https://developer.apple.com/account/ios/device/ipad`

3. You will need to get familiar with making a development (you only get one of these) and Ad-hoc/Store distribution certificates. It's recommended to get started with the development certificate if this is your first time going through the process with an Apple build: `https://developer.apple.com/account/ios/certificate/create`

4. And then similarly, you'll want to get accustomed to making Provisioning Profiles – both a single development one for your team typically, and then one or more for Ad-hoc/Store distribution again: `https://developer.apple.com/account/ios/profile/`

Download these from the links by clicking on them, and import them into UE4. Hopefully all goes well, but for what it's worth, in years of development, I have never seen someone go through this process and have it succeed on the first try. Fortunately, there are thousands of others out there who have probably hit the same snags you will, and after a bit of searching, solutions can typically be found online for whatever issues stop you from having a smooth, successful setup here.

How to build, test, and deploy

This section should move us rather quickly through proper device testing on our mobile (or HTML5 and PC) platforms now that all the setup is taken care of. As noted in the *iOS* section, don't get frustrated if things don't immediately work correctly, every team has pains getting these things setup and working properly initially, but once they are, it's typically a much smoother process to simply maintain and modify those build settings and processes going forward. So let's get to it!

UE4's play options vs package project

OK, one last interruption before we actually make a few builds and test those on their intended platforms: you may be wondering, "What's the difference between just using the Play button in the editor and having it do all the work getting it onto my device compared to this packaging business?" Well in a very rough, very quick nutshell: the Play button will build, cook, and deploy to a platform and does a good job of it, which is very helpful for rapid testing. However, it may put files in a different place than your standalone build does when installed, and uses some specific settings. For example, needing to be able to "attach" to the game from an external debugger for iOS on a Mac. You typically *must* use a developer certificate/provisioning profile in your settings when using the Play button, and specifically don't/can't have that Entitlement setting on a product you upload to Apple to deploy to an audience. So once again, apply common sense here: if you are just making quick changes and want a simple test on the hardware, if the Play button is working for your project and platform, feel free to use it. When you're expecting to actually deliver to a store to deploy, make standalone builds and test with those.

When and how to build and test on device

When your team feels they need to start testing on various platforms is really dependent on your entire development philosophy and process. Most major studios already have these processes in place, and have specific milestone gates to pass, some of which will likely specifically require standalone builds on the platform(s) the game will be run on, other stages may require a simple demonstration of gameplay and art assets, which do not require this. Many independent developers will want to simply have the shortest iteration time possible for getting basic concepts proven out (much like this book had done up to this section), which is by far the most streamlined for simply testing in the editor in PIE on a PC or Mac. However, if you're reading this section at all, it means you have a need and interest in eventually running on devices, and the best advice here is, if at all possible, have those builds working from day one of development, and build, deploy, and test regularly. This is another aspect of development often left neglected, or dormant, for too long, and then when needed most and used, causes unforeseen problems. It's definitely easier to develop day to day without taking the time to make standalone builds (or even use the Play button); but the longer a team goes without doing these, the greater the risk that when they do, there's a problem, and those problems are typically ones that prevent release entirely. So build, deploy, and test as often as possible!

Making standalone builds and installing them

Windows: As there is really nothing to it, building a PC package is as simple as **File ->
Package Project** | **Windows** | **Win32** (or **Win64**) and similar for Mac builds. This gives you
an executable and your built assets in folders, and at this stage, uploading to a product,
such as Steam, for delivery should be very simple. Given this, we won't really spend any
time on it; but if you simply want to test the building process, this is the fastest, easiest,
simplest way to do so. If you check under **Project Settings** | **Platforms** | **Windows**, you'll
also notice very few options, so without further ado, we'll move on to packaging Android
and iOS.

Android: Selecting your preferred texture-compression type under **File** | **Package Project** |
Android (see the picture of the dropdown in the **Setup** section) will generate an .apk file,
by default an .obb file, and two .bat files to the folder specified when you clicked to start
that build. The `.bat` files are very clearly labeled: one for uninstalling the project, the other
for installing it (note that the latter will perform the former to make sure you get a clean
install of a project with the same AppID each time). Assuming you got your device set up
for debugging as `https://developer.android.com/studio/run/device` and can test that it
is being seen in a command-line use of "adb devices," then that .bat file will automatically
install directly to that device (if you have only one device present, which is typically the
case).

iOS: Selecting **File** | **Package Project** | **iOS** will generate a .ipa file for you in the folder you
specified. Typically, this is then simply added to your device in XCode's Devices window
with the + button in the **Devices and Simulators** window.

HTML5 will bundle up all the JavaScript and everything else it uses into a package that can
be dragged into a browser to launch it. How you deliver this to users is up to you from a
web-distribution standpoint, and not explored here further.

Once these builds are on the device, they can be run as any other more traditionally
installed by download from their respective store. Thankfully, both Apple and Google give
staging areas to do test runs of uploaded builds, also, so the whole pipeline for those
platforms can be tested fully before then being sent for live submission/approval.

Avoiding rebuild-hell on platforms near releases

One final note is simply a reminder to use common sense when considering how to test. Are your changes ones that might affect graphics on different platforms (material edits, complex new shader changes, or making changes to project settings that might affect such features)? Then test them on a representative device. Are your changes solely gameplay (note that things such as using the filesystem can be problematic on different platforms, and at this stage of the GitHub project, there is definitely a bug in load/save on devices I can hopefully address soon, for example)? It's typically best to iterate these quickly on your development platform; but when ultimately done, especially at least overnight, build for your actual platform and make sure there are no surprises. On a large project, spending an hour to cook assets every time you want to test any small change is foolish, but neglecting your actual intended hardware platforms is too.

Keep in mind that there are some very good tools and techniques out there for automating a lot of these process and centralizing builds and deployment on a single high-powered machine that can then be readily accessed and used by the whole team any time. For example, see Jenkins and HockeyApp in the *Further reading* section. For a build-automation platform such as Jenkins, setup can often be as simple as watching the Output Window as you package via the Unreal Editor, and copying each of the execution lines it uses into steps there. If you have a large project, large team, or large number of target platforms, this type of automation is highly recommended.

Summary

While far from the most glamorous or exciting fields of game development, building and deploying is absolutely critical for any project that you want to reach an audience outside of your own desk. Writing code and building shaders may be more immediately gratifying areas of game development, but if you can't get building and releasing on a platform right, it's all for naught. Knowing how to set up and maintain these processes is an absolutely critical step in mastering UE4 development. But coming up, a return to some of the beautiful visuals UE4 has to offer!

Questions

1. Why is determining target platforms early a necessary step for any project?
2. What is the reason behind adding maps and content folders to the always-cook lists?
3. What are some risks to adding them?
4. What is the order between iOS, PC, and Android from least setup complexity to highest?
5. What is the advantage to having a single "SKU" for your product? What problems are fixed by having multiple?
6. What four things are needed in order to have the pieces needed for an iOS build?
7. What are some advantages and disadvantages to fixes, such as quality-level switches, in shaders?
8. How can build and iteration time be mitigated for a large project?

Further reading

Building iOS from Windows with a Mac on the network:

`https://docs.unrealengine.com/en-us/Platforms/iOS/Windows`

Jenkins build-automation platform:

`https://jenkins.io/doc/`

HockyApp device deployment:

`https://hockeyapp.net/`

11
Volumetric Lightmaps, Fog, and Precomputing

Introduction

UE4 offers a massive amount of the most cutting edge graphics features developers could hope for. The good news is, for many games on many platforms, with a good set of level designers, this will be handled largely automatically. However, being ignorant of how the systems work in general can have two major drawbacks for a team: not taking advantage of the built-in advanced engine techniques, or you may encounter build time or build size problems and not know where to begin addressing them. While the actual techniques and physics of the lighting available in Unreal could fill books by itself (and does!), our theme of being informed on options and use will be our focus again in this chapter. By the end, confidence in how to best use lighting and how to troubleshoot any problems that arise from it will be assured, to help make a modern beautiful game and guide a team to best practices. This chapter covers:

- Volumetric lightmaps
- Atmosphereic and folumetric fog
- Lightmass (settings and previewing tools)
- Profiling lightmaps

Technical requirements

As is typical, this chapter will use examples from the `Chapter 11` branch of our project on GitHub, but the concepts and techniques are valid in any project:

```
https://github.com/PacktPublishing/Mastering-Game-Development-with-Unreal-
Engine-4-Second-Edition/tree/Chapter-11
```

Engine version used: 4.19.2.

Volumetric lightmaps, lightmass, and fog

In this section, we will briefly go through the three topics listed in the heading, which are often confusing to new or casual game makers:

1. Volumetric lightmaps are a precomputed volume-based set of colors that can be quickly used to determine the bounced lighting in any given area of your map. For those who are familiar with pre-4.18 UE4, this was done via the Indirect Lighting Cache, but that was a fixed sample size. The new lightmaps use more dynamic sampling for added detail. These are different from a plain lightmap, which is color that is directly baked into a scene and applied to objects typically as a blended texture. Another way to think of volumetric lightmaps is as a quick look-up table of complex color information in samples of space.

2. Lightmass is the system name in Unreal that determines your lighting properties, including how (and whether) volumetric lightmaps are computed. To prevent lighting times from being extreme, typically you will add one or more Lightmass Importance Volumes (an actual basic Unreal volume type), to tell the engine and editor where you care about these computations. With as many ways and times light and volume are combined, it's no wonder it can be hard to follow.

3. Atmospheric Fog is a visual effect simulating sunlight (or other light) traveling through the atmosphere of a planet. This is set via an Atmospheric Fog object in the map, as well as the settings on lights set to affect it. And related, but unique, is Volumetric Fog is a visual effect where fog appears to fill a volume in a specified region and is appropriately affected by lighting. While it is another use of the word *volume* in this section, it's defined in Unreal globally via an Exponential Height Fog object in the map, or in a local region via particles. And, like Atmospheric Fog, it is also defined largely by the lights set to affect it.

Adding volumetric lightmaps with lightmass volumes

As noted in the previous section, when adding a Lightmass Importance Volume, the area inside that volume will by default generate volumetric lightmaps. Our FrozenCove map gives an excellent overview of these things. Let's first examine the volume and its placement in the level:

Panning back out of the actual cove/cave playable area, you can see this volume encompasses that playable area entirely, but not much else. This is exactly the practice you should try to employ to keep lighting build times down, to reduce the overall number (and thus memory) of saved out lightmaps, and yet give the player the best visual experience in the areas they will most directly view and interact with. Panning around from that height, you can see there is actually quite a bit of modeled-out geometry in these surrounding rocky crags. Their lighting contribution to the player's scene, though, is not relevant, and other than maybe a lucky long shot with our gun that we added in our game, no dynamic objects are ever intended to be seen closely in these areas.

Why are these things important? Let's take just a quick overview of what pre-built lighting gets us in this example, and what good these lightmaps do us. First and foremost is Diffuse Interreflection. This is the technical term for the main use of Lightmass: taking a very detailed model of how light bounces off of objects and precomputing it into a form usable at runtime. Lightmass does this in two distinct ways: firstly by building lightmaps cooked or baked for all the static objects in your scene that are then rendered directly with the geometry at runtime; and secondly as volumetric lightmaps, the quick look-up table of samples of this bounced color for dynamic moving objects at runtime. Without going too deeply into the computations involved, let's focus on the reasoning this is important: some time spent precomputing this information when doing builds of your game generates a *much* more realistic and visually pleasing scene for your audience at a minimal performance cost at runtime. This interreflection concept, where color bleeds from one object to another near it, may seem a bit extraneous, but take a little time and look up some examples where it is applied and not applied to the same scene, and your brain will immediately choose the scene where it is used as the more realistic and higher-quality rendering. Similarly, Lightmass will compute all manner of shadows, Ambient Occlusion (a technique for shadowing light in nooks and crannies), and much, much more. In the second section of this chapter we'll dig into a lot more of the specifics of Lightmass' settings and how to best take advantage of them. This section was about the most basic way to get Lightmass added to your game (by adding the importance volume) and why adding that importance volume is, well, important!

Using Atmospheric Fog

Epic has done a lot of work over the years (specifically updated in 4.16) on making more complex fog techniques more accessible to developers, and at this stage they are relatively easy to add, at least compared to days past. In our cove map example, first we'll examine its use of the Atmospheric Fog object placed within it, as well as its sky and the sky's corresponding directional light properties. For games desiring a sort of low-lying fog effect, where at low altitudes in the game the fog becomes more thick and pronounced, please do see the next sub-section on *Exponential Height Fog (Volumetric Fog)*. For readers who would like to use localized Volumetric Fog to enhance (or even obscure) an area, have special properties for a localized region, and/or moving/changing dynamic volume fog, the next sub-section will briefly go over this topic as well, and both sections have links in the *Further reading* section.

But, now on to our example here. While it may not have been immediately noticed when jumping in this level, if you remove the effect or exaggerate it (we'll do the later in two shots here) you can easily see what a difference it makes when looking near the sun out of our cave:

Hopefully the haze around the rocks at the top is clear enough, and if you look at the rest of the scene, the area where you can see the sky is noticeably brightened when the sun comes into view, as it is here. Let's look at the settings that generate this. First is the sky sphere, here:

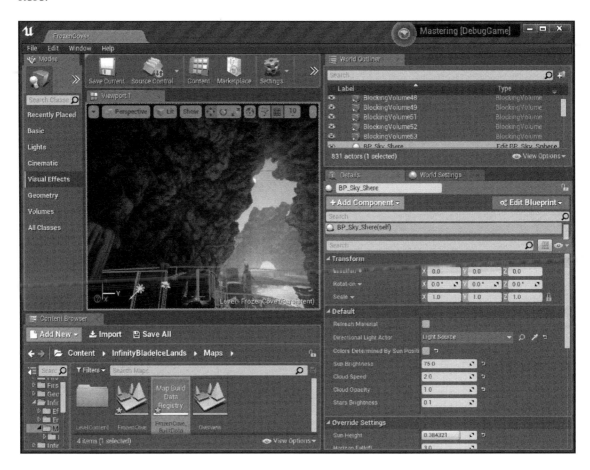

Note specifically that it has a **Directional Light Actor** specified. If we follow that to the one we see there on screen, here are its properties:

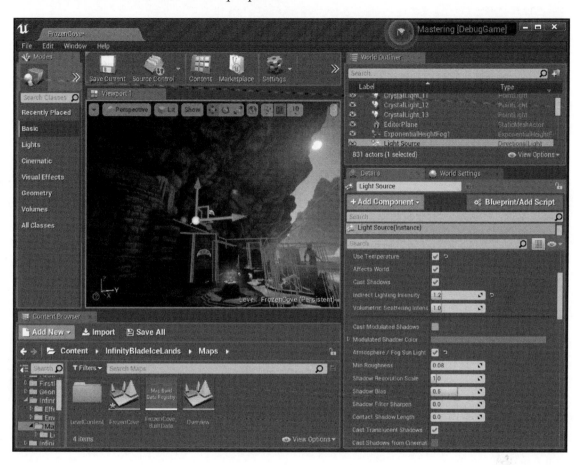

And of course, central to these properties is the **Atmosphere / Fog Sun Light** box, which lets our Atmospheric Fog properties know this is the source of the sun when creating its volume fog:

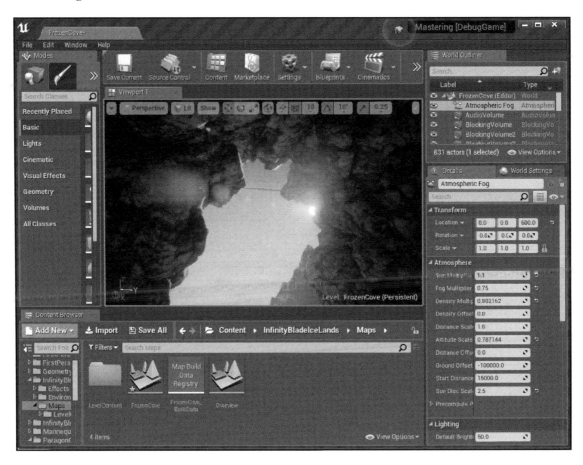

And lastly, let's show how modifying some of these settings on the Atmospheric Fog object (which is found by the Exponential Height Fog object in the Modes pane on the left):

And now it's extreme and you can't miss it! I highly recommend just experimenting with all of these settings. There is so much to explore here, and it's good fun to see just how all the different parameters affect the outcome in real time. Unlike with many of the Lightmass effects and settings, Atmospheric Fog does not require a build (via the **Build** button at the top) to update and is very easy and fast to play with.

Using Volumetric Fog

Volumetric Fog is a great visual effect that currently is very specifically designed for areas a player may be walking in a relatively flat map, or areas they may be looking up from or down to with some elevation changes. Given the difficulty of computation, it's currently not otherwise supported (for example, varying based on camera view-angle), but it is still a very powerful tool and great system to be comfortable with explaining its significance to a team. To start, once more let's take a look at what is already in FrozenCove, and then we'll modify it a bit:

These settings give a nice subtle fog that only begins fairly distant from the placement of the height fog object. So, once again for demonstration purposes, we'll make it a bit more extreme (and the more observant will notice the particles in the foreground that we'll discuss next):

The level uses traditional particles, which we discussed previously due to their blending performance cost, to simulate snow-banks; but as you'll see, we could do this with a Volumetric Fog particle emitter too, which you can view in the map now. However, for this emitter to work, we need to switch the height fog's **Volumetric Fog** setting to be true (currently the box is unchecked). Note that while we'll discuss later how to optimize a bit of your Lightmass output if necessary. If you use Volumetric Fog this way you should remain cognizant of the potential performance costs and use the techniques from Chapter 8, *Shader Editing and Optimization Tips*. So let's take a look at a material we can add to a particle system to get dynamic changing and colored Volumetric Fog:

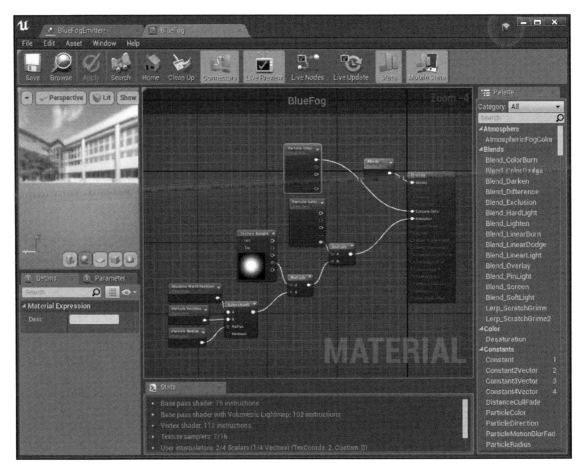

Now, with this material as-is, added to the emitter in the scene, you get a rather hard-to-miss blue (which was the original intent), here:

It turns out, if you disconnect the emissive color, this is a much more subtle effect, matching the fog's natural color. This is what is in the GitHub project presently:

Volumetric Fog both local and global can really make or break the immersion of a scene, so while the whole point here is to be confident using them, it's a big help to have some experienced environmental artists around to make sure they're not *overused* in a scene aesthetically, in addition to possible performance costs already discussed.

Lightmass tools

Now that the basics are out of the way and we've seen the power of Volumetric Fog and a bit of how it combines with lighting in general, it's time to get into a bit more detail with Lightmass itself. There are myriad objects, variables, and endless combinations of the two that can be explored, but to stay focused on our technical confidence, we'll focus on a few key areas here:

- Diffuse Interreflection settings
- The dynamic Indirect Lighting Lightmap and how to visualize and tune it
- Ambient Occlusion and its benefits and drawbacks
- Additional factors that can impact lighting build times
- Quality Modes
- Lightmaps, where to find them, and how to profile your usage of them

Our second sub-section here will deal exclusively with lightmaps, so for our first section, we'll examine a solid subset of Lightmass' defining properties, as well as the impact of Quality Modes.

Learning Lightmass settings and previewing tools

First, let's take a look at the global Lightmass settings, found in **World Settings**:

The first five options affect indirect lighting the most. If your lighting times are very large, setting the static lighting level to greater than 1 can drastically reduce your lighting build times by scaling the sampling size. If lighting build times for various levels or a whole game are becoming a problem, and your game and team can live with the quality reduction in lighting accuracy, try this first. The number of bounces can similarly have a significant impact. The purpose of indirect lighting is to simulate the real world where a fraction of photons (the particles of light our eyes perceive) are deflected or refracted from objects, while some are absorbed. The number of bounces means as each point in space is calculated, an amount of bounced lighting must also be calculated. Naturally, the more bounces, the more work (but also more realistic accuracy). The next three are a bit more esoteric, but feel free to simply mouse over them to see what they entail. Light smoothing, for example, can be a big help in very specific types of maps, but as stated, the cost to indirect shadow detail needs to be weighed. Unfortunately, unlike a lot of the fog settings we previously discussed, all of these will need to be built to be fully appreciated for the changes they make, which can be quite time consuming. Theoretically, if a game has a set style, a few experiments can be done early on, preferred values chosen, and then those are simply locked in for the duration of the project.

To visualize lighting effects, be sure to check out Detail Lighting, Lighting Only, and Reflections under the view options of your viewport:

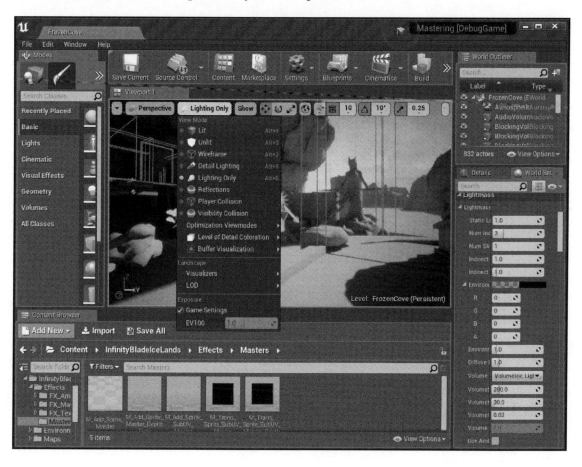

However, of most interest here probably is the volumetric Lightmass, which can be previewed via a viewport's **Show** | **Visualize** | **Volumetric Lightmap**, like so:

These directional lighting samples will be used to move objects at runtime and also for static meshes when moved around before building static lighting again. For experienced UE4 developers, don't forget, since 4.18 this is the default, and a generally better accepted model than the old lighting cache. A detailed description about the changes is in the *Further reading* section.

Quickly touching on Ambient Occlusion (which is actually turned off in FrozenCove), think of it as darkening areas. Concave surfaces block the light bounces in real life. While it adds realism, and adds essentially zero build time to lighting if you're already doing at least one indirect lighting bounce, keep in mind it is modeled on a top-down light to simplify the calculations. So in a sense it's similarly limited to Exponential Height Fog in that if your game is not a fundamentally flat game (for example, a player moving on a similar surface to the Earth, like most of us do), it can lose its realism and value. It is, however, easy enough to turn off in the **Use Ambient Occlusion** setting under your world's Lightmass settings. As with many Lightmass options, it's often best to simply try building lighting with it on, wandering the level, and maybe taking some specific screenshots, then turning it off and repeating this to see if it is of use. You can preview what work is done here in your viewport in its **View Mode | Buffer Visualization | Ambient Occlusion**.

If you find yourself having lighting build time problems, and have adjusted some of the parameters that can impact those build times, it's worth noting that lighting builds use the Swarm Agent system, which can farm the computations out to multiple computers on a network. More on this is also listed in the *Further reading* section. Note also that for many games, purely dynamic lighting is good enough, and much of Lightmass can be turned off for things such as mobile games that require a modest level of dynamic lighting detail but don't benefit from the memory cost and build time of baked/cooked lighting. As always, know your project and its needs, and be ready to do some early experiments and make those calls with your artists on the best options. If eliminating cooked lighting allows your artists to add more detailed textures to environments or characters, this may be a trade-off they're happy to make depending on your game's resolution and other settings, so don't be afraid to experiment and discuss!

And lastly, know your lighting quality levels. They can be selected from the drop-down of the **Build** button like so:

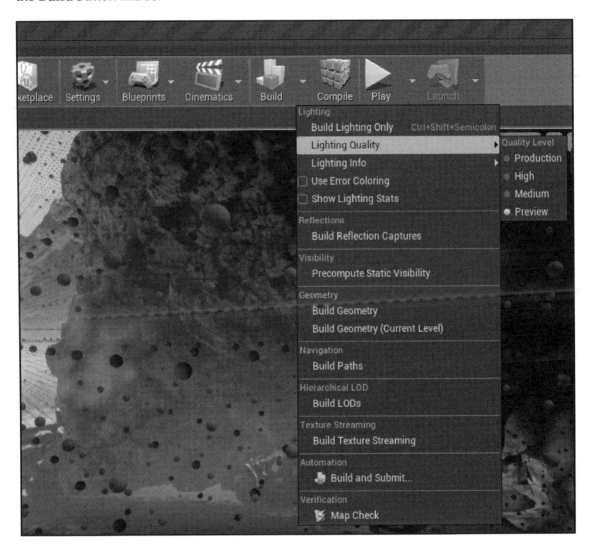

These are really just a high-to-low of build-time versus quality-level at a very high level. If you want to switch in a hurry between these, by all means, this should be your first choice for quality versus time.

Profiling lightmaps

As noted, Lightmass will automatically make lightmaps in all the areas enclosed in an importance volume. But what does that mean for your project's memory? You can always check the built data size for a quick estimate (hint: most of this will be your lightmaps, and maybe a chunk for nav-mesh, and a few smaller necessities internal to the level). For example, look in our project's `Conent/InfinithBladeIceLands/Maps` folder and you'll see frozen cove's built data `.ubulk` file, about 100 MB. This is typical for what we have in our map. However, if you would like some more detail, click the down arrow (more options) in the lightmass world settings, and under that you'll find a **Lightmaps** fly-out like so:

And double-clicking on one of those will give you a lot more detail:

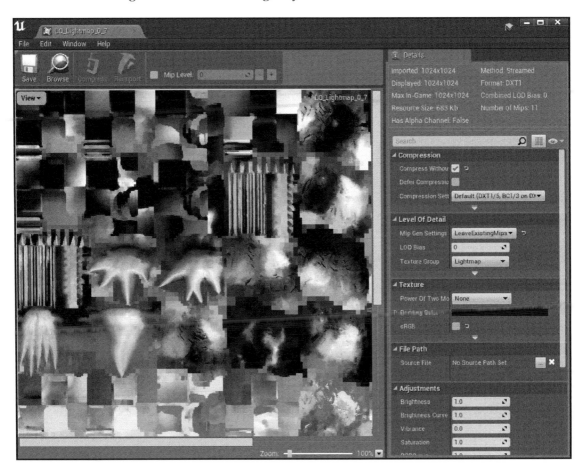

Here you can see compression, size (resolution and memory), and of course, change many of these settings. Individual meshes can change their lightmap resolution in the static mesh editor under their mesh settings. In addition, you can view the texel density of these lightmaps in your viewport via **View Mode | Optimization Viewmodes | Lightmap Density**, as can be seen here:

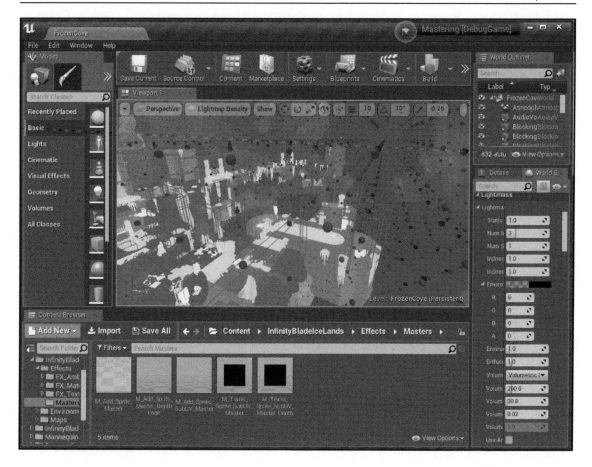

Summary

There is so much here to explore, it is important not to get overwhelmed. At this point, any major questions a team or project may have should be generally answerable. That said, if you finds yourself arguing with artists about visual quality, or arguing with the whole team about build times, the tools should be now in your hands to explore options, tune, tweak, and come to the optimal solution. Lighting in UE4 is amazing and complex, but thankfully, it's not critical to understand the *how* of the entire system, but simply command a mastery of the *what* and *why* to make the right decisions. In the next chapter, we'll have a bit more relaxed time showing off some more cool visual tricks UE4 can do with in-scene videos!

Questions

1. What is the function of volumetric lightmaps?
2. How would you describe the features Lightmass encompasses by default?
3. What is the difference between Atmosphereic Fog and Volumetric Fog?
4. How do you make a localized instance of Volumetric Fog?
5. If you have slow lighting build times, what is the simplest way to alter quality versus time?
6. What are the limitations of Exponential Height Maps and Ambient Occlusion?
7. Where can you find the general size of lightmap data when it's built?
8. What is the difference between a traditional lightmap and a volumetric lightmap?

Further reading

Exponential Height Fog:

https://docs.unrealengine.com/en-US/Engine/Actors/FogEffects/HeightFog

Volumetric Fog (Local Fog via Particles):

https://docs.unrealengine.com/en-us/Engine/Rendering/LightingAndShadows/
VolumetricFog

Indirect Lightmap vs. Lighting Cache:

https://docs.unrealengine.com/en-US/Engine/Rendering/LightingAndShadows/
VolumetricLightmaps

Swarm Agents in Unreal:

https://docs.unrealengine.com/en-us/Engine/Rendering/LightingAndShadows/
Lightmass/Unreal-Swarm-Overview

12
In-scene Video and Visual Effects

Introduction

UE4 has some amazing in-game visual effects. Media Framework is a very cool tool and is used to add in-scene video to a game. Unreal also has some significantly-developed, but not entirely ready-to-go, tools for capturing realtime video. In this chapter, we'll capture a section of video from gameplay, then project it onto a surface as in-scene video playback. Unreal also offers a huge variety of visual FX, and to spice up our weapon impacts, we'll add some impact particles with physics to have a basis for these kinds of options as well. This chapter will focus on:

- Creating an in-game video player with Media Framework
  - Create assets and a material to add this to any actor in the map
  - Triggering and repeating our video
- Adding physics-based particles to the game
  - Creating an emitter for our projectiles and spawning it on hit-events
  - Orienting and modifying particles to have a cool motion/feel

Technical requirements

This chapter will implement its components in the Chapter 12 branch of our project on GitHub: https://github.com/PacktPublishing/Mastering-Game-Development-with-Unreal-Engine-4-Second-Edition/tree/Chapter-12.

We used Engine version 4.19.2.

Playing in-scene video with Media Framework

Media Framework adds several helpful key systems to play videos in-engine. However, the one we will focus on here is playing an in-scene video with audio playback on a "screen" triggered by our player. This is a very common and popular feature in many games, and using Unreal's render target materials, you can put realtime renders of other areas of your map anywhere. The classic example being security cameras showing you other areas. But to reiterate, we're just focusing on how to get a movie into the game to prove what can be done and learn what's involved in adding it to a game. First, however, we'll need a few new items.

Creating our assets

There are several components needed to make a nice in-scene video player, let's quickly enumerate them here:

- The source video, of course! In Epic's documentation, they list supported files, but a nice short version is, when in doubt, use MP4s, as they work across every platform (more on the specific one here in a moment).
- A **File Media Source** object that references, well, this source media (in our case, our video).
- A **Media Player** object that does the work at runtime.
- An associated **Media Texture** asset.
- A **Material** that uses this texture.

Now, the great news about UE4 is that lot of this is automated for you, so don't get intimidated by that list, this will go surprisingly quickly.

As a quick aside, I'll describe generally where this specific video came from, as the actual video file is key to this whole concept. There are, of course, a number of ways to capture video. While this book is not meant to be an endorsement of any specific outside products (other than recognizing what development tools and versions were used), doing an internet search on "Windows screen capture," is an easy solution. Also, using some of the game-streaming tools and apps on mobile devices can do this too: many have a "game mode" that captures the video and saves it.

Check out the Sequence Recorder in the editor (**Windows | Sequence Recorder**), as this may be just what you need. I found a few issues with using it in the past; but there is constant work being done with systems like that, and if you can get comfortable with a supported system built in to UE4, it's the best way to go.

The checked-in asset you can see is literally just me walking over to our Countess introduction in-game scene and capturing it out to an MP4 video that will be uploaded with the branch to GitHub. So with this video file added to our content folder, we can get back to the editor, and making items in our content browser:

The next thing needed, as noted, is a **File Media Source**:

And as you'll see, there's really not much to this particular object, just point it to the source media and note there are options for platform player overrides:

The last thing we'll add here is our **Media Player**. Note that when making a new media player, you'll get this popup and definitely want to check the box (as it is what automates making the media texture and wiring it up for us):

After clicking ok, we can continue:

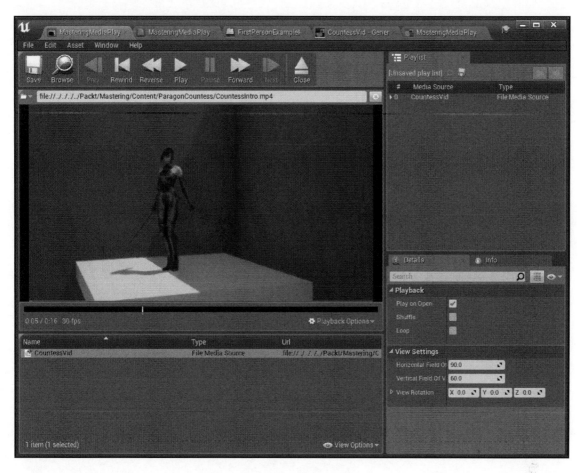

And in here, simply drag and drop the **CountessVid** asset we just made into its list in the bottom left and the player is ready with its default settings. Our texture asset is now automatically created and associated (again, a great streamlining feature of modern UE4!). Now all we need is a material that we can generate by dragging the texture onto an actor, so let's progress to that.

Building and playing the video in-scene

Theoretically, you can now play a video on any static mesh actor or a number of surfaces. Typically, though, it is just a plane, which can be dragged from the modes window right into the level. We'll generate a material by dragging the media texture directly on to the actor we want to use (our plane in this case), and then you can see a dead-simple material is added and is set on the surface. So after doing all of that, as seen here, there's one tricky part left: the audio that will fail to play if we don't right-click the **+Add Component** for our in-scene screen (plane), add a **Media Sound** component, and hook its media to our player:

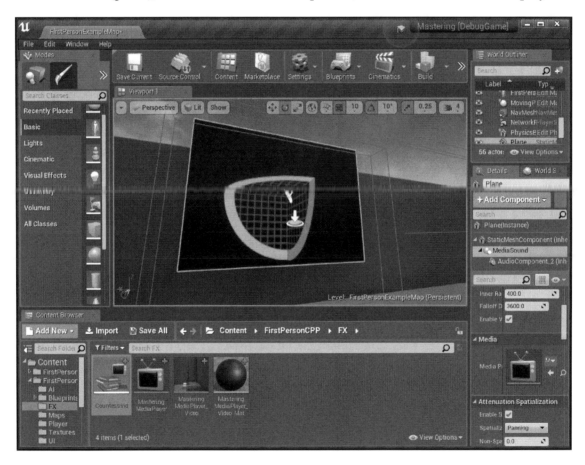

Manually hooking up the audio this way is one of the only complaints I have about the process these days, so now that we're pretty close to having everything we need, it's just a matter of triggering the video and checking it out:

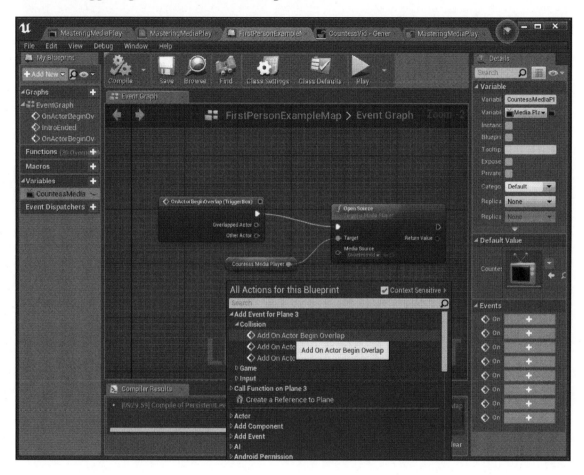

Here a simple trigger volume is added in front of our screen, a blueprint-level variable (of **Media Player** type) is added on the left in the level blueprint, and with the volume selected, right-clicking in the blueprint event area lets you directly drop its on-actor-overlap event in and trigger an **Open Source** node, which is also set to point to our new asset. So note, this logic will trigger any and all instances of this material, which uses our media player, which can be great, but also may not be exactly what you want. There are a number of solutions there – the most obvious, but not nicest for asset cleanliness, is just to duplicate the player for each individual thing you want to play separately. Anyway, there you have it, we can now walk over to the screen to see and hear the Countess' intro sequence as many times as we like, as we trigger our MP4 video thereof!

One last point: when playing, this video comes across pretty dark in the scene:

To correct that, I just did a very simple multiply on the color output in the material. Once again, there are a number of ways you could approach this; I always start with the simplest and if that does the job, move on! You can check that change out here, modify the constant value in the material, see the effect it has on our output in the game:

Now let's check out a couple more great visual FX that can be made with UE4 as we haven't used their particle system much yet.

Adding physics particles

Our goal here will have two parts: first, to add some sparks off of our projectile hits when they impact, but then to get those sparks bouncing around in the physics universe without utterly killing our framerate. One great piece of news is that UE4 supports GPU particles across all kinds of platforms for you, and in general this is where you want to be doing that kind of work. Should you find yourself in a game that is GPU-bound because of its complex visuals (or low-bar for platform hardware specifications), these kinds of things are often the first to go; but let's not worry about that now, let's make some pretty sparks first.

Creating our initial emitter on projectile hit

So some of you may remember way back at the beginning of the book that we added the starter content pack. Well, now we can finally put a bit more of that to use. Scrolling down near the bottom of the folders is **StarterContent/Particles** (or just do a wildcard search for **P_Sparks** in the search box). This is not exactly what we want, but it's close, which is always saves time. Notice that it is already using some spark and smoke GPU Sprite emitters (the other being a flash/burst). It seems pretty close, so why not start here? Similarly for C++ classes and all other aspects of game development, if you can begin with something that is at least partially already doing the job you want, always put that to use and begin modifying from there for efficiency. Now, let's take a look at these sparks:

As we'll be modifying them to behave a bit differently, I simply copy and paste the emitter (**P_Sparks** asset) up to **FirstPersonCPP/FX**. I also renamed it to **P_ImpactSparks** so as to avoid confusion when browsing for it. Now we have our own fresh copy and can begin modifying it. First, though, let's take a step back and just get them to spawn upon projectile impacts. We'll need to add a new variable to our **MasteringProjectile** class and spawn them around where we spawn impact sounds:

First in our projectile's header file we add:

```
UPROPERTY(EditAnywhere, BlueprintReadWrite)
class UParticleSystem* ImpactParticles;
```

Then in `OnHit` down at the bottom in the `.cpp` file we add:

```
const float minVelocity = 1000.0f;
if (cueToPlay != nullptr && GetVelocity().Size() > minVelocity)
{
        UGameplayStatics::PlaySoundAtLocation(this, cueToPlay,
Hit.Location);

        UGameplayStatics::SpawnEmitterAtLocation(GetWorld(),
ImpactParticles, Hit.Location, GetActorRotation(), true);
}
```

And just like that, we have particles spawning at the hit locations. Simply go to each projectile in the `FirstPersonCPP/Blueprints/Weapons` folder and set all of their **ImpactParticle** variables to use the newly copied **P_ImpactSparks** asset. For those going through this step by step, you'll notice some problems at this point:

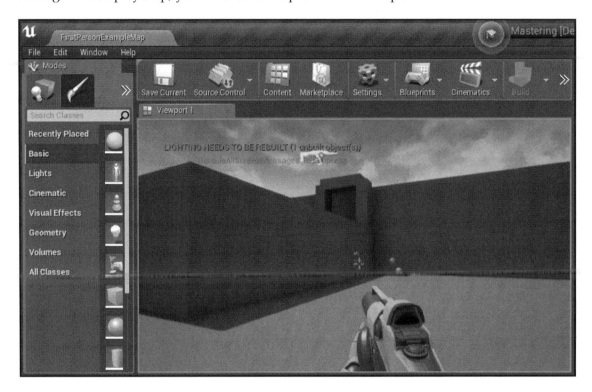

First, our particle systems (emitters) live forever, and second, they always spawn straight up and down with no imparted sense of velocity and simply flow to the ground as a stationary fountain would. The first is trivial to fix: open **P_ImpactSparks** in Cascade (double click the asset) and you'll see three emitters in its main window. Click on the **Required** bar on each and scroll down on the Details menu, and you'll see all three have a looping count set to 0 (loop forever) – set it to 1 as that fixes our infinite systems here:

I'm not a huge fan of the user interface in Cascade, but with practice I have seen FX artists that work in it masterfully and can find and modify systems very quickly. In this case, we'll likely want to increase the sparks' velocity and reduce that emitter's lifetime, but these are all more or less cosmetic things. Our last issues are to get them orienting properly for the way the projectiles hit the surfaces and make sure we can tune the spark behavior coming off of them if needed for performance reasons.

So why not use Niagara, the newer editor for the particles? Honestly, in this instance, it was my own familiarity with Cascade; but of course anyone is welcome to use Niagara and I will add a link to it (which starts with a link to the differences and similarities to Cascade) in Further Reading. Similar to Matinee vs. Sequencer earlier, both will remain and be supported, but long-term, it probably *is* a good idea to move to Niagara.

Orienting and adjusting physics of the particles

Having particle systems just rain down boring-looking sparks is not going to cut it with this type of effect, we need the sparks to align in a way that makes sense from the projectile impact. This will take just a little bit more code work and a little bit more Cascade work; but should come out looking good.

Note: If you use blueprints to spawn various effects, it makes it much easier to hook up outside factors to these emitters and systems. Technical artists often find this invaluable to allow for a quick iteration of systems until they get things looking right. Just be aware that a well-meaning content creator can make one small node that ends up testing a huge amount of physics collisions accidentally, so this kind of experimentation can be dangerous for performance!

First, the quick code change:

```
FRotator rot =  GetVelocity().ToOrientationRotator();
UGameplayStatics::SpawnEmitterAttached(ImpactParticles, GetRootComponent(),
NAME_None, FVector::ZeroVector, rot,
EAttachLocation::SnapToTargetIncludingScale, true);
```

There are a *lot* of options here, you can use **Hit.Normal/Hit.ImpactNormal** instead of the velocity to build your rotation, and not attach the particles if desired, for example. I found here that attaching the system made the particles feel like they were being "pulled with" the projectile and made for a bit of a chaotic look, which I liked, setting the rotation along the velocity as well. In Cascade, only the smoke system was currently set to inherit the parent's velocity; I made the sparks do so as well (right-click in the emitter's column area, add that field, and select it). Note the reduced **Emitter Duration** tuned value on the left:

The end result is not quite ready for professional quality, knowing your limits is an important trait in growing with a team as well. Still, hopefully the journey here helped to boost your confidence in Unreal's awesome visual effects. There's so much more to explore, but having the fundamentals to take a project forward is what this book is all about.

Summary

We've touched on just about all of the major systems traditional UE4 has to offer. While there are a few more specialized systems, at this point, you should be comfortable making a traditional game on whatever platform is desired in UE4. The Unreal community has a huge amount of visual FX that can be downloaded for free, knowing the above you should have the confidence to go explore its deep options! There's only one area we haven't really explored yet; it's one of the newest to UE4 and what we'll cover in the next chapter: AR and VR, Unreal's Augmented Reality and Virtual Reality API and projects. This is also the end of the updates for our main GitHub project: from its humble origins as the FirstPersonCPP template, to FrozenCove, its fog and lighting, to the Countess and her AI, to loading and saving, and effects and optimizations. I hope you have found it an inspiring and meaningful journey. Now on to the new worlds of AR and VR!

Questions

1. Why is MP4 typically the best choice for videos in UE4? (Hint: see the *Further reading* section for some details)
2. If a single Media Player is referenced on multiple actors, what happens when opening that media?
3. What's the quick simple way to get your video texture and video material?
4. Why was the constant multiplier added to color output of the material here?
5. What's a good strategy to save time in both C++ and asset creation that we used with the particle emitter?
6. Why should we attach the emitter to our projectile rather than have it stay still in space, as first implemented?
7. How did we get the emitters aligned with the projectile direction?
8. When is it disadvantageous to have particles simulate on the GPU (which can easily be changed in Cascade)?

Further reading

Supported video types in Media Framework:

```
https://docs.unrealengine.com/en-US/Engine/MediaFramework/TechReference
```

Niagara particle editor:

```
https://docs.unrealengine.com/en-us/Engine/Niagara
```

13
Virtual Reality and Augmented Reality in UE4

Introduction

Two of the newest and most exciting additions to UE4 are its Virtual Reality (VR) and **Augmented Reality (AR)** integrations. While VR has been around for some time, AR was first fully functioning without any need for merging a custom branch or using experimental components mid-summer 2018 in version 4.20. While there is a huge world of both to explore, we'll keep to the focus of this book of building awareness and confidence in Unreal's systems in this chapter by building projects for both and working through some real world additions to them to learn what is involved. So get ready to explore the newest and arguably coolest new platforms in the Unreal world! Our final chapter here covers:

- Creating and modifying a VR project
    - Preparation for and deployment to an Android GearVR headset
    - Adding new motion-based controls to the project
- Creating and modifying an AR project
    - Preparation for and deployment to an Android phone
    - Porting our projectiles from the main project into our new AR game!

Technical requirements

To keep focus on the tech of these new platforms, they will both be created as new standalone projects as noted above. While it is entirely possible to port our existing Mastering project to support VR and even AR, as noted numerous times in this book: major decisions like that are best made at the start of a project so they can be initially proven out, and then maintained throughout development. That said, in the AR project, we'll port over some of our work from the previous project to get a feel for how that goes also, giving a good test of how portable that work was when created. The two respective projects are in these branches in GitHub:

VR:

```
https://github.com/PacktPublishing/Mastering-Game-Development-with-Unreal-
Engine-4-Second-Edition/tree/Chapter-13-VR
```

AR:

```
https://github.com/PacktPublishing/Mastering-Game-Development-with-Unreal-
Engine-4-Second-Edition/tree/Chapter-13-AR
```

In addition, for the AR component, given the GearVR platform used, Google's ARCore app was also installed on my Galaxy Note 8 for Unreal integration without the previous large headache installing custom Google APIs. In this area (AR), 4.20 is a dream compared to previous integrations, both for iOS and especially Android, so it is highly recommended (though not specifically required) to update to at least 4.20 for this chapter.

Engine version used: 4.20.2.

Note: for those using Mac and iOS platforms, while I don't specifically cover those here, these are mainly blueprint project templates and the process will not vary too much, so feel free to go through the blueprint code & code-migration and other points in this chapter, while substituting in "Finder" for "Explorer" and "XCode" for "Visual Studio" and "iPad/iPhone" for "Android," the only parts that might be most difficult were already covered in Chapter 10, *Packaging the Game (PC, Mobile)*.

Making a VR project and adding new controls

VR as I'm sure readers at this stage well know involves the user wearing a headset and the game or app presenting them with a 3D world they can explore immersed completely inside that view.

Making the initial VR project

For those who have been with me the whole journey of this book, there will be a bit of review from Chapter 1, *Making a C++ Project for a First-Person Shooter*. It shouldn't be too much, though; but for those who wanted to skip straight to here, we won't skip any major steps. So first launch the Engine without a project specified, as noted in Chapter 1 this can be done from your engine install directory itself, or hopefully those here since that chapter already have a shortcut built for it. When the Unreal Project Browser comes up, click the **New Project** tab:

And select the Blueprint tab's **VR Project** template, we'll set the content level to **Mobile / Tablet**, and remove **Starter Content** (though I generally recommend keeping this in for prototyping as it gives some fun objects to play with, but does take up a fair deal of extra space). Of course you're welcome to name it whatever you like, but to match GitHub's files, go with the above, MasteringVR. After clicking the create button, it should automatically open up in the editor and for several platforms (PS4-VR, Oculus Rift, etc., the "wired" headsets) it is ready to deploy and test immediately.

For those who have been through the whole book, you'll also know I generally prefer to work in C++ for speed and debugging purposes, however, these templates currently exist for only as Blueprint templates. Now, that said, it's easy enough to add a C++ class and start compiling the project yourself, as will be done in the AR project. *However*, do note that this adds considerable time to your build iterations. In my case, 5-10 minutes *per use* of the Launch button in the editor, as each time it will recompile and re-sign your `.apk`. For those looking closely at GitHub, you'll notice at one point I was going to add code to a pawn class in a .cpp, but after noticing this issue, reverted back to full blueprint. If you stick to blueprint only as we will for this VR section, that iteration time can be less than a minute (total!) so consider wisely before you commit to C++ in projects like these where you are constantly having to deploy to hardware.

And keep in mind the first time you build and deploy for a platform, it will need to compile all of the engine shaders and cook your content. After that first build, iteration times are as I describe above; but that first launch will be a bit slow and painful.

Building and deploying for GearVR

Even with the handy VR project template, there are still a number of steps to get things working on the GearVR platform for those following my lead here and using a Samsung Android device.

I'm a big fan of this platform for a number of reasons. First: no wires! The wired headsets are more powerful and bring some extra capabilities with them, but also that feeling you're tethered to a PC or PS4 all the time which I find distracting. Second: accessibility. While the store and platform are Samsung's and not Google's like other Android apps, a huge number of people own the S7 and on up line which all perform in my opinion very well in GearVR apps. Hopefully it catches on and maybe even Samsung and Google integrate their stores at some point; but for any with the option of trying these projects on such devices, I have had very good results.

So first, for any Android-based app, you need to go to **Project Settings -> Platforms -> Android** and click the **Configure Now** button at the top:

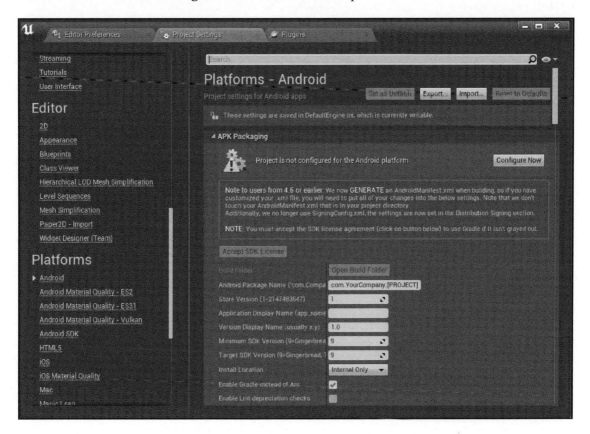

After that, just below in its settings we need a few more things set:

Namely we need to set the SDK versions to 19 and Epic recommends setting the KitKat+ full screen immersive settings to true (though I didn't find this necessary in testing).

Next, scrolling down in the same section to **Advanced APK Settings**, we need one more checkbox checked:

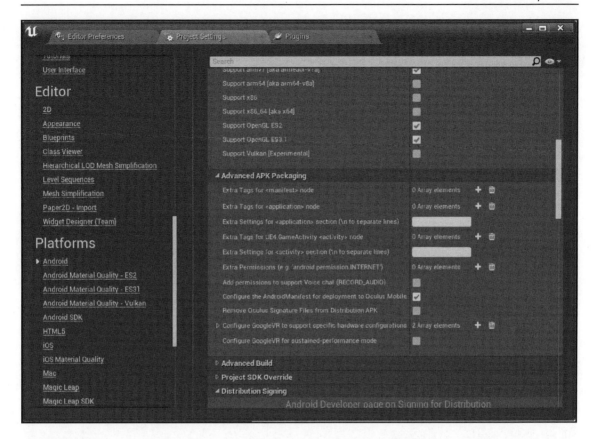

Configure the AndroidManifest for deployment to Oculus Mobile is strictly needed, and for those extra observant, I went ahead and turned on OpenGL ES3.1 as any device that can use a GearVR headset (Galaxy S6+) will support it anyway and there's no reason to limit your shader options nor force yourself to recompile all those shaders later.

 Note also, I tried enabling Vulkan as I am a fan of its hardware acceleration platform, but got a crash on startup with this basic project, so, at least for the moment, save yourself some trouble and leave it unchecked.

And two final minor notes. First, if you are going to launch from the editor as I typically do for iterating, set your startup map to the **MotionControllerMap** as here, not the **StartupMap** default:

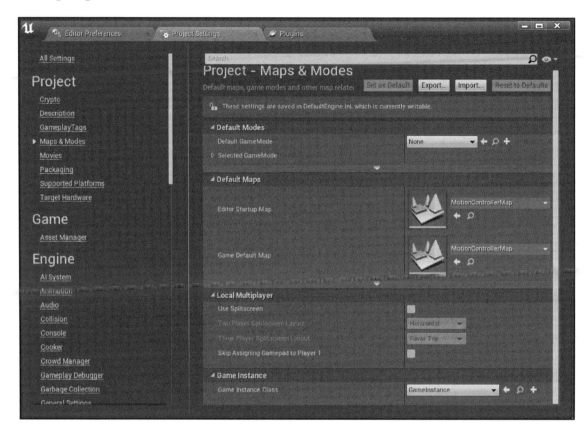

For whatever reason, the GearVR controller doesn't activate in the **StartupMap**, but works as we desire in the **MotionControllerMap** just fine (which is the default game map anyway if you make a standalone .apk and install and run that). Note, you may have to click the tumbstick a couple of times before things show up properly, even here, it seems.

And lastly, you'll need to follow these directions to get a signing key from Oculus, but it's a much simpler process than most of those in the building and deploying chapter we had earlier:

```
https://dashboard.oculus.com/tools/osig-generator/
```

If you don't have that key in the folder it specifies, your app will crash on startup for being unsigned.

Now we can quickly make changes and view those in less than a minute on our GearVR headset!

 For those wanting to use the HMD (Head Mounted Display) pad itself, there's a great guide from Epic in Further Reading at the end.

Adding HMD controls

Now that we're playing in the level and can teleport around with the thumbstick and if you can get close-enough to the blue boxes you can grab them and throw them using the trigger on the controller, it might be nice to move around in the level a bit without having to use the teleport exclusively. One way we could even free up the entire thumbstick for other uses is to make motion based on your head's orientation, using the HMD (Head Mounted Display) orientation itself as a means of conveying input.

However, this means the player can't really look up and down anymore freely without moving; but we'll put in a fix for that too. Let's get the player moving around via blueprint first using some simple logic based on the camera orientation. To do this, we'll do the work in the **MotionControllerPawn** (found in Content/VirtualRealityBP/Blueprints in the content browser). For this to actually work, however, we'll need to convert the pawn to a character. So as we've done in the past, open the blueprint, go to **File | Reparent Blueprint**, and pick **Character**. Now, the default character has quite a tall capsule, and our previous pawn expected its origin to be on the ground, so let's just make its capsule small, doesn't have to be too tiny for this to all work ok, 34cm, its original radius, seems fine for the height too:

Next we'll add a new blueprint function and drag a pin off of the sequence node in event tick to call it:

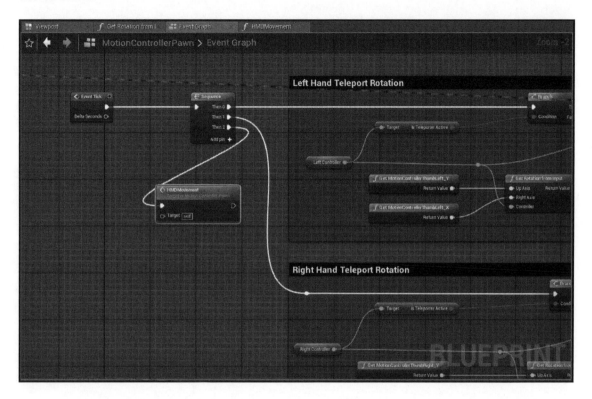

In that function, we'll add some simple logic to move the player based on camera orientation.

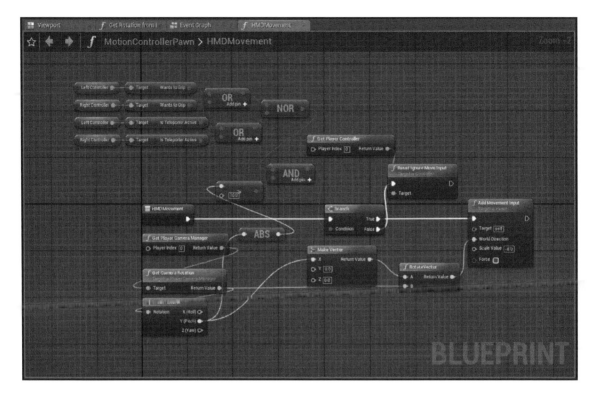

As you can see at the start, the portion I mentioned earlier where we can disable the movement is done whenever any controller is trying to grab or teleport (and also we stop if the tilt is less than 10 degrees either way). This way the player can fully look around while doing those actions, but when not, tilting forward and back will move the player forward & backward, while turning of course changes direction still. If desired, you could easily add strafing left and right by using the same logic with the roll of the camera, and a sideways movement vector.

With this addition, I actually find grabbing those boxes and throwing them around much easier than just by teleporting!

In case you're curious about the screenshot above (which was from device running VR), I simply added an Execute Console Command node to blueprint that was triggered when I pulled the trigger on the controller, and it executed "HighResShot 1920x1280" (but of course you can make that resolution anything you want) and then retrieved them from the phone when it was plugged in
from: `\Phone\UE4Game\MasteringVR\Saved\Screenshots\Android`.

Making an AR project and porting our projectiles

AR is a field that has gained huge popularity over the past year, so it is great to see UE4 finally have a very solid and simple integration path and project template. For those new to it, Augmented Reality is rather different from VR as it does not take the user out of the real world and into a separate one, but rather integrates with the real world through a device which is either worn like the Microsoft's HoloLens, or the newly announced Magic Leap goggles, or held such as many current smartphones and tablets, AR takes real world surroundings and integrates them to the app or game so the user can combine real world objects with in-game interactions. We'll get this started with its new project and then pull some code and assets from previous work into this branch to show that process now.

Making the initial AR project

So much like in our first chapter and directly above in the VR section, this will be a bit of review; but since it's a project starting from scratch, it's always best to go through each step (so be ready for the Unreal Project Browser one more time!) So launching the engine without a project once more, gets us to the browser, where under the **New Project** and **Blueprint** tabs, you'll now find **Handheld AR** as a template, select that, we set the content to **Mobile / Tablet** again and no **Starter Content** (unless you want it of course).

And as usual, this should now be opened up in your editor so we can begin work right away!

Android deployment specifics

There was much less to do here than in the VR section, but the same critical start has to be made, configuring for Android:

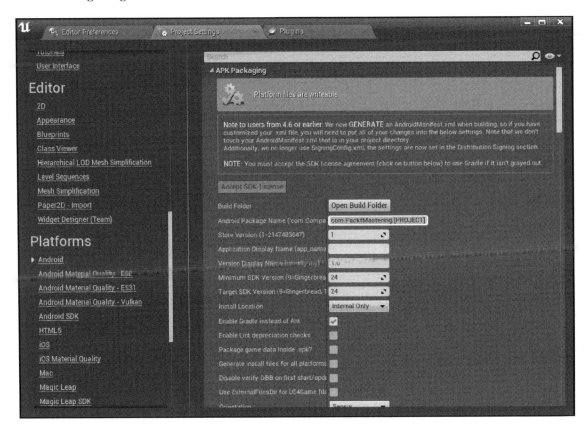

Like in VR or again, any Android project, be sure to head to **Project Settings** | **Platforms** | **Android**, and click the **Configure Now** button. As you can see below that in this template, it has already done other work we had to do for VR like setting APK versions for you.

In truth, this was all that was needed to get the basic AR game running on my device, from there you can tap to add some shapes to the world and use the debug menus to get a feel for what work UE4 AR is doing and visualize how well it is doing it.

Porting our projectiles and firing them in AR

Now we'll make things more interesting by pulling our projectiles from the earlier project in to this AR demo in all their glory. First, though, we'll need to add the source files to the proper folder and then generate project files. To do this, I've made two copies of the project on my local hard drive (which makes GitHub a bit tricky to handle as they're both branches in the same repository); but to keep things simple, I'll work locally with a copy of this branch (simply cut & paste to a new folder):

```
https://github.com/PacktPublishing/Mastering-Game-Development-with-Unreal-Engine-4-Second-Edition/tree/Chapter-13-AR
```

And have `chapter 12`'s branch here in my normal GitHub local drive location:

```
https://github.com/PacktPublishing/Mastering-Game-Development-with-Unreal-Engine-4-Second-Edition/tree/Chapter-12
```

This way I can cherry-pick items from `chapter 12` into the AR project. In the end, it's a bit complicated, but I'll simply delete my local `chapter 12` files and folders when done, *except* the `.git` hidden folder for git's information, then move (or rename) the local AR to that location and switch branches back to the AR project and check in those specific changes. Git can be tricky in cases like this, but right now we're just trying to have some fun in an AR environment and see what we can do, so let's get to it!

Copying the source files as noted was the first step, just simply take `chapter 12`'s `MasteringProjectile.h` and `.cpp` files, and move them in to the `MasteringAR/Source` folder. Once that's done, we can right click on the `MasteringAR.uproj` file and generate project files with our UE4 version, or use a batch file as we have in the past to make sure we have VS 2017 files. Now we can build and run the editor as normal and deploy the project as well. Keep in mind, though, as a C++ project now, iteration times will increase significantly between runs on the device as it will compile code each time it deploys; but that's what we need to do here to get our projectiles firing with all their code of course we built over previous chapters.

 In full disclosure: I actually had to, from the UE4 AR project here, name it Mastering.uproject, add a new C++ class of MasteringProjectile (based on the Actor class), and then copy-paste the code from the main project into this one for the migrated assets to find their parent class properly. In the past, the copy-paste file-version above has worked fine, but in case anyone has trouble, try this one as a last resort as I did.

A bit unfortunately, we actually need to launch the `chapter 12` project to migrate the assets from there, to our AR project. So open it in the editor and we'll browse to the projectiles section of our blueprints and right click on one of them. You'll see this pop-up and under **Asset Actions** is **Migrate**.

The next thing that will pop-up is a list, basically, of all the dependencies that Unreal is telling you it will copy, just click **ok**:

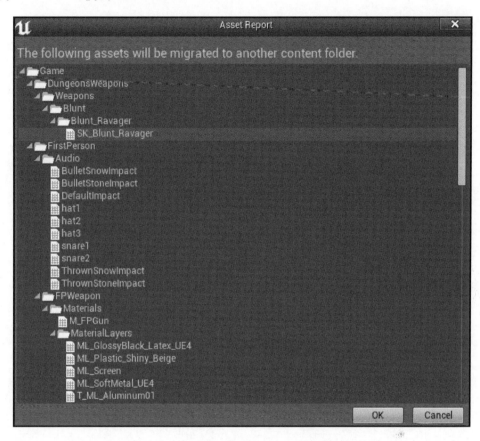

Now we just need to point to our Content folder in the AR project's Content folder, and those projectiles and all their asset dependencies (the special FX we did in `Chapter 12`, *In-Scene Video and Visual Effects*, and so on, will all be brought with it). Migrating assets like this is a huge time saver between projects that share them, so I'm glad to finally get a chance to share its use here.

With that done, we can get back to the AR project in the editor once more, make an array of our projectiles, and spawn those instead of the test geometry the project starts with:

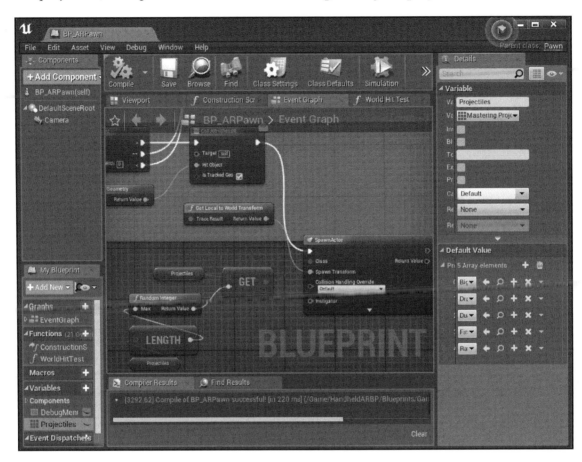

And that's it, now we have our core project's projectiles spawning in the AR world with special FX and all!

Summary

Through this journey, we've gone from the most basic starting point in UE4 to building and modifying some of its latest and greatest technologies. There's nothing quite as satisfying as seeing your work on your target platform and knowing it's only a matter of time before the rest of the world gets to share in it too. VR and AR are exciting new areas and UE4 is a leader in their development we are lucky to have. Having the know-how to get these technologies up and running and the myriad of new projects and games they bring to possible makes this a very exciting time, and can allow us to feel we're truly mastering UE4!

Questions

1. What advantages and disadvantages does including starting content in a new project entail?
2. When making a VR or AR project, what is the primary reason to keep it blueprint only as long as possible?
3. What step is necessary to getting every Android project to build and deploy?
4. What are some advantages and disadvantages to the GearVR platform over the current PC/Console versions?
5. When adding movement via the HMD, what problems could it cause a user? How was it mitigated?
6. Which basic Android settings for the AR template are already set that we had to set for the VR template?
7. When converting from blueprint only to a C++ project, what two steps are taken?
8. How are assets migrated from one project to another with full dependencies?

Further reading

GearVR HMD touchpad in UE4:

```
https://docs.unrealengine.com/en-us/Platforms/GearVR/HowTo/HMDTouchPad
```

Google's supported Android AR devices:

```
https://developers.google.com/ar/discover/supported-devices
```

Other Books You May Enjoy

If you enjoyed this book, you may be interested in these other books by Packt:

Godot Engine Game Development Projects
Chris Bradfield

ISBN: 9781788831505

- Get started with the Godot game engine and editor
- Organize a game project
- Import graphical and audio assets
- Use Godot's node and scene system to design robust, reusable game objects
- Write code in GDScript to capture input and build complex behaviors
- Implement user interfaces to display information
- Create visual effects to spice up your game
- Learn techniques that you can apply to your own game projects

Mastering C++ Game Development
Mickey Macdonald

ISBN: 9781788629225

- Work and communicate effectively in the modern games industry
- Develop simple and advanced gameplay systems
- How to leverage the standard core C++ libraries
- Use modern real-time rendering techniques to achieve immersive 3D visuals
- Achieve a narrative-driven game experience using a variety of data management techniques
- Implement scripting using LUA
- Learn AI algorithms and concepts for handling motion, behavior, and decision making
- Implementation of the OpenGL, Bullet Physics, GLM, SteamVR and other common libraries

Leave a review - let other readers know what you think

Please share your thoughts on this book with others by leaving a review on the site that you bought it from. If you purchased the book from Amazon, please leave us an honest review on this book's Amazon page. This is vital so that other potential readers can see and use your unbiased opinion to make purchasing decisions, we can understand what our customers think about our products, and our authors can see your feedback on the title that they have worked with Packt to create. It will only take a few minutes of your time, but is valuable to other potential customers, our authors, and Packt. Thank you!

Index

A

A1
  loading/saving 146
AI controller
  creating 118
animation
  sounds, triggering 183, 186, 190
Atmospheric Fog
  about 274
  using 277, 281
Augmented Reality (AR) project
  Android deployment specifics 330
  creating 328
  projectiles, firing 331
  projectiles, porting 328, 331

B

basic brain
  creating 118
behavior tree
  C++ decision making, adding 123
blueprint variables
  overview 76
blueprint visual scripting (BVS) system 56
blueprint-only games 56, 62
blueprint
  overview 56, 57, 61
  performance 63
  performance tips 74
  scripting 63
  scripting example 64, 67, 70, 72

C

C++ profiling tools
  reference 76
C++

  used, for managing FPS C++ 14
character
  swapping of weapons, adding 51
cycle weapons
  controls, adding 51

D

data
  loading, from menu 108, 115
  saving, from menu 108
device
  building on 268
  testing on 267, 268
Dialog Voice 181
Dialog Wave 181
dying 141, 146

E

enemies
  spawning 139
existing gun
  converting 28
Exponential Height Fog
  reference 296

F

first-person shooter (FPS) 12
FPS C++ project
  building 9, 13
  character class, overriding 14
  class, editing in VS 19, 22
  editor, executing 12
  editor, hot-reloading 19, 22
  executing 13
  managing, with C++ 14
  template, picking 12

UE4, building 9
UE4, installing 9

G

game save slots
  about 100
  widget, creating 101
GearVR
  building for 318
  deploying for 318
Git LFS
  reference 202

H

hit reactions 141, 146

I

icons
  building, for inventory with captures 78
in-game scenes
  blueprint 250
  Dialog system 250
  simple sequences 250
in-scene video
  assets, selecting 298
  building 302
  playing 302
  playing, with Media Framework 298
Inventory class
  adding 26
inventory, with screen captures
  icons, building 78
inventory
  creating 30, 33, 38
  default gun, adding 30, 33, 38
  summarizing 53
  synchronizing, with HUD 94, 99
  using 50

L

level loading
  about 152
  basics 152
  load/save, used for transition 155, 158, 164,
    170
lightmaps
  profiling 293, 294
lightmass 274
lightmass tools
  about 286
  previewing tools 287
  settings 287

M

Mastering Unreal Engine 4 7
materials
  at runtime 217
  at various platforms 217
  building 206
  instance creation 207
  networks, working on 210
  overview 207
  performance tips 210
Matinee editor 251
Media Framework
  supported video types, reference 313
  used, for playing in-scene video 298

N

non-player characters (NPCs) 117

P

physics particles
  adding 305
  adjusting 310
  initial emitter, creating on projectile hit 306
  orienting 310
platform
  Android, setting up 260, 266
  exploring 220, 230, 256
  general settings 257
  installable PC version, setting up 257
  iOS setup 266
  rebuild-hell, avoiding 270
Play In Editor (PIE) 13
player
  attacking 127, 133, 135, 138

R

Reverb Effect 181

S

save game file
  creating 104, 107
sequencer
  about 234
  Actor to Sequencer Track 235
  alternatives 249
  level sequences 235
  master sequences 235
  scene, adding 240
  scene, triggering 240
  shot track 235
  takes 235
  using 234
shaders
  adapting 220, 230
  iterating, with untime tools and techniques 218
Sound Attenuation 181
Sound Class 182
Sound Concurrency 182
Sound Cue 182
Sound Mix 182
Sound Wave 181
sound
  adding 190
  different surfaces 194
  different surfaces, hitting 190
  environment FX 196, 201
  player footfalls 196, 201
spawn points
  used, for enemy replacement 139
standalone builds
  creating 269
  installing 269
streaming
  about 170
  advantages 170
  best practices 172

disadvantages 170
example 172

U

UE4 audio
  channels 180
  cues 180
  dialog 180
  FX volumes 180
  sound 180
  triggering, from animation 178
UE4
  play options, versus package project 268
UMG
  integrating, into player's HUD class 78
  used, for displaying inventory icons on screen 93
  using 100
Unreal Dialog system
  reference 202

V

Virtual Reality (VR) project
  creating 317
  HMD controls, adding 323
  new controls, adding 317
Volumetric Fog
  reference 296
  using 282, 286
volumetric lightmaps
  about 274
  adding, with lightmass volumes 275

W

Weapon class
  adding 26
  creating 26, 27
WeaponPickup class
  adding 39
  blueprints, setting up 43
  code, executing 46, 49
  new actor class, creating 39